GOLFER'S GUIDE

SCOTLAND

150 COURSES AND FACILITIES

DAVID J. WHYTE

NEW
HOLLAND

To my father and my uncles who attempted to acquaint me with the game of golf at an early age but had to wait some three decades before I finally discovered its delight for myself.

First published in 2001 by
New Holland Publishers (UK) Ltd
London • Cape Town • Sydney • Auckland

Garfield House
86 Edgware Road
London, W2 2EA, UK

80 McKenzie Street
Cape Town 8001
South Africa

14 Aquatic Drive
Frenchs Forest, NSW 2086
Australia

218 Lake Road
Northcote, Auckland
New Zealand

1 3 5 7 9 10 8 6 4 2

ISBN 1 85974 276 9

A Kinsey & Harrison Production

For New Holland Publishers
Commissioning editor: Tim Jollands
Design concept: Alan Marshall
Cartographer: William Smuts
Production controller: Joan Woodroffe
Indexer: Patricia Hymans

Reproduction by Pica Colour Separation Overseas (Pte) Ltd, Singapore
Printed and bound in Singapore by Kyodo Printing Co (Singapore) Pte Ltd

Photographic Acknowledgements
All photographs taken by David J. Whyte (Scottish Golf Photo Library)
except pages 10 (Cowie Collection and St Andrews University)
and 109 (Frank Christian/Historic Golf Prints)

Front cover: *Cruden Bay*
Spine: *Colin Montgomerie*
Back cover (anti-clockwise from top left): *Duff House Royal, Dufftown,
Braemar Gathering, Durness, Caerlaverock Castle*
Title page: *St Andrews*

Publisher's Note
While every care has been taken to ensure that the information in this book
was as accurate as possible at the time of going to press, the publisher and author
accept no responsibility for any loss, injury or inconvenience sustained by
anyone using this book.

Contents

HOW TO USE THIS BOOK

Finding Your Course

The 150 courses in this book are presented by their geographical location, on a region-by-region basis. To find a course, use the contents list, or the index, or go to each regional map located in the relevant regional chapter introduction. Within each of the eight major Scottish regions presented here, the courses are arranged loosely by their geographical proximity and, where appropriate, by a possible itinerary. Use the regional map to locate your course and then go to the appropriate number within the chapter for a full course description.

You will also find that some major Scottish courses, such as Gleneagles or St Andrews, have been given more in-depth descriptions including a diagram of the course layout and a full card with yardages.

The selection of the 150 courses here reflects the author's opinion of those that you should try to visit. However there are now over 500 golf courses in Scotland and most are worthy of playing.

Golf Course Yardages

All Scottish courses are measured in Imperial yards and this is the information that is presented in this guide (with metric equivalents also given). Overall course yardages are for the maximum length of the course either from the white (medal) tees or from the championship (tiger) tees. The usual set-up of tee markers for the majority of Scottish courses is white for medal tees (competition), yellow for visitors' tees, red for ladies' tees.

Occasionally a blue juniors' tee is added between the men's visitors and the ladies tee. Tiger tees are a phenomenon of newer courses intended for professional golfers only. Visitors are rarely allowed to use the white competition tees, which are reserved for club members' competitions.

Club Facilities

Most clubs offer a range of facilities and it is only the more remote or smaller clubs that do not cater for the usual golfing requirements. Changing rooms are commonly provided, usually with a separate area for visitors. Showers are available at most clubs although it is a good practice to take a towel with you as not all clubs provide this service.

Scottish golfers traditionally carry their bags out on the course with older golfers using a pull or electric trolley. Sit-on golf buggies are now increasingly available at many clubs.

Visitors' Restrictions

Visitors' golf is often restricted to certain times especially at the weekends (often Saturdays) or early weekday mornings when club members hold their competitions. There are a few clubs that do not allow any visitors to play at the weekend. For example, the Old Course at St Andrews is closed on Sundays but this is a perfect time to walk through the course using the paths provided. However, most golf clubs will allow tee times – often later in the day – at weekends.

There are also a growing number of pay-and-play facilities with no weekend restrictions. In any event, always try to make a telephone booking in advance.

You will find, in practice, that handicap certificates are rarely requested on the majority of Scottish courses, although it is by far the best policy to keep your certificate and/or a letter of introduction from your club with you.

Key to Green Fees

For each course we have provided a rough guide to green fees to play a round of 18 holes, as follows:

£	=	*up to £19 ($31)*
££	=	*£20 to £29 ($32 to $48)*
£££	=	*£30 to £39 ($49 to $65)*
££££	=	*£40 to £49 ($66 to $81)*
£££££	=	*£50 to £59 ($82 to $99)*
£££££+	=	*£60 or over ($100 or over)*

Bear in mind, however, that clubs will offer a day rate (usually a bit more expensive, but you have the chance to play two or more rounds) as well as a single round rate. Concessions are also often available for mid-week, late afternoon and out-of-season rounds, as well for touring groups, parties, senior citizens, packages and the like.

Introduction

Golf in Scotland

The very notion of Scotland carries with it potent images, a country steeped in history, intense in visual splendour and stocked by a determined and assiduous folk. The strength of these images has transcended the country's modest dimensions and around the globe people hold Scotland and the Scots in high regard. None more so than golfers. Anyone who has taken up the 'cleeks' (the Scotish word for the old hickory-shafted clubs) will, on a visit, soon perceive the intimate bond between Scotland and the game of golf. For it was here that the game first took hold and was nurtured.

Centuries of Golf

It is generally agreed that the game of golf which we recognise today was established some 600 years ago in Scotland, probably in the area of coastal Fife and particularly on the wide expanse of links adjacent to the

Left: Carnoustie, in Angus, has been the setting for several Open Championships, most notably in 1999, and is a must for any visitor, as are Scotland's famous malt whisky distilleries (above).

ancient ecclesiastical and university centre of St Andrews. This is according to surviving written records. It is quite probable that the game was established before this time and indeed had spread to other areas along Scotland's east coast. The history may be hazy but, by the 15th century, golf along with football, was so popular it had been banned by the Scottish Parliament because it interfered with military training for the wars against the English.

Rail and Royal links

It was the Victorian era that witnessed golf's first boom. The sport had been gradually gaining popularity through the first half of the 19th century with clubs opening throughout Scotland. The discovery of Scotland's health-giving airs lead Queen Victoria and her ailing consort, Prince Albert, to became frequent visitors particularly to the Highlands, travelling extensively and eventually spending much of their time at Balmoral in Deeside. With their patronage, Scotland became fashionable and middle-class Victorians made use of the extensive new

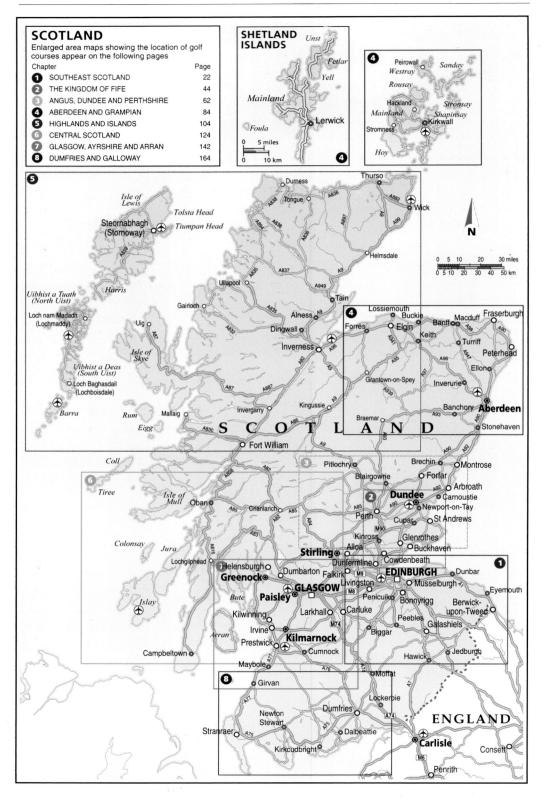

SCOTLAND

Enlarged area maps showing the location of golf
courses appear on the following pages

SHETLAND ISLANDS

Unst

Fetlar

Yell

Mainland

Foula

Lerwick

0   5 miles

0   10 km

4

Peirowall
Westray   Sanday

Rousay

Hackland   Stronsay
Mainland   Shapinsay
Stromness   Kirkwall

Hoy

railway systems to reach places previously only available to locals.

Helping to further spread golf's popularity was the advent of the gutta percha ball in the mid-1800s. This new rubberised sphere was far less expensive than the previous feathery ball and it flew much further. New courses sprang up on the back of this ball throughout Scotland and indeed the UK and beyond.

Scottish Golf Today

Today there are more golf courses in Scotland per head of population than in any other country. In all of its 30,500sq miles (79,059sq km) – about the size of South Carolina – there are over 500 courses. Golf is as popular here as it ever was, probably more so, a game played by every section of Scottish society. As such it is probably more egalitarian here in its place of birth than in any other golfing nation. Although the majority of the courses cater for a strong membership they also welcome visitors, and players no matter what their handicap will find a venue that suits them. We have selected 150 courses of varying landscapes and degrees of difficulty – but all of which you will be able to book and play on.

TRAVELLING TO SCOTLAND

By Plane The main cities of Edinburgh, Glasgow and Aberdeen all have international serving airports and are well provided with motorway and rail links. Glasgow and Edinburgh Airports are the main air gateways with land or air connections available to most outlying areas. Many visitors also choose to come to Scotland via London and fly into one of the UK's southern airports such as Heathrow or Gatwick. This allows sight-seeing in London and the south-east before catching a shuttle flight or train up to Scotland. There are now many international carriers flying directly to Scotland so check with your local travel agent.

The Scottish border is around six hours driving time from London and approximately four and a half hours on a train to Edinburgh or Glasgow. Most shuttle flights from London airports to Glasgow or Edinburgh take just over one hour with other domestic flights further north to Aberdeen, Inverness and Dundee taking just a little longer. Shuttle flight fares are competitive between operators and services are frequent – usually several from each operator per day. Booking ahead is unnecessary (except on national holidays, and sporting events) as tickets can be purchased on the day of travel at the airport or on board the plane.

By Rail Travelling by train is a comfortable and scenic way of reaching Scotland from the south. You will also arrive fresh and ready for golf rather than fatigued from an arduous drive. The extra cost of a sleeping compartment is little more than a night's B&B (bed and breakfast) on top of your regular fare if two people share a berth, and a light breakfast is served shortly before arrival. On the downside, the small sleeping compartments can prove quite crowded with golf clubs and luggage for two. Single first-class sleeping compartments are an alternative but quite expensive option. Still, bear in mind the benefits of a good night's sleep to your golf game the next day as well as the time-saving aspect of covering the miles to Scotland overnight possibly allowing an extra day's golf.

By Car The main motorway connections into Scotland are the M6 across the west side of England and joining the M73/74 at the Scottish Border or on the east, the A1(M) road system via Newcastle. The

SCOTTISH GOLF TIMELINE

1457
King James II bans the playing of golf along with football as it is interfering with archery practice and other military training.

1502
The ban is lifted and James IV makes the first recorded purchase of golf equipment, a set of clubs from a bow-maker in Perth.

1553
The Archbishop of St Andrews issues an edict allowing locals the right to play golf on the links.

1567
Mary Queen of Scots gives golf a go.

1618
The feathery golf ball is invented.

1621
Golf on the links at Dornoch is recorded.

1744
The first golf club is formed, the Honourable Company of Edinburgh Golfers, playing at Leith Links.

1754
The first *Rules of Golf* is published by the St Andrews Golfers.

1764
St Andrews becomes the first 18-hole golf course. The first four holes are combined into two, reducing the round from 22 to 18 holes.

1780
The Aberdeen Golf Club (later Royal Aberdeen) is founded.

1817
Scotscraig Golf Club is established, making a total of 13 golf courses in Scotland.

1826
Hickory imported from the USA is used to make golf shafts.

Old Tom Morris, world-famous Scottish player and architect.

1834
William IV bestows the title Royal & Ancient to St Andrews Golf Club.

1836
The Honourable Company of Edinburgh Golfers moves to Musselburgh due to overcrowding and poor conditions at Leith.

1848
The longer flight and cheaper cost of the gutta-percha ball opens up golf to all.

1851
Prestwick Golf Club is founded. Old Tom Morris leaves for Prestwick to create the first purpose built golf course.

1852
The railway comes to St Andrews, opening up the course to Sassenachs (Southerners). Allan Robertson, the first great professional golfer, records a 79 on the Old Course, St Andrews becoming the first to break 80.

1860
The first professional championship is held at Prestwick Golf Club (which only had 12 holes). Willie Park wins by two strokes from Old Tom Morris.

1861
The Professional Championship is opened up to amateurs. The first competition is won by Old Tom Morris.

1869
From the age of 17 Young Tom Morris wins the first of four successive British Opens. His third consecutive win entitles him to keep the ornamental belt trophy.

1870
The gutty ball, using cork and leather in a rubberised compound, is credited by some to Dr Paterson of St Andrews who melted his shoe soles to ply around a gutta percha ball.

1872
A new claret jug trophy is offered for the British Open championship by Prestwick, St Andrews and the Honourable Company of Edinburgh Golfers.

1873
The British Open is held at St Andrews for the first time and won by Tom Kidd, a local caddie.

1880
Dimples are designed for gutta-percha balls, helping them to fly better.

1919
The R&A undertakes control of the British Open and British Amateur Championships.

1920s
James Braid designs many of Scotland's finer courses including Lanark, Stranraer, Golspie, Brora, Taymouth Castle, Kirriemuir, Forfar, and Scotscraig (all featured in this book).

1999
There are over 500 golf courses open to visitors in Scotland, including Carnoustie, where Scots Paul Lawrie wins the Open.

RAIL DEALS

ScotRail's Caledonian Sleeper service offers two services from London's Euston Station at 2130 nightly Monday to Friday 2110 Sundays for Aberdeen, Inverness and Fort William and at 2355 Mondays to Fridays/2325 Sundays for Glasgow and Edinburgh

The National Railways Enquiry Scheme (Tel 08457 484950) offers a variety of tickets to reach Scotland from the south and for travelling around Scotland. Cheaper fares (Apex and Super Apex) can be obtained if you book in advance. Sleeper tickets can be booked by credit card through ScotRail Telesales on 08457 550033.

M6/M74 is preferred for rapid, motorway travel to Glasgow or Edinburgh following the M8 and all points north, but the A1(M) may offer a more relaxing journey. Both routes however have splendid scenery to drive past, especially when you cross the border into Scotland. On crossing the border you may wish to use alternative A routes such as the A7 or the A68 both of which pass through attractive countryside.

By Coach Coach travel, from the main terminus at London's Victorian Bus Station (and also from other major UK cities) is available throughout each day and overnight. This is the cheapest but not really the most comfortable way of travelling to Scotland from the south.

By Ferry Ferries are available mainly from Northern Ireland to Stranraer or Troon on Scotland's southwest coast. Scandinavian, Low Countries and German visitors might find the ferry services into Newcastle from the Hook of Holland and Rotterdam useful if they wish to bring their own vehicle.

TRAVELLING WITHIN SCOTLAND
Travelling by Plane Flights within Scotland are generally confined to the outer islands such as Shetland, Orkney, Islay, Tiree, or from Edinburgh and Glasgow to Inverness.

Airports include
Glasgow Airport 0141 887 1111
Edinburgh Airport 0131 333 1000
Aberdeen Airport 01224 722331
Dundee 01382 643242
Inverness 01463 232471
Gatwick Airport 01293 535353
Heathrow Airport 0181 759 4321

Travelling by Train or Coach Internal distances are relatively short and best traversed by car, train or ferry. Trains and coaches are an option for internal travel throughout Scotland but for golfers they lack the required flexibility especially when trying to reach the golf course from the station or bus terminal.
National Rail Enquiries 0345 484950
International Rail Enquiries 0900 848848
Channel Tunnel Rail Enquiries 0990 186186
National Coach Enquiries 0990 808080

Travelling by Car The most popular and versatile way of visiting Scotland on a golf vacation is by car. The advantages of having a vehicle at your disposal are obvious including transporting your clubs and luggage directly to the hotel door or clubhouse car park.

Fly-drive tickets purchased in your home country are possibly the most economical way of hiring a car, as prices in the UK tend to be comparatively expensive. Internationally known car-hire companies are found at all airports, railway stations and most towns.

Driving in Scotland – Essential Tips
• *Left-side drive* Vehicles in the UK use the left side of the road. This can prove daunting to drivers who have spent their driving

careers on the opposite side. Local authorities have tried to help by posting *Drive on the Left* reminders at, for instance, exits of service areas, rest areas and ferry ports.

• *Negotiating roundabouts,* or 'circles', at first might be the most hazardous problem. These are intended to slow traffic and provide a safe entrance or exit to or from busy roads. Stay to the left and give way to traffic coming from the right.

•*At T-junctions* look to the right first for oncoming traffic. It is not permitted to turn left at a cross-roads with traffic lights at red if the way is clear as it is in some other countries such as the USA.

• *The wearing of seat belts* is compulsory in the UK, both front and rear. A fine can be imposed if any occupants of a vehicle do not comply with this.

• *Speed limits* are posted in miles per hour. Hire car speedometers display in miles per hour though kilometre equivalents are usually also indicated. Speed limits on motorways might seem fast for North American drivers but 60 mph/100 km/h in the nearside lane is acceptable, with most traffic cruising around 70mph/112 km/h. Urban areas are restricted to 30mph/50km/h.

• *Parking* a car in Glasgow and Edinburgh city centres is a trying experience for everyone so, if you have a hire car whilst visiting these cities, leave it at your hotel car park and use public transport. 'Park & Ride' bus facilities are often available where the car is left at the city perimeter and a regular bus takes you to the centre for an all-in price. These will prove cheaper in relation to parking charges and a lot less hassle. Traffic wardens, while looking to fine illegally-parked cars, will also assist you with directions.

• *Driving hazards* in rural parts are likely to be roaming sheep, checking the grass from one side of the road to the other.

CAR HIRE IN SCOTLAND

International Reservations Numbers

Hertz 0990 99 66 99
Avis 0990 900 500
Budget 0541 56 56 56
Europcar 0870 607 5000
Arnold Clark Tel: 0141 848 0202

Although the major international car hire companies all have outlets in Scotland, the largest car rental fleet in the country is Arnold Clark. They have 33 branches throughout Scotland and are ideally placed to provide vehicle rental to golfers. They also operate a complimentary collection and delivery service from all main Scottish airports and railway stations.

Car rental companies offer a wide range of vehicle types from hatchbacks to space cruisers. Prices start from under £20 per day and under £100 per week for a Group 1 car such as a compact Ford.

For those looking for something larger, a Group 4 Car such as a Toyota saloon offers excellent value for money between £30 to £40 per day and £160 per week. A people carrier will provide adequate room for a small group with a Group 9 car such as the Volkswagen Caravelle being extremely cost effective at under £70 per day and around £330 per week.

All rates usually include VAT (Value Added Tax, the local sales tax which is currently at 17.5%) as well as insurance. When hiring a car, you should also bring with you a driver's license, passport, and a copy of your own car insurance details.

• *Single-track road etiquette* is needed in the most rural parts of the mainland and on many of the islands. The vehicle that is closest to a provided *Passing Place*, and these are most frequent, pulls over and allows oncoming vehicles through. You will find that drivers tend to signal with a one-hand salute or wave to one another to indicate thanks at these passing places. This greeting carries on, especially on the islands so that every car that passes waves as a matter of routine. Being courteous and patient are the code for these roads.

• *Fuel* is predominantly unleaded or diesel, and is easily available even in remote areas. Some of the Western Isles such as Lewis and Harris, strongholds of staunch Presbyterianism, do not open garages or most other services on the Sabbath.

• *Security* should be taken in keeping your golf bags or cameras out of sight in the trunk of a car and keeping the passenger compartment free of other tell-tale signs that the car is being used for golf touring. In prime golfing areas, such as St Andrews or East Lothian, vehicles have been targeted by organised thieves. So take your clubs with you wherever you go and be sure to store your clubs in your accommodation while not using them.

Travelling by Ferry Most of Scotland's islands, both north and west, have attractive golf courses and indeed these offer an experience of how golf might have been played in its earliest history. To explore the islands off the west coast or north to Orkney and Shetland you need to use a ferry or plane to reach them. Caledonian MacBrayne offers frequent sailings to the west coast islands for both cars and foot passengers, and P&O operate between the mainland and Orkney and Shetland while smaller operators ply the short distance between the mainland and Orkney on the north coast near John o' Groats. If you intend to take a vehicle on to the islands the best advice is to book well in advance especially through the busier summer months as space can be rapidly booked up.

Ferry reservations and information
Caledonian MacBrayne 0990 650000
Brittany Ferries 0990 360360
Colorline 0191 296 1313
Hoverspeed 0990 240241
P&O European Ferries 0990 980555
P&O Stena Line 0990 980980
Scandinavian Seaways 0990 333000
Sea France 0990 711711
Stena Line 0990 707070
Irish Ferries 0990 171717
Sea Container Ferries 0990 523523

Scotland's Climate
Scotland's northern latitude – in line with Norway, Labrador and Moscow – should make it much colder than it is, but the Gulf Stream, a warm flow of water crossing the Atlantic from the Caribbean, has a warming effect. This is most noticeable in parts of the west coast where palm trees and other exotic vegetation grow. Many of the coastal golf courses of the west are playable all year as there is very little winter frost. The warming effect extends along the north of Scotland via the Pentland Firth and then turns down the east coast to the Moray Firth area, again keeping the coastal links quite playable throughout the year.

With such a temperate climate, rain is a common feature at any time of the year, hence the lovely green vegetation through the high summer months.

When to Play Golf
Generally the Scottish golfing season commences the first weekend in April, although some courses start a little earlier depending on their location. Often the best weather is found in the months of May and September when clear skies and moderate temperatures are ideal for golf. These are busy months with golf visitors, with the countryside often at its best with either new spring growth or the colours of early Autumn gracing the trees. October is still a reasonable month to play golf although many courses begin their winter programmes of course maintenance.

Through the winter months many inland courses will close temporarily if there has been a frost to avoid damage to the grass. A recent trend has been to have golfers use

There are some superb golf courses right in the heart of the 'precipitous city' of Edinburgh such as Braid Hills.

little, portable mats on the fairways to avoid divots. This has resulted in a great improvement in course conditions.

Scotland's Daylight Hours

Visitors to Scotland are often surprised to see how much daylight Scotland enjoys through the summer months. Scottish daylight hours begin to extend noticeably by May and continue well into the evening through August. It is light by 5am and does not get dark until 10pm through the summer.

For golfers this means their playing time can be extended and it is perfectly feasible if you are keen enough to go out for a round after an early dinner. In the most northerly parts such as Shetland, the sun only sets for around two hours near the summer equinox.

Golf Club Opening/Closing Times

Generally golf clubs open for business between 7.30 and 8am. Some of the first morning tee times are reserved for members and this might be the same in the early afternoon. But unless it is one of the more serious members' clubs, there is usually a degree of flexibility, and green fee paying visitors are fitted in as soon as possible.

Although most Scottish clubs are termed 'private' this is a slight mis-labelling as they are generally open and welcoming to the public with only some time restrictions. Members of the club enjoy slightly cheaper drinks in the 'Member's Bar' but other than that, as long as they have paid their green fees, visitors enjoy the privileges of the club for that day.

Weekends are a different case. Most clubs hold club competitions on Saturday and Sunday mornings. If there is large number taking part, tee times could be booked off for members until well into the afternoon and therefore some clubs do not allow any visitors, especially on a Saturday. Through the week also there can be ladies afternoon and medal competitions. The golden golfing rule is to always telephone ahead, even if it is on the day, and the club professional or starter will try to accommodate you.

Municipal courses are public courses (normally run by the local council) and are open to all at a set fee. You can still book tee times and it is advisable to do this rather than just turn up.

What to Wear at the Golf Club

Despite images that golfers might see on television during major Scottish golfing events, the weather during the golfing season is not all that bad. Most foreign visitors are glad of cooler conditions in which to enjoy their rounds and the average summer temperatures run from around 65–75°F/47–57°C. Bring a woollen sweater and rain proofs however. The trend towards soft-spikes has not caught on in Scotland although it ultimately will. As most visiting golfers are already wearing these, it is not much of a problem.

Dress codes associated with most golf clubs and even municipal (public) courses expect a sensible turnout of clothing style which is fairly universal and definitely means no jeans or collarless shirts. There are one or two more traditional clubs that insist on gentlemen wearing a jacket, collar and tie in the main lounge. Such clubs often also feature wonderful golfing paraphernalia of the club's history so it is worth the extra effort.

Accommodation

Throughout Scotland, there is a high standard of accommodation including B&Bs (bed and breakfast), guest houses, country house hotels, large hotels and self catering cottages. You will find each region is highly accustomed to dealing with golfers and their specific requirements. Many golf-oriented hotels will even book your tee times for the days that you are staying with them and suggest or even provide excursions for non-golfing guests.

If you are travelling independently and looking for accommodation, a useful tip is to call in at the local Tourist Information Office (listed at the end of each regional chapter). Here, they can find suitable accommodation at short notice through their *Book-A-Bed-Ahead* scheme. This, of course, depends on availability and, in popular areas, can occasionally lead to disappointment if all rooms are taken. There is a 10 % booking charge on the *Advanced Booking Service* as well as the *Book-A-Bed-Ahead* scheme, but this is deducted from your accommodation bill.

To help you plan your trip in advance, each area tourist board publishes accommodation guides to their region which list a wide range of places to stay. Regional tourist boards can be found in each regional directory. Telephone their

ACCOMMODATION AGENCIES

Beyond the recommended establishments in the individual sections of this book, there are several agencies offering properties of all kinds throughout Scotland.

Holiday Cottages (Scotland) Limited Lilliesleaf, Melrose, Roxburghshire RD6 9JD. Tel 01835 870481

Scottish Farmhouse Holidays Drumtenant, Ladybank, Fife KY7 7UG. Tel 01337 830451

The Landmark Trust Shottesbrooke, Maidenhead, Berkshire SL6 3SW. Tel 01628 825925

Scotland's Heritage Hotels 2d Churchill Way, Bishopbriggs, Glasgow G64 2RH. Tel 0141 772 6911

Scottish Country Cottages Suite 2d, Churchill Way, Bishopbriggs, Glasgow G64 2RH. Tel 0141 772 5920

Scottish Tourist Board 23 Ravelston Terrace, Edinburgh EH4 3EU. Tel 0131 332 2433

helpline numbers and ask for their golf and accommodation guides to be sent to you well in advance of your trip.

The Scottish Tourist Board inspects hotels and guest houses which are members of their scheme and grades them annually so this is a useful indicator to help your choice. Grades and classification are included in their accommodation guides and also indicated by blue oval plaques placed outside an establishment with information such as whether it is Approved, Commended, Highly Commended or Deluxe. Recommended accommodation is also listed in each regional directory.

B&Bs Generally the best value for accommodation in Scotland is found in the numerous B&Bs throughout each area. These are not like the grandiose establishments now referred to as B&Bs in North America but usually a room in someone's home with good facilities such as en-suite bathroom, TV and tea/coffee making facilities. While these are very competitively priced they may not suit groups of golfers who would rather have the communal facilities of a bar in which to recount the day's action. Recommended B&Bs are also listed in each regional directory.

Hotels There is a view that Scottish hotels are on the slightly expensive side. So, in order to get the best value from this type of accommodation, it might be better to book a golfing package from a travel agent or dedicated tour operator. However, it is also worth doing a little homework to see if it is worthwhile to organise your own trip.

Self Catering Cottages For small groups of golfers wishing to stay in one area for an extended period, it might be worth considering a self catering cottage. The advantage is that for a group of four or more it can prove most cost effective. Again, their level is dictated by the local tourist boards' commended scheme. There are companies that specialise in this type of accommodation such as Country Cottages in Scotland (Tel 01328 851155).

Booking your Golf Vacation

Most first-time visitors are advised to purchase a package from a recognised golf tour operator specialising in or including Scotland in their brochure. These tend to use more pricey hotels and courses where the operator makes most profit. If you wish to sample the great links and upmarket resort courses this might well be acceptable but the overall package price is likely to be costly.

Tour operators

If your budget is tight, there are still tour operators who can help. These are often best found on the Internet. There are several reputable Scottish golf tour specialists dealing with travel packages to Scotland. The advantage of booking a trip through a golf tour operator is that most elements of your visit are prearranged. The disadvantage is that the vacation might be slightly more expensive than if you book a holiday directly yourself. Tour operators however can negotiate lower rates on accommodation, car hire and sometimes golf so their comprehensive service is actually good value.

Packages from some tour operators such as Linksland Golf Travel include cultural, educational and gastronomic elements that you may find difficult to organise yourself and yet can make a great difference to your overall experience of golfing in Scotland.

- Linksland Golf Travel
(44) 1575 574515
www.linksland.co.uk
Email: travel@linksland.co.uk
- Wilkinson Golf & Leisure
(44) 1383 861000Email:
wilkinsongolf@easynet.co.uk
- Executive Golf & Leisure
(44) 1786 832244
Email: Graeme@executive-golfleisure.com
- Golf Scotland
(44) 1382 454035
Email: tours@golfscotland.co.uk
- Adventures in Golf
(44) 1334 479500
Email: info@aigscotland.sol.co.uk
- Best of Scotland
(44) 1333 360395
Email: 100670.1521@compuserve.com
- Links Golf St Andrews

The Queen's View is a famous outlook over Loch Tummel, visited by Queen Victoria in 1866. Royal Family links and stunning landscapes combine especially in the Royal Deeside area of Northeast Scotland.

(44) 1334 478639
Email: lgtsta@aol.com
• Perry Golf
(44) 1436 671763
Email: perrygolf@golftravel.co.uk
• Celtic Links
(44) 292 511133
Email: celticlinks@easynet.co.uk
• Morton Golf Holidays
(44) 1738 626701
Email:
mortongolfholidays@compuserve.com

Day to Day Essentials

• *Currency* The basic unit of currency in Scotland and throughout the UK is Sterling which is based upon 100 pennies to the £. Coins in circulation are 1p, 2p, 5p, 10p, 20p, 50p, £1 and £2. Notes come in £5, £10, £20, and £50. There are still £1 paper notes circulating in Scotland but the £1 coin is now more common. £1 notes have been discontinued in England. Scottish banks such as the Royal Bank of Scotland, Bank of Scotland and Clydesdale Bank issue their own sterling notes which are legal tender throughout the UK, although occasionally you will find reluctance to have these accepted should you take them to England.

• *Traveller's cheques* are accepted in most city outlets but occasionally these might prove difficult to use in smaller establishments located in outlying areas, especially if the traveller's cheque is more than £20. In the north or the more remote west be sure to obtain cash, especially before the weekend when banks are closed. Banks are open Monday to Saturday morning and in most cases later on Thursdays. Bureau de Changes are found in larger towns only and have longer opening hours than banks.

• *Credit cards* Credit cards are widely accepted with Visa and Mastercard the most established. Small hotels, restaurants and B&Bs in the north might not be equipped to accept credit cards so cash will be required. Filling stations almost always accept credit cards. Using your credit card to obtain money from a bank's external cash dispenser is a simple and often most cost-effective method (depending on exchange rates and bank charges). This avoids the double fee paid on obtaining and cashing travellers cheques. Cash dispensers are found throughout Scotland.

• *Electricity* The electrical current throughout the UK is 240V/AC using a large 3-pin plug. An adaptor is required for Australasian appliances. Both adaptor and transformer are needed for North American appliances. Most hotels provide hairdryers and irons but it might prove useful to buy your own hair-dryer in Scotland, especially if you intend to stay in B&Bs.

• *Passports* Visitors from all European countries except Poland, Albania and Bulgaria require only a passport and no visa. This is also the case for citizens of North America, Australia and New Zealand. Generally, a stay of 3 months is allowed but stays of a duration longer than 6 months will require a visa. There are no vaccination requirements.

• *Embassies* The are no Embassies in Scotland. British Embassies abroad include:
USA, 3100 Massachusetts Avenue NW, Washington DC 20008.
Tel 202 462 1340
Canada, 80 Elgin Street, Ottawa, Ontario, K1P 5K7. Tel 613 237 1530
Australia, Commonwealth Avenue, Yarralumia, Canberra, ACT 2600.
Tel 062 270 6666
New Zealand, Reserve Bank Building, 2 The Terrace, PO Box 1812, Wellington.
Tel 04 726 049
Ireland, 31-33 Merrion Road, Dublin 4.
Tel 01 695211
South Africa, Dunkeld Corner, 275 Jan Smuts Avenue, Dunkeld West 2196, PO Box 1082, Parklands 2121.
Tel: 011-327 0015 Fax: 011-327 0152
Netherlands, General Koningslaan, 44, Amsterdam.

• *Festivals and Public Holidays* The only statutory public holiday in Scotland is New Year's Day. Bank holidays are frequent and include 2 January, the Friday before Easter, the first and last Friday in May, the first Monday in August, 30 November and 25 and 26 of December. Besides banks, many offices close on these days but most retailers, accommodation and visitor attractions are open. There is a booklet printed by Glasgow Chamber of Commerce detailing local holidays. Write to them at 30 George Square, Glasgow, G2 1EQ.

• *Health Care* Most travel agents offer health insurance along with your other travel arrangements, and this is recommended. If you need to attend a doctor in Scotland, many nationals of EEC countries as well as others are treated free of charge under the NHS scheme. Residents of countries such as the USA and Canada and several others, are treated as private patients and a consultation with a GP will cost around £30. In emergencies patients will be seen as soon as possible or sent to a hospital with an Accident & Emergency Unit.

• *Maps and Brochures* Maps are always a good investment and the best for general touring purposes is the Scottish Touring Map published by the Scottish Tourist Board. It includes most of the important attractions and facilities in each area and is accompanied by a useful little book, *1001 Things to See in Scotland*. Every Tourist Information Office carries copious amounts of brochures and flyers on attractions in their own and other areas, mostly free of charge.

• *What's On Guides* are useful indicators of events as well as places of interest in each town or region and can be obtained in the local Tourist Information Office. Occasionally, free maps are available and come with adverts for tourist attractions, accommodation and local restaurants. Some newspapers produce a yearly publication such as *Welcome to the Highlands and Islands* published by the Highland News Group, available free at Tourist Information Offices throughout the North.

• *Newspapers* For a broad view of what is going on in Scotland as well as the rest of the world, the *Glasgow Herald* or the *Scotsman* newspapers are the best buy. Local newspapers are useful for local information or events.

If you are looking to take home a kilt or a set of bagpipes, it might be worth looking in the classified sections of local papers for a second-hand version, as these items are quite expensive new.

Foreign papers and magazines can be purchased in some shops in Edinburgh or the larger chain stores such as Menzies or WH Smith. *The European*, *Time* and *Newsweek* are quite widely available as are some American golf magazines.

There are magazines such as *Scottish Field* or the *Scots Magazine* that visitors might find interesting, although the features are written mainly for those who know the country well or for expatriate Scots.

• *Shopping and Souvenirs* Scotland's best buys are probably woollens, smoked salmon and whisky although the latter may be cheaper in your home country as taxes make spirits quite expensive in Scotland. Having said that, the choice of malts is greatest here, so it is probably worth purchasing some of the less exported brands. Some clothes items can be of a superior quality.

VAT (Value Added Tax currently at 17.5%) is added to most purchases with the exception of food and books but this can be claimed back on goods taken out of the country by non-nationals. Not all shops participate in this 'Retail Export Scheme' so, before purchasing, look for a sign or enquire.

• *Shop Opening Hours* Opening hours for shops and most relevant facilities are generally 9am to 5pm, as is the case with offices and other places of employment. Banks have outside cash-points that can be used at all hours. Convenience stores open from 8am until late.

Pubs typically are open 11am to midnight. Businesses in the north-west and especially the Western Isles (including filling stations and stores) are usually closed on Sundays.

• *Telephones* Public phones take coins (usually 10p, 20p, 50p £1) or cards which you can purchase from newsagents and kiosks and hotel lobbies. All country and area codes are found in the front part, (section 3), of British Telecom's telephone directory or by dialling 153.

• *Emergency phone number*
To summon the police, ambulance or fire brigade, telephone 999 on any phone. There is no charge. It must only be used in genuine emergencies.

• *Useful Operator numbers*:
100 for the UK Operator
155 for the International Operator
192 for UK Directory Enquiries
153 for International Directory Enquiries

• *Call charges* The cheaper rate for making international calls is 8pm to 8am through the week and all day Saturday and Sunday. To instigate a call routed through your own telephone credit card company dial 155, British Telecom's international operator and they will connect you.

International reverse charge calls (Collect) are also available through 155.

Chapter 1

Southeast Scotland

Between the Firth of Forth and the English border, the area comprising Edinburgh, the Lothians and the Scottish Borders holds many attractions for the golfing visitor. Not only is the region rich in courses of great character and scenic beauty, but it is also home to the Scottish capital, Edinburgh.

'Auld Reekie'

Highly cultured and cosmopolitan, Edinburgh is undoubtedly one of Europe's most exciting cities. Along with its mighty castle, charming cobblestoned lanes and cosy coffee-shops there is a real contemporary buzz. From Princes Street to the Mound and down the Royal Mile, travellers from the world's four corners congregate to enjoy the capital's many cultural delights, culminating in the Edinburgh International Festival which includes jazz, film, fringe (comedy and arts) festivals and the Military Tattoo

Left: Edinburgh Castle towers commandingly over Princes Street Gardens. Bass Rock (above) is a landmark along East Lothian's golfing shoreline.

complete with kilts and bagpipes in the atmospheric setting of Edinburgh Castle Esplanade.

Dubbed 'Auld Reekie' because of the smell and smog produced there in its industrial heyday, Edinburgh today is a bright and breezy city with numerous courses for the visiting golfer within the city limits offering spectacular views over its Georgian and earlier architecture and the Firth of Forth shoreline beyond.

For a capital city the golfing choice is hard to beat. There are seven council-run courses within the city boundaries, each representing extraordinary value for money and deserving of a round no matter what your handicap. There are a further 20 clubs in and around the city. Duddingston, just to name one, lies below Arthur's Seat, in the east of the city, and is a superb parkland course. Edinburgh is also the perfect base to sample Scotland's most famous and historic courses. The premier golfing area of East Lothian is only an hour's drive away.

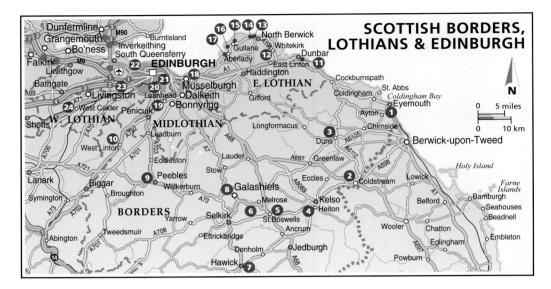

East Lothian

The coastal strip and hinterland immediately east of Edinburgh boasts world–famous courses including Muirfield, Gullane, North Berwick and Dunbar. A regular train service takes only half an hour from Edinburgh to this stretch of Scotland overlooking the Firth of Forth to the Kingdom of Fife. Its proximity to Edinburgh makes East Lothian one of Scotland's most popular golfing venues so visits should therefore be planned well in advance, especially if you wish to play at Muirfield where bookings may need to be made at least a year before your visit. East Lothian's finest courses are links but there are several newer courses which have taken advantage of the rolling hinterland overlooking the coast.

When relaxing away from golf, you can take in historic castle ruins such as at Dunbar, Dirleton and Tantallon. These ancient structures were once strategic in the long wars between the Scots and English. Other outdoor leisure pursuits include birdwatching, beachcombing and fishing.

Accommodation in East Lothian is geared for golfers, with many hotels and

A cluster of golf courses lie within Edinburgh, and to the east in East Lothian, including the championship course at Muirfield, and to the south in the Scottish Borders.

guesthouses just a short distance from the clubhouses. The main towns of Dunbar, North Berwick and Gullane are full of fine guesthouses and hotels but there is also plenty of quality accommodation to be found in the hinterland (*see pages 40-41*).

The Scottish Borders

The rolling, hilly terrain was originally more suitable for sheep farming than golf. In fact golf has not traditionally been the Borders' main sport – fishing and rugby maintain equal local favour. At the beginning of the 20th century several courses were built, often on or near hillsides, and it is only recently that there have been extensions to 18 holes or complete new courses built. The golfing stock is now at an excellent level.

In spite of its turbulent history during the wars between Scotland and England, the Scottish Borders is now an area that combines the quiet pleasures of country life with a wide array of golfing opportunities. Championship-level venues are restricted to the magnificent new Roxburghe course near Kelso. The course is owned by the Duke of Roxburghe who also owns nearby Roxburghe Hotel, one of the finest country house hotels in Scotland which caters for many other sports such as trout and salmon fishing, clay pigeon shooting and off-road driving. However, there are several other 18-hole courses of good standard in the Borders as well as a host of exceptional 9-hole courses. These may seem short but all are a pleasure to play twice round.

The Borders' scenery is exceptional with rolling moorland cut through by delightful valleys containing some of Scotland's finest salmon rivers such as the Teviot and the Tweed. It is also the centre of the Scottish woollen industry and bargains can be purchased at the mill shops which abound in the area, particularly in the towns of Hawick, Jedburgh and Selkirk.

Just a few miles from Muirfield, The Glen offers all year round golf with every hole giving a different perspective of the Firth of Forth and the dominating Bass Rock, one of the world's largest bird sanctuaries. This is the par-3 13th Sea Hole.

DISCOUNT PASS

The Lothians & Edinburgh Golf Pass offers a discount on every round on 20 courses in the area. Buy this pass from any Edinburgh and Lothians Tourist Board information centre, or, to purchase a pass in advance, telephone 0131 4733838 or via the Internet on *www. edinburgh.org/golf*

The Scottish Borders *Freedom of the Fairways Passport* offers 3- or 5-day packages at greatly reduced prices, from any tourist information centre in the Borders or on the Internet at *www.scot-borders.co.uk*. By telephone contact 0870 6070250 or write to Scottish Borders Tourist Board Scottish Admail-2193, Jedburgh, Scottish Borders, D8 6ZY.

1 Eyemouth

Eyemouth Golf Club, Gunsgreen House, Eyemouth,
Scottish Borders TD14 5SF
TEL: *01890 750551*
LOCATION: *6 miles/10km north of Berwick-on-Tweed, off*
the A1
COURSE: *18 holes, 6472yd/5915m, par 72, SSS 71*
FEES: *£*
FACILITIES: *Changing rooms and showers, full catering,*
bar, pro shop, teaching pro, trolley hire
VISITORS: *Welcome everyday though pre-booking is advised*

The building of a super-harbour at
Eyemouth took away 8 of the original 9
holes at Eyemouth Golf Club but gave the
opportunity to create a brand new, 18-hole
layout. The new course stretches south from
the town along the rocky North Sea coast.
From the splendid new clubhouse you can
watch lobster boats and diving vessels ply their
trade – Eyemouth is a centre for off-shore
diving.

The 1st and 2nd holes are mild openers,
with the 3rd, a good par 3 over a small pond,
giving an excellent view to the harbour. From
the tee, the 13th seems a daunting par 5, with
a pond in front of the green, but it plays more
comfortably than it appears. The toughest
challenge is the long par-4 15th, Bain's
Brawest. In a wind it needs two spectacular
blows to get near the green with the added
danger of both a burn and a ditch coming
into play. Indeed, winds can severely hamper
progress on any of the doglegs of this course.

2 The Hirsel

The Hirsel Golf Club, Kelso Road, Coldstream, Scottish
Borders TD12 4NJ
TEL: *01890 882678* **FAX:** *01890 882233*
LOCATION: *Off the A697 at the west end of Coldstream*
COURSE: *18 holes, 6111yd/5585m, par 70, SSS 70*
GREEN FEES: *££*
FACILITIES: *Changing rooms and showers, full catering,*
bar, pro shop, teaching pro, club hire, buggy hire, trolley hire
VISITORS: *Welcome everyday though pre-booking is advised*

Drive through the sandstone gates of the
Hirsel estate and you are impressed by
the grandeur. Stepping on to the course that
has been created within the estate's wide
boundaries is no less inspiring. This fine

parkland course is in part still relatively new,
but you would not notice this as most of the
holes blend so well into the mature woodland
of the estate.

The 1st hole doglegs slightly into a tree-
backed hollow where the River Leet can be
seen. The river meanders along much of the
course although it presents little danger unless
you are seriously wayward off the 2nd tee.
The 6th is the most difficult par 4 on the
front 9 while the 7th presents an excellent par
3 with a long carry over the river to the
green. The back 9, more open and longer,
creates an impression of increasing challenge
– the mark of good course design – with the
12th to 17th all daunting golf holes.

3 Duns

Duns Golf Club, Hardens Road, Duns, Berwickshire
TD11 3NR
TEL: *01361 882194*
LOCATION: *1 mile/3km west of Duns off A6105 signposted*
COURSE: *18 holes, 6209yd/5675m, par 70, SSS 70*
GREEN FEES : *££*
FACILITIES: *Basic changing facilities, full catering, bar, club*
hire by arrangement, trolley hire
VISITORS: *Welcome everyday although there are restrictions*
after 4pm Monday, Tuesday and Wednesday

Duns offers a newly extended upland
course with views south to the Cheviot
Hills and north to the Lammermuirs. The
original course offered a few good holes but
now, with the new section occupying a
pleasant wooded rise to the west, the entire
layout has achieved a good balance.

The original Duns golf course was known
for the quality of its compact greens and this is
still the case throughout, although the new
greens are still a little firm. Challenge comes
on the new 9 with length and accuracy being
frequently tested. The 2nd hole, Cheviots, is
398yd/364m from the back tee; it is probably
the best on the course. It plays into the
woods, a dogleg requiring a decent drive for
position, then a good strike over a burn to the
raised green. The wooded 6th is a long par 5
climbing to the highest point on the course at
the Gully. Back at the clubhouse, an
extension has added an enjoyable dining area
catering for visitors and larger parties.

The Roxburghe

The Roxburghe Golf Club, Heiton, Near Kelso, Scottish Borders TD5 8JZ
TEL: *01573 450333* **FAX:** *01573 450611*
LOCATION: *From Kelso, A698 for 2 miles/3km to village of Heiton. Signposted from road*
COURSE: *18 holes, 7111yd/6500m, par 72, SSS 74*
GREEN FEES: *££££*
FACILITIES: *Changing rooms and showers, full catering, bar, pro shop, teaching pro, club hire, buggy hire, trolley hire*
VISITORS: *Welcome everyday though pre-booking is advised*

The completion in 1997 of the Roxburghe course at last provided a top grade championship course in the Borders for serious golfers to test their metal. From the many elevated tees, visitors can admire the exquisite scenery as the River Teviot ambles by on its way to join the Tweed (both offering some of Scotland's finest and most expensive salmon fishing beats).

The raised tees also expose golfers to the elements, and, although the area is protected by the hills and fine groves of deciduous woodland, there is often a breeze following the river to affect many holes. The course is crafted to perfection by designer Dave Thomas with well-defined cross-cut fairways. The putting surfaces are also artfully moulded and sometimes two-tiered, with notable slopes but often imperceptible borrows that carry the ball away.

For long drivers, the course can yield results, but loose tee shots will be punished in the snarling rough. The par 4s may not be over-long, but the many deep greenside bunkers require a good set-up position and precise approach.

The short and long game come into play on the 14th. From the elevated tee, a steep bank, thick with the worst kind of grass, threatens from the right while the river and a thin strip of graded rough guard the left. There is often a tail wind here to assist the drive and fairway shot, but few will be confident enough to look for a birdie. To avoid the two wide bunkers at the entrance to the green it is much wiser to play a safe pitch on to the putting area.

Roxburghe's premier hole, the par-5 14th, runs parallel to the River Teviot and is backed by the magnificent Roxburghe Viaduct, which once carried the railway from St Boswells to Kelso (and on to Edinburgh).

5 St Boswells

St Boswells Golf Club, Braeheads, St Boswells, Scottish Borders TD6 0DE
TEL: *01835 823527*
LOCATION: *Turn off A68 at St. Boswells Green, ¼ mile/ 0.5km and signposted*
COURSE: *9 holes, 5274yd/4820m, par 66, SSS 66*
GREEN FEES: *£*
FACILITIES: *Changing rooms and showers, full catering if booked in advance, bar, trolley hire*
VISITORS: *Welcome everyday up to 4pm although pre-booking is advised*

There are many 9-hole courses in the Borders, laid out attractively and making good use out of limited land and ideal for holiday golf. Of these, the course at St Boswells is probably the most pleasing. It is a flat course – and in the Scottish Borders flat is something of a novelty – where each hole presents a challenge.

The view from the 2nd tee looking down to the River Tweed with the course in between is one of the finest sights in the area. The nearby ruins of Dryburgh Abbey, burial ground of Sir Walter Scott, can be seen above the trees on the opposite bank of the river with the Eildon Hills forming a backdrop. The river runs parallel to holes 4, 5 and 6, and it has spilled on to the course in the past but, like a links course, the built-up alluvium soil drains extremely quickly.

6 Melrose

Melrose Golf Club, Dingleton Road, Melrose, Scottish Borders TD6 9HS
TEL: *01896 822855*
LOCATION: *Off the A68 to the south of Melrose village square following Dingleton Road*
COURSE: *9 holes, 5562yd/5084m, par 70, SSS 68*
GREEN FEES: *£*
FACILITIES: *Changing rooms and showers, full catering if booked in advance, bar*
VISITORS: *Welcome weekdays, and Saturdays after 5pm although pre-booking is advised*

From the north slopes of the Eildon Hills, scenery much favoured by Sir Walter Scott, this 9-hole course overlooks the delightful Borders village of Melrose.

From the relatively new clubhouse the course climbs for the first four holes but is not over strenuous and offers magnificent views to the north. The 4th, a short par 4 uphill to a ledge of a green, calls for accuracy with short irons. The 5th booms out and down to the valley floor again with the green being almost driveable especially in a following wind.

The final hole is most deceptive because there is a great temptation to go for the green which stands downhill, but with bunkers on either side, the road out-of-bounds on the right, and a prevailing crosswind many a good score has been lost by such a lure.

The view from the 2nd tee at St Boswells: eight of its nine holes are set on the flat plain or haugh of the River Tweed.

Hawick

Hawick (Vertish Hill) Golf Club, Vertish Hill, Hawick, Scottish Borders TD9 0NY

TEL: *01450 372293*

LOCATION: *Above the town of Hawick on A7, 40 miles/ 64km from Carlisle or south on A7 from Edinburgh for 50 miles/80km*

COURSE: *18 holes, 5933yd/5423m, par 68 SSS 69*

GREEN FEES: *££*

FACILITIES: *Changing rooms and showers, full catering, bar, trolley hire*

VISITORS: *Welcome weekdays anytime; after 3pm on Saturday, after 10.30am on Sunday; pre-booking is advised*

In 1993, Nick Faldo and Colin Montgomerie played a Medal exhibition match on this testing, upland course and both were generous in their praise. Nick Faldo was no stranger as he had previously played with Tony Jacklin in 1989 and shot a 4-under-par 64, the pro course record to this day.

The opening three holes climb and are fairly tight with a road to the right signifying out-of-bounds and it is a difficult start for anybody's game. The course then opens out to play over Vertish Hill with magnificent views of the surrounding hillsides and the town of Hawick itself which is best seen from the 15th green, a par 4 of 437yd/399m called The Gallery. On a windy day this hole can prove exceptionally testing.

Many of the hill-top holes are equally trying because the thick copses of trees do not offer protection from the wind's effects once the ball is lofted. Finally, the par-3 18th travels rapidly downhill to a Troon-style 'Postage Stamp' green with the road behind as out-of-bounds. The gully in front of the green is also reminiscent of the Valley of Sin on St Andrews Old Course.

The 2nd hole (Thorntree) at Hawick is a 350yd/320m par 4 presenting a tight target with out-of-bounds on the right, while the upgraded mock-Tudor clubhouse (inset) offers splendid views across to Vertish Hill.

8 Torwoodlee

Torwoodlee Golf Club, Edinburgh Road, Galashiels, Scottish Borders TD1 2NE
TEL: 01896 752260
LOCATION: 1¼ miles/3km north-west off Galashiels on the A7
COURSE: 18 holes, 6200yd/5667m, par 70, SSS 69
GREEN FEES: ££
FACILITIES: Changing rooms and showers in gents only, full catering, bar, buggy hire, trolley hire, club hire
VISITORS: Welcome weekdays though telephone ahead for times, and Saturdays between 10.15am to 12.15pm and 3 to 4pm. Sundays are the same as weekdays

Torwoodlee, just outside Galashiels, once existed as a sleepy, tree-gladed 9-hole course where Sunday golfers enjoyed lush, parkland fairways. An abundance of trees still exists but they are now spiced with an additional layout making up 18 holes and a course with two very different aspects.

The opening three holes of the new course play over original land while the 4th opens out onto airy Border hillsides. It is a steady progression up to the 5th green and an inspiring viewpoint before zig-zagging back to the valley floor. Having to play uphill and hit long fairway shots makes the 5th a 'double whammy'.

There is a double green joining the 7th and 13th, unusual for this part of the world, while the par-4 11th is a difficult dogleg that could upset some scores. Then it is back into the trees to a fine finish alongside the River Gala. After a round at this friendly club you could try the excellent catering at the new clubhouse bar, lounge or restaurant from bar snacks to 3-course dinners.

9 Peebles

Peebles Golf Club, Kirkland Street, Peebles, Scottish Borders EH45 8EU
TEL: 01721 720197 **FAX:** 01721 720197
LOCATION: On the west side of Peebles town centre just off A72 and well signposted from both main approach roads
COURSE: 18 holes, 6160yd/5630m, par 70, SSS 70
GREEN FEES: £
FACILITIES: Changing rooms and showers, full catering, bar, buggy hire, trolley hire, club hire, pro tuition, pro shop
VISITORS: Welcome weekdays and Sunday, but not Saturdays. It is advisable to make your booking in advance

Peebles is one of the better favoured of Scottish Border courses. From the 1st tee the uphill prospect may seem a little daunting but the gradient for the first four holes is mild and hardly taxing (though the same cannot be said for the calibre of the golf holes). Moreover, the views over this magnificent, historic Border town and its surrounds, including the River Tweed, are reward enough. Once the 5th green has been reached, there are no more noticeable climbs.

The outstanding set of holes comes at the finish from the 14th to 18th. The par-3 16th is a memorable hole with out-of-bounds left and rear of the green. It also has a delightful burn crossed by a centenary bridge not unlike St Andrews's Swilcan Bridge at the 17th. The remaining holes offer a testing finish.

Peebles is renowned for its quality greens but it is reaching them in par that presents the challenge. It is not a long course but the combination of rising fairways, elevated greens and a regular crosswind will often conspire to make a well-conceived shot fall short.

The attractive backdrop of Peebles town and the rolling Border hills from the not so appealing bunker at the 2nd.

10 *West Linton*

West Linton Golf Club, West Linton, Scottish Borders EH46 7HN
TEL: *01968 660256* **FAX:** *01968 660256*
LOCATION: *17 miles/27km south west of Edinburgh on A702 and signposted west from village of West Linton*
COURSE: *18 holes, 6132yd/5605m, par 69, SSS 70*
GREEN FEES: *££*
FACILITIES: *Changing rooms and showers, full catering in summer, bar, trolley hire, pro tuition, pro shop*
VISITORS: *Welcome everyday but advance booking advisable*

Etched out of the base of the Pentland Hill, this course huddles on a plateau over 1000ft/330m above sea level, yet it remains fairly level. Moreover, despite its wild setting on natural moorland, it is kept in immaculate condition by the greenkeepers. Therefore golfers tend to find West Linton a fairer test than they might have imagined.

There are two outstanding holes. The 14th, a 376yd/345m par 4 crosses a 200yd/183m wide chasm from the medal tee, but this is generally manageable unless the wind is coming out of the Mendick Valley to the south-west. Putting is also problematic as the green slopes from back to front making 3-putts common. The 18th is one of the best par-3 finishes with out-of-bounds to the right, a small burn to the left and a large drop at the front that forces a carry to the green.

11 *Dunbar*

Dunbar Golf Club, East Links, Dunbar, East Lothian EH42 1LT
TEL: *01368 862317* **FAX:** *01368 865202*
LOCATION: *On the coast, ½ mile/¾km east and signposted from Dunbar town centre*
COURSE: *18 holes, 6404yd/5853m, par 71, SSS 71*
GREEN FEES: *££*
FACILITIES: *Changing rooms and showers, full catering, bar, trolley hire, teaching pro, pro shop*
VISITORS: *Welcome throughout the week but not before 9.30am nor between 12 to 2pm or all day Thursday. This is a very popular course so book well in advance*

Dunbar nestles in a predominantly flat strip of seaside turf. It is in wonderful condition and makes a worthy qualifying venue when the Open is held at nearby Muirfield. Wind is the major factor golfers

Bunkers are a key element in Dunbar's armoury, a variety of configurations placed to wreak the most damage. These are on the 2nd and 3rd holes.

have to contend with – the course being exposed to every breeze that blows along the Firth of Forth or in off the North Sea.

The 1st, 2nd, 3rd and 18th holes travel inland but are just as exposed to the prevailing elements. The seaside 4th to 17th holes give the course its character with some being laid out hard by the beach. The best challenge on the course is the 12th, a difficult par 4 of 460yd/420m and usually influenced by a crosswind. In moderate conditions, two good shots are required to reach the green in front of the beach. The 16th is an outstanding par 3 of only 166yd/152m but depending on the wind the choice of club can vary in the extreme. The beach lies to the right hand side with the wind usually blowing against while a wall lies to the rear of the green similar to the St Andrews Road Hole.

The beach is always in play at Dunbar and there are many holes, especially on the back 9, that will lure wayward golf shots on to the sand. More sand awaits on the bunkers surrounding the large greens, many of which have subtle swells that offer further challenges when putting from a distance.

The 14th at North Berwick West Links with its low-lying green next to the beach and the Bass Rock in the distance.

12 Whitekirk

Whitekirk Golf Club, Whitekirk, North Berwick, East Lothian EH39 5PR
TEL: *01620 870300* **FAX:** *01620 870330*
EMAIL: *golf@whitekirk.u-net.com*
LOCATION: *4 miles/6km south-east of North Berwick on the A198*
COURSE: *18 holes, 6526yd/5965m, par 72, SSS 72*
GREEN FEES: *££*
FACILITIES: *Changing rooms and showers, full catering, bar, buggy hire, trolley hire, club hire*
VISITORS: *Welcome throughout the week although on weekends not before 9am. Telephone to book in advance*

Though only a few miles from the sea, Whitekirk Golf Club (1995) offers golfers a rugged, heathland test. There is a links feel too, with several humps and bumps to encounter as well as magnificent views to the Bass Rock and the Forth Estuary.

The high, rocky outcrops and deep, grassy hollows of the course call for a target approach with emphasis placed on position off the tee to allow an accurate approach to the greens which can be small and fairly fast. The long par-4 5th, Cameron's Test (named after Cameron Sinclair, the course designer), is the best example. Many have dubbed it Cameron's Nest as the hole perches on the side of a steep rise and is surrounded by gorse. The tee shot must first carry 200yd/183m to be safe on the fairway (avoiding a cluster of bunkers) for a second shot to cross a deep canyon in front of the green. The par-4 18th provides downhill drama through a fertile valley between rocky outcrops.

13 North Berwick West

North Berwick Golf Club, New Clubhouse, Beach Road, North Berwick EH39 4BB
TEL: *01620 892135* **FAX:** *01620 893274*
EMAIL: *nbgc_sec@compuserve.com*
LOCATION: *At the centre of town and towards the foreshore*
COURSE: *8 holes, 6420yd/5868m, par 71, SSS 71*
GREEN FEES: *£££*
FACILITIES: *Changing rooms and showers, full catering, bar, trolley hire. club hire*
VISITORS: *Welcome 10am to 4pm weekdays and after 10.20am Saturday and Sunday. This is a very popular course so book well in advance*

For many golfers, this is the most esteemed course in all of East Lothian. Perhaps they have not had the honour of playing at Muirfield (sometimes not an easy proposition) but for the thousands of low-handicapped golfers who find their way to this attractive part of Scotland, the West Links at North Berwick usually wins their hearts. Perhaps it is the views across the Firth to Fife, the near proximity of Fidra or Craigleith, or the many tiny skerries (islands) that lie just off the coast, or the fine stretch of beach so close to the links. Or the fact that it starts and finishes so close to town.

Like so many of Scotland's premier courses, the West Links has its idiosyncrasies: blind shots into a green and a wall or two crossing holes at rather awkward spots. But such course 'signatures', however unusual, were as nature, and the first course architects, designed them. They have since been copied or have inspired holes throughout the world.

The 1st hole at North Berwick West is an excellent example of nature and designer working together: the green is raised and not far off, but putting the drive on the beach is all too easily managed. The angle of flight is often crossed by a stiff westerly forcing a second shot to be taken from amongst seaweed and sand. This threat exists even more so at the 2nd hole, appropriately called Sea.

There are many fine holes to savour on the course but the most delightful is the run from 13th to 15th. The 13th, at 365yd/334m, is not particularly long but that does not make the hole, called Pit, easy. A dry stone wall runs along the edge of the green, but you have to play as close to the wall as possible, probably laying up, as the beach is close on the left side, and it is a very narrow green to hit on to.

The 14th is called Perfection and has two blind shots. Then comes the famous short hole 15th, Redan. This is the most flattered hole in the world if, as they say, imitation is the sincerest form of flattery. To stand under the twin, towering bunkers that defend the green and flag 190yd/174m away with a steady crosswind is as unnerving as you would wish golf to be.

14 *The Glen*

The Glen Golf Club, East Links, Tantallon Terrace, North Berwick EH39 4LE
TEL: *01620 895288* **FAX:** *01620 895447*
EMAIL: *secretary@glen.gowf.net*
LOCATION: *Off A198, 1 mile/1.6km east of town and signposted*
COURSE: *18 holes, 6043yd/5523m, par 69, SSS 69*
GREEN FEES: *££*
FACILITIES: *Changing rooms and showers, full catering, bar, trolley hire, pro shop*
VISITORS: *Welcome weekdays except between 12am to 1pm and 5pm to 6.30pm. Saturday and Sunday as available. This is a popular course so book well in advance*

On the eastern side of North Berwick, The Glen is both testing and beautiful – on a clear day you can see Tantallon Castle from the course's eastern extremity. Originally a 9-hole course designed by Ben Sayers and James Braid, it has developed into an engaging mix of inland turf and traditional links. The first and last holes stand out as both negotiate the escarpment that much of the course is laid out over. The par-4 5th is a most deceptive hole having a large, concealed drop in front of the green. The short 13th has claims to be one of Scotland's finest holes: it plays down to sea level and may require a pitching wedge one day and a 3-iron the next.

Rewarding views of North Berwick and its long cambered beach and Bass Rock greet players on the 1st green at The Glen.

15 The Honourable Company of Edinburgh Golfers (Muirfield)

Muirfield, Duncur Road, Muirfield, Gullane EH31 2EG
TEL: *01620 842123* **FAX:** *01620 842977*
EMAIL: *hceg@btinternet*
LOCATION: *On A198, on the east side of the village of Gullane with entrance adjacent to Greywalls Hotel*
STATISTICS: *18 holes, 6970yd/6370m, par 71, SSS 73*
GREEN FEES: *£££££+*
FACILITIES: *Changing rooms and showers, full catering, bar, trolley hire*
VISITORS: *Tuesday and Thursday morning only; contact well in advance and have handicap certificate (18 for men and 24 for ladies) as well as a letter of introduction. Bookings are currently being taken for about a year in advance*

Muirfield is home to The Honourable Company of Scottish Golfers – perhaps Britain's most exclusive golf club – yet it is possible for visiting golfers to play what is regarded as the fairest links test on the Open championship rota.

A fine balance of testing design and incredible condition has brought 14 Open championships to Muirfield with some of the game's greatest heroes battling each other and the course. Braid, Vardon, Hagen and Cotton all took on the course to win and

THE HONOURABLE COMPANY OF EDINBURGH GOLFERS, MUIRFIELD							
HOLE	YD	M	PAR	HOLE	YD	M	PAR
1	447	408	4	10	475	434	4
2	351	321	4	11	385	352	4
3	379	346	4	12	381	348	4
4	180	164	3	13	159	145	3
5	559	511	5	14	449	410	4
6	469	429	4	15	417	381	4
7	185	169	3	16	188	172	3
8	444	406	4	17	550	503	5
9	504	461	5	18	448	410	4
OUT	3518	3215	36	IN	3452	3155	35

6970 YD • 6370 M • PAR 71

Nicklaus, Player, Trevino, Watson and Faldo followed in later years. All have the greatest respect for the place. 'The course is built to the right proportions,' said Nick Faldo, Open winner here in 1987 and 1992. 'When you have a long shot to the green, the green is generous enough. When you face a small shot, the target is small too.'

Compared to many of the true Scottish

Muirfield's impressive clubhouse viewed from the 18th, with the typical ensnaring bunkers that act as a magnet for wayward golfing shots.

links, Muirfield is more inland in character with fewer of the characteristic swells and dips. The course relies mainly upon its punishing rough and bunkers for defence. Jack Nicklaus describes these as 'the most fastidiously built bunkers I have ever seen, the high front walls faced with bricks of turf'. The skill therefore, perhaps more than at any other Open venue, is to keep the ball in play. This in turn can often require the use of a driving iron or 3-wood, picking your way towards the pin along the slender avenues between swathes of wafting grass and avoiding, at all costs, the bunkers.

The 10th is recognised as one of the outstanding holes in Scottish golf, a long par 4 playing away from the clubhouse towards the sea, and usually crossed by a west to east wind. A second shot, whilst still long, is also blind. But the real test is in the crafty green, whose subtle movements have fooled many good putters.

The closing two holes are generally regarded as the most demanding. It was here that Lee Trevino and Tony Jacklin struggled for supremacy in the climax of the 1972 Open. Trevino was 1-up at the 17th following a brace of birdies but then

proceeded to throw the game away with a series of wild shots. Meanwhile, Jacklin played straight up the middle. At the green, Trevino had rolled through and was looking at a possible 6 or 7, but his pitch back on was perfect and fell into the cup for par. Jacklin, on his turn, 3-putted. It was on the 18th that, arguably, Faldo's greatest moment came – his most emotional at least. In 1987, following two years of reassembling his swing, Faldo had trailed Paul Azinger through a chilling sea-mist. On the home stretch, at the 17th and 18th, Azinger's game came up on the rocks and Faldo, with his unadulterated application to basics, sailed out of the fog into the home port scoring, that round, an impeccable string of 18 pars.

Muirfield, in spite of a rather aloof reputation, is a course that is loved by many and scorned by few. There is nothing cryptic about the place – you get what you play and, should you get the chance, it is a test of the highest calibre. Its lack of device is, for many, a great part of its appeal, especially to foreign visitors who have not yet learned to relish the rock and roll of a true links.

There are many stories about golfers of the highest ranking being turned away from the gates but the moral is simple; book well in advance and meet the various visitor requirements, and you will have a round of golf to cherish.

16 *Gullane No 1*

Gullane Golf Club, West Links Road, Gullane, East
Lothian EH31 2BB
TEL: *01620 842255* **FAX:** *01620 842327*
EMAIL: *gullane@compuserve.com*
WWW: *113566.754@compuseve.com*
LOCATION: *At west end of village on A198. Both
clubhouses are on the main route/entrance to town*
STATISTICS: *18 holes, 6466yd/5910m, par 71, SSS 72*
GREEN FEES: *££££*
FACILITIES: *Visitors may use the more formal facilities of
the Members Clubhouse, or the new Visitors Clubhouse
across the main road offers changing rooms and showers, full
catering, bar, pro shop, trolley hire, buggy hire, teaching pros*
VISITORS: *Welcome on weekdays from 10.30am to 12pm
and 2.30pm to 4pm. At weekends 4pm tee times are made
available, 2 in the morning and 2 in the afternoon. Booking
in advance is advisable and handicap certificates required –
24 for men and 36 for ladies.*

One of seven courses around the East
Lothian town of Gullane, the No 1
course is the best test for big hitters, after
Muirfield, and those wanting the challenge of
an Open qualifying layout. Gullane Hill plays
a prominent role shaping the front inland
seven holes before the course meanders down
to the Firth shore.

At the 7th tee, the Muirfield coast is visible
to the east. But the most impressive view is
the expanse of golf holes below you and
toward Aberlady Bay, home to Gullane's
shorter but equally interesting No 2 and 3
courses.

Gullane No 1 is actually fairly manageable
despite its length. The 2nd, Windygate, is a

*The finishing hole to Gullane's No 1 Course, the
par-4 355yd/325m Kirklands.*

great par-4 driving hole. But the second shot
has to climb a valley into a long elongated
green and the wind tunnelling down the
valley can add considerable yardage. The
par-4 7th faces downhill and often straight
into the wind, requiring full-blooded strikes
to cover the distance. The green is well
bunkered and difficult to hit accurately from
the downhill fairway.

The start of the back 9 is one of the longest
consecutive runs in Scotland from the 10th to
the 12th. You will be doing well to record 5,
5, 5 here. There is some respite with the 13th,
a delightful par 3 raised at both tee and green.

Gullane No 2 has also been an Open
qualifying course, and may appeal more to the
average golfer. No 3 is a supreme short course,
well-bunkered with small, undulating greens.

17 *Longniddry*

Longniddry Golf Club, The Clubhouse Links Road,
Longniddry EH32 ONL
TEL: *01875 852141* **FAX:** *01875 853371*
EMAIL: *secretary@longniddrygc.sol.co.uk*
LOCATION: *From Edinburgh by A1, left for Longniddry,
A198 golf course signposted*
COURSE: *18 holes, 6220yd/5684m, par 68, SSS 70*
GREEN FEES: *£££*
FACILITIES: *Changing rooms and showers, full catering,
bar, buggy hire, trolley hire, club hire, teaching pro, pro shop*
VISITORS: *Welcome weekdays and limited at weekends.
Telephone well in advance to make a booking*

This course presents itself in two distinct
halves: the front 9 holes being tighter and
more enclosed than the back 9, which opens
out and is susceptible to the wind that prowls
the south shore of the Firth of Forth. A
course so close to the sea has obvious links
features, but there are also mature trees and
many newer plantings next to lush grass
which give the course a parkland feel too.

The 3rd hole is on the par 4 limit at
460yd/420m and one of the more stretching
tests especially into the noticeable westerly
wind. The course has many tricky par 4s with
fairly wide fairways, but desperately tough
rough, and a host of bunkers for the unwary.
The dogleg 5th has a two-tier green and was
highly rated by golf anchorman Peter Alliss.

18 *Musselburgh Old*

Musselburgh Old Course, 10 Balcarres Road, Musselburgh
East Lothian EH21 7SD
TEL: *0131 665 6981*
EMAIL: *mocgc@breathmail.net*
LOCATION: *7 miles / 11km E of Edinburgh on the A1 on the
east side of Musselburgh*
COURSE: *9 holes, 5380yd / 4917m, par 66, SSS 67*
GREEN FEES: £
FACILITIES: *Changing rooms, snacks, refreshments*
VISITORS: *Welcome everyday to play the 9-hole course.
Clubhouse has restricted viewing times, telephone to check*

One course you should visit, if not to play
then just to come and pay homage to, is
Musselburgh Links, the world's oldest golf
course. Golf has been played here since at least
the 16th century with visits from Mary Queen
of Scots and James VI as well as Willie Park Jr
and Tom Morris. The world's first women's
golf competition (between local fishwives) also
took place here.

This council-run course was long neglected
while attention was paid to the surrounding
racetrack. Under new East Lothian Council
management, this has now all changed.

The course, which was never easy, is well
maintained while the pavilion-style Starter's
Box has been refurbished and includes a
displayed history of the course. You can even
hire a reproduction set of hickory clubs for a
taste of how the game used to be played. At
the 4th, Mrs Forman's Public House, they
used to serve golfers a warming draught
through a hole in the wall, now sadly sealed
up. There are two other fine courses a short
drive from the Old links: Royal Musselburgh
and Musselburgh Golf Club.

*The 4th green on the world's oldest golf course, where
(inset) hickory-shafted clubs can be hired.*

19 Kings Acre

Kings Acre Golf Course, Lasswade, Midlothian EH18 1AU
TEL: *0131 663 3456* **FAX:** *0131 663 7076*
LOCATION: *Off Edinburgh City by-pass A720 and exit Lasswade Junction ¼ mile/1km; follow brown tourist road signs*
COURSE: *18 holes, 5935yd/5425m, par 70, SSS 68*
GREEN FEES: *£*
FACILITIES: *Changing rooms and showers, full catering, bar, buggy hire, trolley hire, club hire, teaching pro, pro shop, golf academy*
VISITORS: *Visitors welcome all week with no restrictions. Please book in advance*

A new (1997) 18-hole facility, grandly designated Kings Acre Golf Course, lies south of Edinburgh towards the village of Lasswade. The lush parkland course is maintained to the highest standards.

The first 12 holes are generously proportioned covering rolling pastureland artistically carved into a flowing and challenging layout. The introduction of semi-mature trees has noticeably tightened this aspect of the course. The 3rd, a long-haul par 5, is a superb hole with excellent shaping to its dogleg and six bunkers surrounding the green.

Moving into the more mature trees on the back half, the 15th is a difficult dogleg playing through a gap in the trees and down to the River Esk valley. Additional trees have made it nearly impossible to cut the corner here.

The 18th is an excellent finish with two ponds coming into play. Aptly named The Last Splash, a carry of 220yd/201m is required from the back tees over the first pond with out-of-bounds down the right hand side. The second pond awaits at the left of the green. The restored sandstone clubhouse looks over this pond and has a restaurant and bar open to visitors and non-golfers. Kings Acre also offers a 4-hole, par-3 course and an excellent Golf Academy with well arranged teaching areas.

20 Braid Hills No 1

Braid Hills No 1, 22 Braid Hills Approach, Morningside, Edinburgh EH10 6JY
TEL: *0131 447 6666*
LOCATION: *From Edinburgh city centre follow A702 – Comiston Road to Braid Hills on south side of city*
COURSE: *18 holes, 5692yd/5202m, par 70, SSS 68*
GREEN FEES: *£*
FACILITIES: *Changing rooms, trolley hire, club hire*
VISITORS: *Welcome everyday; telephone ahead to book*

Almost in the heart of Edinburgh, this municipal course is a true gem of Scottish golf. It has no connection with James Braid, the famous course architect, but it does have

Edinburgh Castle towers over 'Auld Reekie' – one of the superb views from Braid Hills No 1.

views over Edinburgh that are simply stunning. Bring your camera and take a few snapshots of Edinburgh Castle from one of the many vantage points before getting back to this excellent golfing challenge at a very reasonable price.

Diversity is the name of the game here and the course presents a wide variety of playing situations. Gorse, one side or the other of every fairway, and hills and dales continually threaten safe passage, so knowing where to place the ball is critical. There are two excellent par 3s at the 2nd and 13th, while the 10th and 11th are a couple of straight par 5s, but unexpectedly hard work especially into a wind. The best hole is undoubtedly the par-4 14th that drives from an elevated tee with rocks on the right and oceans of gorse to the left, before doglegging into a flat green with further punishment behind it.

Braid Hills No 2, a council course, is a shorter and tighter course with, in many instances, even better greens than No 1.

21 Duddingston

Duddingston Golf Club, Duddingston Road West, Edinburgh, Lothian EH15 3QD
TEL: *0131 661 4301* FAX: *0131 661 4301*
LOCATION: *In southeast Edinburgh – adjacent to A1 – Willowbrae Road, turn right at Duddingston crossroads then 1 mile/1.6km on Duddingston Road West*
COURSE: *18 holes, 6420yd/5868m, par 71, SSS 71*
GREEN FEES: *£££*
FACILITIES: *Changing rooms and showers, full catering and bar, buggy hire, trolley hire, teaching pro and pro shop, practice area*
VISITORS: *Welcome everyday after 1.30pm*

Edinburgh appears to be supplied with better golf facilities than any other major European centre. The Scottish capital boasts an amazing array of courses, many council run, as well as some of the finest private courses, most of which warmly welcome visitors.

Only five minutes' drive from the city centre is one of the best parkland layouts available within the bustling metropolis. Duddingston is a slightly sterner test than its

EDINBURGH SITES

The capital city of Scotland is one of the most beautiful cities in Europe. It is often referred to as the Athens of the North due to its fine, Palladian architecture and general air of education and refinement.

The topography of the town is remarkable with several elevations breaking the city's slate-grey, chimney-potted expanse. Robert Louis Stevenson declared 'No situation could be more commanding for the head of a kingdom and none better chosen for better prospects'.

Edinburgh, like most of the Lothians, is set on the wide plain of the River Forth with volcanic left-overs such as Castle Rock and Arthur's Seat being the most prominent natural landmarks. Around these hills 'Auld Reekie', as it was known before the days of smokeless fuel, grew and prospered.

For exploration, the city is best divided into three sections, the Old Town, the New Town and the outskirts. Each section would need at least a day to best appreciate its character, so a minimum of three days should be allowed. The Old and New Town are essentially walking propositions with most places of consequence within easy distance of one another. Parking a car anywhere near the city centre is very difficult, especially during the Edinburgh Festival (August-September) but public transport is effective both into the centre and to outlying parts.

nearby neighbours such as Braid Hills, and it is a fine configuration playing through a lovely tree-lined park artfully intersected by a gathering burn.

There are several long par 4s, an excellent example being the 11th where a drive must thread through an extremely narrow gap in the trees. This is the toughest hole on the course. The 4th is a death or glory hole, changed from a par 5 to a par 4, and requiring full conviction to reach the green in regulation. On the back 9, the 14th is an excellent par 3 called High and Dry which is where you want to be as the hole is surrounded by water. The best of golfers would come off Duddingston well satisfied.

THE WORLD'S OLDEST GOLF CLUB?

Royal Burgess is said by many to be the oldest golf club in the world with a continuous history. The club that disputes this is Royal Blackheath in east London which claims to have originated in 1608. There is no doubt that golf was played there at that time but there are no formal records as such. The Royal Burgess Golfing Society originated in 1735 and came to its present course from nearby Bruntsfield Links in 1896.

22 The Royal Burgess Golfing Society of Edinburgh

The Royal Burgess Golfing Society of Edinburgh, 181 Whitehouse Road, Barnton, Edinburgh EH4 6BY
TEL: *0131 339 2075* **FAX:** *0131 339 3712*
LOCATION: *From Edinburgh follow the A90 Queensferry Road to Barnton Roundabout and turn right down Whitehouse Road. The club entrance is immediately on the right*
COURSE: *18 holes, 6494yd/5935m, par 71, SSS 71*
GREEN FEES: *££££*
FACILITIES: *Changing rooms and showers, full catering and bar, pro shop and teaching pro, trolley hire, club hire*
VISITORS: *Welcome weekdays; weekends on request*

On the northwestern edge of Edinburgh, just off the Queensferry Road, Royal Burgess is a lovely parkland trail winding through a variety of tall, mature woodland with lush fairways and exceptional greens, large and at the same time quite fast. The course is generally long and flat and therefore fairly forgiving on the fairways. Playing on these fairways you feel you are in the heart of the countryside, but in fact you are only minutes from Edinburgh's hustle and bustle.

The 4th hole is a long par 4, and has bunkers threatening on the left side of the fairway and out-of-bounds to the right. The elevated green presents a tight entrance with two large trees either side. All in all this a classic hole and one of the best in Scotland.

The 7th is a medium-to-long par-4 dogleg right that requires a carefully placed tee shot to avoid hazards on the right and yet be near the right side to approach the green on the next shot.

The back 9 is defined by an exceptional par 3 at the 13th to a well-bunkered green that cuts from front left to back right. This is a narrow target to hit over 190yd/174m. The 18th, an even longer par-3, has out-of-bounds only two paces off the large two-tiered green to the rear. This final hole presents quite a challenge even if you reach the green from your tee shot.

23 Marriott Dalmahoy

Marriott Dalmahoy Hotel & Country Club, Kirknewton, Edinburgh, EH27 8EB
TEL: *0131 333 1845* **FAX:** *0131 335 3203*
LOCATION: *On the A71 approximately 8 miles/13km west of Edinburgh*
COURSE: *18 holes, 6638yd/6067m, par 72, SSS 72*
GREEN FEES: *£££££*
FACILITIES: *Changing rooms and showers, swimming pool, jacuzzi, gym, full catering, bar, buggy hire, trolley hire, teaching pro, pro shop*
VISITORS: *Welcome throughout the week but phone in advance for competition days*

Set in a mature country estate, the East Course at Dalmahoy is without doubt one of Scotland's finest parkland courses. This is a championship course which has played host to many major events such as the European Ladies Solheim Cup in 1992 and the Scottish Seniors Open in 1998. It is also the home venue for the Scottish PGA Championships. Dalmahoy's East should be on every visitors golf list. James Braid designed the course in 1927 and it bears all his hallmarks.

The impressive Dalmahoy Golf and Country Club with 36 challenging holes over rolling parkland.

Off the tee there is usually plenty of room, but it is the famous Braid bunkering and large undulating greens that add the spice. The course can have added infringing rough in the summer months, and landing in this will force a dropped shot in most instances. The greens are generally big and very fast, calling for great concentration on every putt.

While the front 9 is testing, it is the back 9 that is longest and more difficult. A tremendous run of challenging golf begins at the 11th and runs though to the 17th. The par-3 15th is a little terror aptly named the Wee Wrecker. Deadly little pot bunkers surround the green and a visit to any one of them could spell disaster. To negotiate the notable par-4 16th you need your tactical wits about you. If you strike the drive successfully you may have the opportunity to go for the green otherwise lay up and avoid the penalties of landing in trouble.

The nearby West Course offers a shorter, but still tight and testing challenge, and has a great finish around the Gogar Burn.

Whichever course you play, guests can also sample the Leisure Club's sauna, steam room and swimming pool afterwards, as well as the two restaurants – one smart, one casual.

24 *Harburn*

Harburn Golf Club, Harburn, West Calder, West Lothian EH55 8AH
TEL: *01506 871256* **FAX:** *01506 871131*
LOCATION: *14 miles / 22km west of Edinburgh and 2 miles / 3km south of West Calder on B7008*
COURSE: *18 holes, 5921yd / 5412m, par 69, SSS 69*
GREEN FEES: *££*
FACILITIES: *Changing rooms and showers, full catering and bar, pro shop and teaching pro, driving range, short game practice, trolley hire, buggy hire, club hire*
VISITORS: *Welcome weekdays except Wednesday. Saturday and Sunday bookings as available. Please phone in advance*

The mainline Edinburgh-to-Glasgow railway passes the southern side of this moorland-parkland course, which was once considered for the site of a most prestigious golf resort. Instead, quite by chance, the Caledonian Railway found a spot further north in Perthshire and Gleneagles was created. But Harburn needn't be put out: the

The inland tree-lined course at Harburn in West Lothian, just a few miles from West Calder, is some 600ft / 183m above sea level. Wind can be a critical factor here.

course is splendid, with an abundance of beech, oak and pine trees along many of the holes. The course is not long but a prevailing wind from the west makes up for this.

Challenging tests start at the outset. The first four holes play into the wind, and an average player reaching the railway bridge (5th tee) in 20 is doing well. The 15th is a cunning par 3 of 127yd / 116m where club selection is critical.

The par-4 16th makes an excellent challenge: tall trees stand either side of the teeing ground and are quite intimidating at the address. The hole immediately presents a narrow fairway for average drives (though big hitters could clear this challenge). To the right of the fairway is also a line of trees and at the left a bank running down to the burn. If this hole is not played strategically double bogey scores and worse can easily happen.

REGIONAL DIRECTORY

Where to Stay

Edinburgh **Prestonfield House** (0131 668 3346) is a fabulous 17th-century country house set only 10 minutes away from Edinburgh's busy Princes Street within its own elegant estate. Prestonfield Golf Club can be seen outside the windows and guests enjoy reduced green fees there. Both food and accommodation are expensive but worth it. **The Balmoral Hotel**, 1 Princes Street (0131 556 2414), is right in the middle of town, opulent and costly with a great restaurant called the No 1 as well as the less formal Hadrian's Brasserie. Less pricey but very handy for the Old Town pubs is the **Crowne Plaza** on the High Street (0131 557 9797). In Rothesay Terrace, **Melvin House Hotel** (0131 225 5084) is more economical set in a Victorian building with evocative decor. **Southside** B&B (0131 668 4422), not far from Commonwealth Pool, is a non-smoking B&B, quite exceptional with natural floors, open fires and home cooking. Another excellent 4-star B&B is **Mrs Elizabeth Smith's** (0131 337 1979) close to Murrayfield Golf Club (Mrs S and her husband are both keen golfers).

Lothians The majority of golfers wishing to play on the area's best courses will base themselves in East Lothian. The **Marine Hotel** overlooks the West Links but can be disappointing. Some of the B&Bs in the area are exceptional, rated with 4 stars and geared for golfers. The **Dirleton Open Arms Hotel** (01620 850241) is a 4-star establishment between North Berwick and Gullane and well worth considering as a base. **Faussetthill House** (01620 842396), just off the main street in Gullane, is a fine detached Edwardian house, conveniently situated for all the courses in this area. Back from the coast yet still easily accessible is **Brown's Hotel** (01620 822254) in Haddington, a regency house full of elegant furnishings as well as an attached restaurant with contemporary Scottish art. **Hopefield House** (01620 842191) in Gullane is a charming guest house set in a secluded garden, while **Springfield House** (01368 862502) in Dunbar is a good base for that side of the region. The premier golf accommodation on the west side of Edinburgh is **Marriott Dalmahoy Hotel & Country Club** (0131 333 1845) which has superb leisure facilities and two top-grade golf courses.

Borders There are few finer country house hotels anywhere than **Roxburghe Hotel** (01573 450331), near Kelso, not least since it has a premier 18-hole championship golf course in its ground. Less expensive but set in a lovely village square is **Burt's Hotel** (01896 822285), which also offers fine food. In St Boswells the best place

to stay is **Dryburgh Abbey Hotel** (01835 822261) overlooking the 12th-century Dryburgh Abbey and including an indoor pool as well as a putting green. The **Peebles Hotel Hydro** (01721 720602) is 4-star, set in a stunning location, serves excellent meals and has a brand new leisure centre with a generously-sized swimming pool. Also in Peebles is the **Cringletie House Hotel**, (01721 730233), a 4-star Scottish baronial mansion designed by famous Scottish architect David Bryce. Near Selkirk is **Philipburn Country House Hotel** (01750 720747) where garden rooms are also available by the outdoor heated pool.

Where to Eat

Edinburgh **Igg's** (0131 557 8184) in the heart of Edinburgh Old Town offers quality Scottish cuisine while, next door, **Barioja** (same management) serves excellent Spanish tapas. On the Royal Mile itself is **Jackson's**, (0131 225 1793), another good outlet for fine Scottish cuisine. If you are looking for a spell-binding meal seek out the **Witchery** and **Secret Garden** restaurants (0131 225 5613) on Castlehill at the beginning of the Royal Mile – also handy for pre-theatre suppers. Perhaps the best for Scottish fare is **Dubh Prais** (0131 557 5732) in the High Street. The **Tower Restaurant** (0131 225 3003) on the top floor of the Museum of Scotland is noted for its contemporary styling, modern food and pleasing views towards the castle. In Leith, at the Shore, is **Restaurant Martin Wishart's** (0131 553 3557) which is mostly seafood including the most amazing shell fish dishes.

Lothians North Berwick is quiet at night-time so go out and make a meal of it. One of the best restaurants in town is the **Joypur** (01620 895649) on the High Street, an exceptional Indian restaurant producing exquisite, authentic flavours. The **Tantallon Inn** is a small restaurant serving good bar food using local produce. **Poldrates** (01620 826882) in Haddington is a converted mill of the 1750s. Its décor is basic but the Scottish cuisine is exceptional, often using unusual berries and fruits. The clubhouse at **Whitekirk Golf Club** (01620 870300) has established itself as an excellent restaurant and is worth considering even at night-time. Another good find is the **Drover's Inn** in East Linton, a country pub with a low-beamed dining room upstairs with a remarkably good menu. The best place to eat in East Lothian is **La Potiniere** (01620 843214) but it is expensive and booked well in advance. Try the **Old Clubhouse**, a pleasant little haven just off Gullane's main street. South of Edinburgh in Dalkeith is the **Water Tower** (0131 660 4865).

Borders Burt's Hotel and Roxburghe Hotel (for details see 'Where to Stay') both have excellent restaurants. The **Wheatsheaf Inn** in Swinton near Duns is a small country inn with a big reputation for its food. The **Hoebridge Inn Restaurant** in Gattonside near Melrose (01896 823082) serves modern Scottish cuisine in a stylish but casual atmosphere whose specialities include seasonal game, duck and lamb dishes. The **Cringletie House Hotel** (01721 730233) in Peebles is a fine baronial mansion set in 30 acres of gardens, which uses vegetables from the walled garden and is constantly recommended.

What to Do

Edinburgh **Edinburgh Castle** is one of the most popular tourist attractions in Europe so be prepared for the throngs. Highlights are the Scottish Regalia, or Crown Jewels, and the Stone of Destiny. Many visitors come to Edinburgh specifically for the **Edinburgh International Festival**, **Military Tattoo** and **Edinburgh Fringe Festival** which are held for three weeks every year in August when the town is taken over by performers (and audiences) of every nation. Walk the **Royal Mile** which links the Castle with the royal **Palace of Holyroodhouse** (taking in four separate streets including the High Street). The **Museum of Scotland** is a must, while **Dynamic Earth** at the foot of Arthur's Seat tells the story of the creation of the earth. Hogmanay in Edinburgh is becoming as popular as The Festival. It lasts seven days over New Year and has street theatre, food, fireworks, and 1000 pipers .

Lothians East and West Lothian are rather overshadowed by the near proximity of Edinburgh when it comes to excursions or entertainment. Local museums such as the **Museum of Flight** at

Preston Mill near Dunbar in the Lothians is a charming example of rural Scotland and within striking distance of Dunbar, an exceptional example of links golf.

East Fortune are interesting and the ruined castles at **Tantallon**, **Dirleton** and **Dunbar**, are worth a visit. **Glenkinchie Distillery** (01875 342004), just off the A68, is one of the most southerly malt whisky distilleries. To the west of Edinburgh are **Linlithgow Palace** and **Hopeton House**, both worth visiting for their ancient architecture and history.

Borders Local museums offer a good insight into the woollen industry. **Robert Smail's Printing Workshop** in Innerleithen is an unusual diversion as is nearby **Traquair House**. The 13th-century Borders abbeys at **Dryburgh**, **Jedburgh**, **Melrose** and **Kelso** are testament to the vicious attacks by English armies in this area. Floors Castle near Kelso is where they shot part of the Tarzan movie, *Greystoke*. **Mellerstain House**, north-west of Kelso is impressive for its Adams architecture and paintings by Allan Ramsay, Gainsborough and Constable. For a breath of fresh air and birdwatching, head for **St Abbs Head** near Eyemouth with stunning coastal views.

TOURIST INFORMATION CENTRES
Open all year
Edinburgh & Lothians Tourist Board: Edinburgh & Scotland Information Centre, 3 Princes Street, Edinburgh, EH2 2QP, Tel : +44 (0131) 557 1700 Email : esic@eltb.org
Scottish Borders Tourist Board: Tourist Information Centre, Murray's Green, Jedburgh, TD8 6BE, Tel : +44 (01835) 863435 / 863688 Email : sbtb@scotborders.co.uk

Chapter 2

The Kingdom of Fife

When King James VI of Scotland (later also James I of England) called the Kingdom of Fife a 'beggars mantle fringed with gold' he was referring to the wealthy fishing and trading ports found along the Forth and East Neuk (or corner) of Fife. But 'gold' might have been a prescient misprint for 'golf' because it was in the Kingdom of Fife that the game first took hold and flourished, and indeed James himself took the game with him south of the border.

The fringe of truly exceptional links courses includes St Andrews, the Mecca for golfers all over the world. But also dispersed along the Fife coast are some other classic courses without equal in the whole country. Moreover, the golfing tradition is not confined to the coast. There are as many excellent courses throughout Fife's rolling interior, some lauded as Open qualifying venues while

Left: Pettycur Bay near Kinghorn presents scenes typical of the traditional fishing villages found along the Neuk of Fife, as does Crail Harbour (above).

others are park or heathland courses where the average player can enjoy both fine scenery and sport.

Planning an itinerary

When planning your visit to the Kingdom of Fife it is worth noting that Edinburgh airport is only 15 minutes drive away. Either by car or train you will cross the River Forth to enter Fife. An itinerary could start in the southwest corner of the area with excellent courses such as Dunfermline Golf Club in the village of Crossford. Alternatively, follow the A92 coast road and start at Aberdour Golf Club. There are excellent links courses intermittently spaced along the Forth Estuary and two or three fruitful days could be spent visiting Leven Links, Lundin Links, heading inland to play Ladybank and back to the coast for Elie and Crail and finally St Andrews. While St Andrews is no doubt the biggest draw in the area, each of the 'second-string' courses in Fife is of the highest standard.

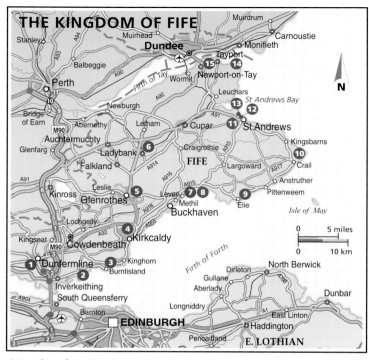

There are six superb courses to choose from in St Andrews alone, with new developments on the town's outskirts, and over 40 courses throughout Fife.

North of St Andrews, Scotscraig should be sampled before moving into Tayside and Carnoustie country.

St Andrews: the home of golf

St Andrews lies at Fife's golfing epicentre. The game's history is uniquely linked with the town: some 600 years ago, 'gowf' was a favourite pastime for St Andrews' citizens, who played for free over the wide links or common land on the north edge of town. St Andrews residents still enjoy the advantage of cheap golf on the five municipal links courses that are owned by them through their town council.

If your heart is set on the Old Course and you have not managed to book in advance, you can join the daily ballot or, if you are a single golfer, go along and announce yourself to the Old Course starter as early in the morning as possible. He will try to fit you in with a two or three ball, an excellent way to meet and play with new people.

While golf is the magnet, St Andrews is also home to Scotland's oldest university (co-founded by Mary, Queen of Scots) and the town is similar in feel to Oxford and Cambridge south of the border. St Andrews Castle stands on a rocky promontory, close to the impressive cathedral ruins. As the residence of the bishops and later Archbishops of St Andrews, it was also used as their palace, fortress and prison. First erected around 1200, the ruins seen today date back to 1571. This is an absorbing town to explore on foot, and it also boasts Scotland's oldest surviving medieval market, the Lammas Fair in mid-August.

The Royal and Ancient Golf Club of St Andrews (R&A), set in its honey-coloured citadel overlooking the 1st and 18th holes of the Old Course, is the ruling body of golf world-wide outside North America and Mexico. The men-only clubhouse, built in 1854, may only be entered by invitation. It may be hard for non-golfers to fully grasp the significance of St Andrews to the game of golf, but most will enjoy a tour around the British Golf Museum, situated behind the Royal & Ancient clubhouse. The museum has taken the fascinating history of the game and brought it to life with the use of audio-visual and hands-on presentations.

The Neuk of Fife

Fife's other main population centres include Dunfermline, Kirkcaldy, Cupar, Kinross and Glenrothes. Each of these is well-provided with golf with a total of 40 courses scattered throughout the area. Dunfermline is noted both for its political and ecclesiastical history while Kirkcaldy had mainly an industrial base. Away from the towns, the East Neuk of Fife is dotted with picturesque, ancient fishing villages well worth exploring with camera or, if you are inclined, easel.

The northern border of Fife is set apart from bordering Tayside by the silvery River Tay. This area is mainly agricultural land and was once a stronghold of the early Celtic Pictish people. In more recent years it has become the home of the Scottish National Golf Centre, at Drumoig, Scotland's showcase golf-teaching academy. With excellent indoor and outdoor practice facilities and a surrounding championship course, the centre is open to both visitors and professional golfers seeking to improve each and every aspect of their game.

There is no shortage of delightful accommodation along the coast in such charming spots as Lower Largo or Aberdour. The wide interior Howe of Fife is mainly agricultural but there are one or two excellent farmhouse B&Bs that are worth a detour.

Playing on the Old Course at St Andrews is not impossible, but it does take patience and planning. There is a handicap limit of 24 for men and 36 for women.

1 Dunfermline

Dunfermline Golf Club, Pitfirrane, Crossford, Dunfermline
KY12 8QW
TEL: *01383 723534*
EMAIL: *pitfirrane@aol.com*
LOCATION: *2 miles/3km west of Dunfermline by village of Crossford on A994*
COURSE: *18 holes, 6121yd/5595m, par 72, SSS 70*
GREEN FEES: *££*
FACILITIES: *Changing rooms and showers, full catering, bar, pro shop, teaching pro, trolley hire*
VISITORS: *Welcome weekdays and Sunday between 10am to 12pm and 2 to 4pm although pre-booking is advised*

Notwithstanding a fascinating history involving moving locations, changing course designers (including James Braid) and an ornate 600-year old Tower House (the current clubhouse) that really must be seen, Dunfermline can also boast the fact that members of this club established the first golf club in America: the St Andrews Club in Yonkers, New York.

That aside, the course is one of the finest parkland courses in Scotland. Unusually it consists of five par 5s and five par 3s with a group of relatively easy par 4s. It is the par 3s

Teeing off at the 2nd hole at Aberdour which plays over a bay and is both charming and testing in windy conditions.

that are most testing with for instance the 208yd/190m, 2nd, presenting a stiff challenge early in the round. The beautifully-maintained course harbours trees of great maturity and the walled garden of the old Pitfirrane estate forms out-of-bounds on three holes. Cutting across the 4th fairway you can still make out the old drovers trail that ran from Stirling to Dunfermline, a main thoroughfare in the 15th century.

2 Aberdour

Aberdour Golf Club, Seaside Place, Aberdour, Fife KY3
0TX
TEL: *01383 860256* FAX: *01383 860050*
LOCATION: *From centre of Aberdour take Shore Road south towards the Firth; about 4 miles/6km from Forth road and rail bridges*
COURSE: *18 holes, 5460yd/4990m, par 67, SSS 66*
GREEN FEES: *£*
FACILITIES: *Changing rooms and showers, full catering, bar, pro shop, teaching pro, trolley hire, club hire*
VISITORS: *Welcome weekdays and Sunday except after 4pm. Saturday is limited. Pre-booking is advised*

Easily accessible from Edinburgh, Aberdour begins a fine chain of courses along the north Firth of Forth shoreline. For inspiring backdrops, there are few holes that can compete with Aberdour's 1st. A par 3 of only 159yd/148m, the elevated tee looks down onto the green which is flanked by an ancient sea wall and 14th century watchtower to the right. Behind this the grey-blue waters of the Firth of Forth lap along Inchcolm Abbey. Attractive as it may appear, in a headwind it is not an easy start. Unusually, the course continues with another par 3 of the same distance. Away from these shoreline beginnings the course turns into parkland by the 5th, with further splendid views over the Forth to the city of Edinburgh and the dominant landmarks of Arthur's Seat, Salisbury Crags and Edinburgh Castle clearly visible.

The 7th to 9th are newer holes; the par-4 8th of 458yd/419m presents the greatest challenge on the course. A good drive will avoid trouble to the left yet be long enough to give a good line into the green which is defended by a noticeable mound to the right.

3 *Burntisland*

Burntisland Golf House Club, Dodhead, Kirkcaldy Road, Burntisland Fife KY3 9EY
TEL: *01592 874093* **FAX:** *01592 874093*
EMAIL: *wkthghc@aol.com*
LOCATION: *On B923, approximately ½ mile/0.75km east of Burntisland town centre*
COURSE: *18 holes, 5965yd/5452m, par 70, SSS 70*
GREEN FEES: £
FACILITIES: *Changing rooms and showers, full catering, bar, pro shop, teaching pro, trolley hire, club hire*
VISITORS: *Welcome everyday though pre-booking is advised*

If you've been playing on the nearby coastal courses such as Leven or Lundin Links it is a refreshing change to mount Burntisland's broad, lush parkland fairways and rise to a test of a different nature. Yet Burntisland, set above its busy Fife holiday town namesake, is not totally a parkland course. With a sandy subsoil on some of the higher holes (8th through 14th), it can play like a links.

A favourite hole with a view is the 4th which plays slightly downhill and takes a line off Edinburgh Castle away in the distance. Another tester is the 12th, a slightly uphill par 4 of 455yd/416m. The 9th and 10th are strategy holes, best tackled with a view to the second shot and not necessarily with a driver.

Looking back at the refurbished Kirkcaldy clubhouse from the 1st green. There are some hill climbs on this well kept course, but not enough to put you off.

4 *Kirkcaldy*

Kirkcaldy Golf Club, Balwearie Road, Kirkcaldy, Fife KY2 5LT
TEL: *01592 203258* **FAX:** *01592 205240*
LOCATION: *At the back of Beveridge Park on the south-west side of town (off A910)*
COURSE: *18 holes, 6038yd/5519m, par 71, SSS 69*
GREEN FEES: £
FACILITIES: *Changing rooms and showers, full catering, bar, pro shop, teaching pro, practice area, trolley hire, club hire, buggy hire*
VISITORS: *Welcome weekday, though pre-booking is advised. At weekends, no play for visitors on Saturday before 3pm*

Known locally as Balwearie, this course sits neatly on a lovely, rolling piece of countryside only minutes from Kirkcaldy. The clubhouse and surrounds have benefitted from a major overhaul making for a welcoming start and finish to a round on one of the best conditioned parkland courses in Fife. Established in 1904, it offers a very well kept mature layout. The fast greens are exceptionally smooth and the fairways well-defined. Kirkcaldy opens up to players who can steer their tee shots onto the short grass.

The course commences with one of its best holes, the par-4 1st with a 180yd/165m carry to clear the burn. The hole then turns uphill to the left and on a windy day this can be quite daunting. Once on the upper level the course continues evenly until the 4th and 5th which again climb slightly. A Kirkcaldy version of Augusta's Amen Corner takes place at the 7th, 8th and 9th with the burn running all the way down the right and out-of-bounds on the other side. If you are not accurate off the tee this could be the most costly stretch.

On the back stretch, the 17th stands out as an excellent par 5 that can change dramatically according to wind conditions. With a tail wind it is possible to drive to the down slope and roll close to the burn, leaving a short pitch on and a birdie opportunity. Otherwise it might be a drive and a 3-wood to lay up, then a pitch over the burn.

The Firth of Forth can be seen from several points on the course. The club offers a a good all-round package including buggy, green fees and meal.

⑤ Balbirnie

Balbirnie Park Golf Club, Balbirnie Park, Markinch, Fife
KY7 6NR
TEL: *01592 612095* **FAX:** *01592 612383*
LOCATION: *Turn towards Markinch off A92 near
Glenrothes*
COURSE: *18 holes, 6214yd/5680m, par 71, SSS 70*
GREEN FEES: *££*
FACILITIES: *Changing rooms and showers, full catering,
bar, pro shop, teaching pro, trolley hire, club hire, buggy
hire, practice area*
VISITORS: *Welcome weekdays except Thursdays from 4pm
to 6pm and weekends from 10am onwards; pre-booking is
advised*

The course at Balbirnie Park is a long-established parkland located at the centre of the Kingdom of Fife. It winds its way through a leafy, well-manicured estate. In fact the course is itself relatively new but makes excellent use of the mature, tree-lined estate surrounding the luxurious Balbirnie House Hotel.

The rolling parkland course is a little hilly, especially at some of the green approaches, but never strenuous. The layout rewards direct hitters and can frustrate those who end up with trees between them and their target. This is the course's main defence but if the trees and rough can be avoided, golfers should be able to play close to their handicap.

The 12th presents a good test, a lengthy par 4 to a tight fairway. The premium test however comes at the final hole, a par-5 requiring two strokes of at least 200yd/183m with the second shot usually blind. A pretty burn runs across the front of the green forcing a lay-up and carry to the flag.

The clubhouse has recently been updated throughout making it an inviting conclusion to a lively round.

⑥ Ladybank

Ladybank Golf Club, Annsmuir, Ladybank, Fife KY15
7RA
TEL: *01337 830814* **FAX:** *01337 831505*
LOCATION: *South of A91 on A914 and on north side of
village of Ladybank*
COURSE: *18 holes, 6641yd/6043m, par 71, SSS 72*
GREEN FEES: *£££*
FACILITIES: *Changing rooms and showers, full catering,
bar, pro shop, teaching pro, trolley hire, club hire, buggy hire*
VISITORS: *Welcome weekdays between 9.30am to
4.30pm. Weekends are limited. Pre-booking is advised*

An exemplary qualifying course when the Open is held at St Andrews, Ladybank is long and challenging, but mainly flat and so not overtaxing. Playing through avenues of beech trees, Scots pine and silver birch you might consider it parkland but with swathes of heather and gorse, and firm, short grass on the fairways it is most definitely heathland in nature.

Old Tom Morris was responsible for designing the first six holes: the 2nd is a long par 5 running along the course's perimeter. It is straightforward and yielding to those who stick to the fairway though three good strikes are required.

The 9th is Stroke Index 1, a dogleg left with a huge Scots pine blocking the fairway. Percentage players tend to take an iron off the tee for position and expect a longer second shot into the green. But that shot must then negotiate a large unseen dip just before the green.

After the short 10th, the back nine has a number of doglegs. These holes turn in opposing directions, with the exception of the14th, which is both long and straight and plays into the wind with 180yd/165m to carry to reach the fairway. The 16th arches radically left, and the driver is best left in the bag.

*Teeing off from the 7th on Ladybank's exceptional
heathland course with views to the Lomond Hills.*

Leven Links

Leven Golfing Society, Links Road, Leven Fife KY8 4HS
TEL: *01333 428859* **FAX:** *01333 428859*
LOCATION: *9 miles/14km east of Kirkcaldy on the A955*
COURSE: *18 holes, 6436yd/5883m, par 71, SSS 70*
GREEN FEES: *££*
FACILITIES: *Changing rooms and showers, full catering, bar, pro shop, trolley hire, club hire on request*
VISITORS: *Welcome weekdays 9.30am to 4pm and weekends 10.30am to 4.30pm though pre-booking is advised*

Leven Links is a no-frills, natural sweep of links set on a wide sandy bay of the Firth of Forth. The old dunesland is hard packed, rippling and more pronounced than most links. The course is built on limited acreage yet it still presents a tract that is used as an Open qualifier when it is held in St Andrews.

Starting out at the 1st or finishing off the 18th can leave one confused as it appears the same fairway is being utilised. There is certainly little definition between the two fairways. The way forward is clearer at the 2nd and 3rd where the fairways form channels between the compacted dunes and rough grass banks. There is not much room for manoeuvre but the rough remains thin for most of the year and stray balls are not usually lost.

The 4th hole, aptly entitled Sea, clears the

The 18th at Leven is a great green to play on if you can get onto it: it is defended by a wide burn that almost creates an island.

caravan park, built rather close to the course, and gives wide open vistas of the Firth of Forth and East Lothian to the south. It is a long par 4, but in typical summer links conditions this can be covered quite easily especially with a following wind.

The course turns inland at an old dry-stone wall that lies between Leven and Lundin Links. These two courses were originally one when Leven continued out along the beach before turning homeward in the traditional links manner. A famous competition is held yearly for the McDonald Trophy combining part of both courses to emulate the original layout.

The 5th is a quirky par 3 while the 6th is an outstanding par 5: horses graze close-by in fields on the right, and it can be most difficult to play here against a wind.

Players not used to Scottish links golf will find Leven especially testing for its fast fairways, haphazard bounces and difficult, running approaches. But Leven also offers an excellent opportunity to hone new skills dictated by a links setting that is as traditional as one could hope to find.

8 *Lundin Links*

Lundin Golf Club, Golf Road, Lundin Links Fife KY8 6BA
TEL: *01333 320202* **FAX:** *01333 329743*
WWW: *www.lundingolfclub.co.uk*
LOCATION: *West side of village of Lundin and off A915*
COURSE: *18 holes, 6394yd/5844m, par 71, SSS 71*
GREEN FEES: *£££*
FACILITIES: *Changing rooms and showers, full catering, bar, pro shop, teaching pro, trolley hire, club hire*
VISITORS: *Welcome weekdays and Saturdays although pre-booking is advised*

The opening holes at Lundin Links have impressive undulations – ancient dunes worn down by the footfall of many generations of golfers – leaving shots little chance of a smooth journey. The par-4 4th in particular has a deep hidden drop just before the green laced by the Silver Burn. First timers seeing only the green can fall foul of this hazard and add several strokes to a promising start.

Like a mirror image of its neighbour across the wall, Leven Links, Lundin takes a turn inland at the 5th, a short hole well defended by seven bunkers. The 9th is a long par 5

Lundin is a quirky course, a pure seaside course like its next-door neighbour Leven Links.

and, although sheltered by a rise to its right, can be devastating in a headwind.

At the short 12th Lundin changes character completely and rises onto a parkland plateau. The long 13th doglegs slightly towards a green that is obstructed by a stand of a dozen pines. This usually means laying-up to the right in order to strike the green squarely. The 175yd/160m 14th, aptly called Perfection, offers views of every green and tee, the Firth of Forth, and the hills beyond Edinburgh and East Lothian.

The homeward stretch is of a links nature but not as pronounced as the first holes. The climax is left to the par-4 442yd/404m final hole whose long, narrow green can prove difficult to judge especially towards the back of the green.

Like all links courses, the pace of Lundin's greens and their approaches, and the fairways themselves, is often dictated by the wind. Take account of this, and you can enjoy a worthy pre-qualifying Open course (when it is held at St Andrews).

9 *Golf House Club*

Golf House Club Golf Course Lane Elie, Fife KY9 1AS
TEL: *01333 330301* **FAX:** *01333 330895*
LOCATION: *10 miles/16km south of St Andrews on A917*
COURSE: *18 holes, 6273yd/5734m, par 70, SSS 69*
GREEN FEES: *£££*
FACILITIES: *Changing rooms and showers, full catering, bar, pro shop, teaching pro, trolley hire, club hire, buggy hire*
VISITORS: *Welcome Monday to Saturdays after 10am, although pre-booking is advised. During July and August there is a daily ballot system*

Of the many excellent natural links courses south of St Andrews, the Golf House Club at Elie is possibly the most enjoyable and memorable. On a course abounding with unusual features, the first oddity is the periscope dismantled from *HMS Excaliber* in 1966 and presented to the club. Protruding from the middle of the starter's hut adjacent to the 1st tee, it is used to check that the fairway is clear. Distance is easily covered at Elie as the ball rolls far over the hard-packed fairways covered in thin grass burned by sun and wind.

The 13th hole at Golf House Club, Elie – one of the most striking of this course's holes.

But sensitive touches are called for at Golf House, to stop the ball running through the firm approaches and lightening-fast greens. A classic example of this lies on the slope down towards the beach at the picturesque 10th.

10 Crail Golfing Society

Crail Golfing Society, Balcomie Clubhouse, Fife, Crail KY10 3XN
TEL: *01333 451414* **FAX:** *01333 450416*
EMAIL: *crailgolfs@aol.com*
LOCATION: *11 miles/17km south-east of St. Andrews on A917 through to village centre and left for 3 miles/5km*
COURSE: *18 holes, 5922yd/5413m, par 69, SSS 69*
GREEN FEES: *££*
FACILITIES: *Changing rooms and showers, full catering, bar, pro shop, teaching pro, trolley hire, club hire*
VISITORS: *Welcome everyday though pre-booking is advised*

Ancient cobble-stoned wynds and perhaps the most delightful harbour in Scotland are at the centre of the enchanting village of Crail on Fife's East Neuk. Painters and landscape photographers spend hours here. A few minutes' drive north of the village brings you to Crail Golfing Society, and to its Balcomie course – one of the best in Fife.

The clubhouse and course occupy the easternmost tip of the Neuk in a commanding position overlooking the Firth of Tay, Firth of Forth and the North Sea. The 1st hole drops to sea level from a high vantage point that should give you an indication of the strength of the day's wind. The beach to the right of the 2nd is out-of-bounds and a prevailing westerly wind can easily carry your ball there. The most demanding hole on the course is the par-4 5th (Hell's Hole), a right dogleg playing over the jagged rocks of Tullybothy Crags. It generally pays to lay up safely here, resisting the temptation to drive for the pin, attractive though it might seem.

A second newer course, Craighead, is longer and more demanding than Balcomie with snarling rough that has been cut back of late to provide for easier passage. The closing holes are the most demanding especially the par-3 17th, which plays onto a multi-level green, and a long par-4 final hole.

11 St Andrews Old Course

St Andrews Old Course, St Andrews Links Trust, St Andrews Fife KY16 9SF

TEL: *01334 466666* **FAX:** *01334 477036*

EMAIL: *linkstrust@standrews.org.uk*

WWW: *standrews.org.uk and www.linksnet.co.uk (for bookings)*

LOCATION: *Follow the A91 to St Andrews. The courses are well signposted via Golf Place; follow the beach road towards West Sands, parking and St Andrews Links Clubhouse*

COURSE: *18 holes, 6566yd/6002m, par 72, SSS 72*

GREEN FEES: *£££££+*

FACILITIES: *Changing rooms, showers, full catering, bar, pro shop, golf practice centre, caddies, trolley hire after 12pm*

VISITORS: *Golfers should go to the Links Clubhouse at least half an hour before your tee time and then catch the shuttle buggy to the 1st tee. A handicap certificate is required and no visitors are allowed on Sunday on the Old Course*

ST ANDREWS
OLD COURSE (MEDAL TEES)

HOLE	YD	M	PAR	HOLE	YD	M	PAR
1	370	338	4	10	318	291	4
2	411	376	4	11	172	157	3
3	352	322	4	12	316	289	4
4	419	383	4	13	398	364	4
5	514	470	5	14	523	478	5
6	374	342	4	15	401	366	4
7	359	328	4	16	351	321	4
8	166	152	3	17	461	421	4
9	307	280	4	18	354	324	4
OUT	3372	2991	36	IN	3294	3011	36

6566 YD •6002M • PAR 72

There is little doubt that St Andrews has the most famous strip of golfing ground in the world. The coastal margin, created over the millennia by alluvial deposits, receding sea and hammering wind, is undoubtedly where the game of ball and stick developed into the sophisticated sport we know today. The links land to the north of ancient St Andrews town was originally used by locals for the grazing of animals or drying clothes, but here, by the 16th century, 'gowf' was well established.

The sandy peninsula, despite being sold at one time by an unscrupulous and bankrupt town council for rabbit breeding, remains the property of St Andrews' citizens today. St Andrews' golf courses are, therefore, essentially municipal allowing anyone to play providing they can obtain a ballot or tee time and, for the Old Course, have a handicap certificate. Over the years, the Old Course has seen the world's best golfers grace its hallowed turf, from Allan Robertson, Tom Morris and his son Young Tom onwards. So one of the hardest tests of golf for the average player must be teeing off at the 1st for the first time on the Old Course. The gallery comprising (in the mind at least) scratch golfers waiting to play off behind you, members of the R&A peering from their clubhouse window, and several coach-loads of holiday makers can be intimidating but try not to let this put you off.

The Old Course does not favour any particular type of player as it demands a wide variety of shots and will test every part of your game. Its characteristically wide fairways and double greens (for instance the 3rd and 15th share the same green) can lead some to think that the tee shots and approaches to the green are easy, but with some 150 bunkers scattered around the course there is a definite prescribed route to every hole, generally to

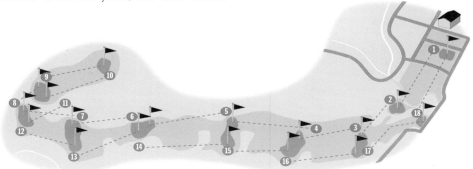

The final hole at St Andrews is an elegant if somewhat surprisingly easy finish by the old clubhouse (inset). In the foreground is Swilcan Bridge, once the route to the ancient city. Aside from this hazard, and the Valley of Sin which does make it deliberately difficult to roll on to the flag, the fairway is wide enough to land a jet, and there is little to trouble an experienced golfer.

the left (the locals or caddies will tell you), and deviation from this can cause many extra strokes.

The first hole on the Old Course is the par-4 Burn. There is little that can go wrong with such a wide fairway. Aim slightly left of centre to cross Granny Clark's Wynd, the road that crosses the fairway 150yd/137m out. The Swilcan Burn and clumps of gorse come into play for the second shot. The burn can be hazardous if the pin is set close to the front of the green.

Fourteen of the holes are par 4s and the course overall looks deceptively flat, but all have subtle undulations which rarely give the chance to play a fairway shot from a level stance. The pitch and roll of the greens, strategically protected by gaping sand bunkers, also begin to wear down the already hard-pressed player.

All St Andrews' foibles come in to play at the par-4 17th Road Hole. The Old Course Hotel (once a goods station and coal yard)

plays a major role with the Black Sheds protruding into the fairway to create a blind approach which you can either play over or around. The classic line is to play a draw out-of-bounds and bring it around to find the fairway aiming for the letter H on the Hotel sign. The green is tight and set just before the road with the notorious Road Bunker hard in at its left. It is best to lay up with your second shot and pitch on to hold the green.

HOW TO GET A GAME AT ST ANDREWS

Although you might be booking a year in advance to play on the Old Course in the peak months, the procedure is straightforward. Check the web site and phone or email your request to the reservations office and they will try to meet your needs. You must have a handicap of 24 (men) and 36 (women).

For those who wish to take a chance and turn up with the hope of having a round then and there, a daily ballot system has stood the test of time as being the fairest way of allocating playing privileges. To enter the ballot golfers should contact the Starter or telephone 01334 466666 before 2pm on the day before they wish to play. Your name is added to the hat and the ballot is drawn after 2pm each day for play the next but on Saturday for Monday as the Old Course is closed for play on Sunday. The ballot results are posted at several sites near the course including the tourist information office.

Scotland's Unique Links

Many golfers come to Scotland in order to experience true links golf and several adjustments are necessary to get the best out of your game. While no two links courses are the same (some may run parallel to the beach while others will turn inland from the shore and offer softer parkland loam), generally the terrain is markedly undulating with a firm, sandy subsoil covered with fine, fescue grass.

The earliest courses evolved from common grazing land and employed the natural contours formed between the dunes. Bunkers are a particularly distinctive feature. Back in the mists of time livestock would have sheltered in these natural hollows, and on the first links, golf balls would roll into them, repeated divots would be taken, and a crude, sandy bunker would be formed. Mainly in the interest of improved maintenance, greenkeepers through the years have developed the distinctive links pot bunkers we find today. Their steep turf walls, laid in brick fashion, prevent sand being blown out of the bunker and subsequently deteriorating the surrounding grass.

Burns or ditches are another fairly common feature. These natural water outlets usually find their way – several times – into strategic positions in a course's design, forcing golfers to consider whether to brave a full strike to carry the hazard or lay up safe.

Designed by Harry Colt, the Eden Course at St Andrews is one of the milder tests of links golf and great fun to play.

The 14th at Crail – seashore, prevailing winds, large bunkers, fast wind-burnt grass all await.

However, of all the elements that make up a good links test, wind is the most significant factor. You will notice on most links that trees are not generally a feature – indicating that wind is. This calls for new tactics such as low tee hits, punchy iron play, and chip and run shots to roll the ball into the green. The strength of the wind will determine club selection both into and down wind. It is often the case that a 150yd/137m seaside par 3 will call for a pitching wedge one day and a 3-iron or more the next.

If you manage to combat the sand, turf and coarse grass, you will still have an array of challenging approaches to the greens to contend with. Indeed you may be better off trying to bump-and-run the ball, playing short and using the contours of the ground to slow the ball before it enters the green. Some old Scottish golfers use a putter from as much as 50 yd/45m out. Wind can effect a putt as well as a drive on a links, making it more difficult to judge how much to borrow. It is an old golfing adage that most putts will run towards the water.

12 Duke's Course

St Andrews, Duke's Course, Craigtoun Park, St Andrews, Fife KY16 8NS
TEL: *01334 474371* **FAX:** *01334 477668*
EMAIL: *ldcoursehotel@standrews.co.uk*
WWW: *www.oldcoursehotel.co.uk*
LOCATION: *From St Andrews take the Craigtoun Road for 2 miles/3km and the course is well signposted on the left*
COURSE: *18 holes, 7271yd/6646m, par 72, SSS 75*
GREEN FEES: *££££+ Apr-Oct; ££+ Nov-March*
FACILITIES: *Changing rooms and showers, full catering, bar, pro shop, teaching pro, driving range, golf academy, trolley hire, club hire, buggy hire, shoe hire*
VISITORS: *Welcome everyday though pre-booking is essential*

Owned and operated by the Old Course Hotel in St Andrews, this is a beauty and a beast of a course. The beauty comes with the views over the town to the Old Course and West Sands as well as the gorgeously shaped holes that abound throughout. The beast comes out when you play them.

It is a magnificent parkland course with beautifully sculpted holes laid open to pitch and run, each exploiting the natural features of a stunning woodland setting. The front 9, weaving through trees opens early with a testing 2nd, a slight dogleg right best played up the left to gain sight of the green. Another tester is the 212yd/194m par 3, 8th called Fair Dunt, which is Scottish for a sound strike and is sound advice if facing the wind.

Compared to the tree-lined avenues of the front 9 with relatively flat greens, the back 9 drops down to a lower level and offers links-like rolling fairways and undulating greens. The 13th aptly entitled Braw View gives a refreshing glimpse of the Grampian Mountains away to the north but you are spoilt for choice here when it comes to panoramas.

The par-4 472yd/431m, 14th incorporates a natural spring emanating from a stone mound while the 18th is an exceptional finish rising gradually from tee to green with a large oak tree on the right at 280yd/256m. Handicap limits are not required to play the Duke's Course, and it remains less demanding than the Old and New Courses.

13 St Andrews New Course

St Andrews Links Trust, St Andrews Fife KY16 9SF
TEL: 01334 466666 **FAX:** 01334 477036
EMAIL: linkstrust@standrews.org.uk
WWW: standrews.org.uk and www.linksnet.co.uk
LOCATION: Follow the A91 to St Andrews. The courses are well signposted via Golf Place and follow the beach road towards West Sands, parking and St Andrews Links Clubhouse
STATISTICS: 18 holes, 6604yd/6036m, par 71, SSS 72
GREEN FEES: £££
FACILITIES: Changing rooms and showers, full catering, bar, pro shop, teaching pro, trolley hire, buggy hire, club hire
VISITORS: Welcome everyday though pre-booking is advised. Handicap certificates required (24/men, 36/women)

The New Course at St Andrews is well over 100 years old, but compared to the Old Course (now in its sixth century as a golf venue) it is an adolescent. Even in the 1880s the demand to play the Old Course was outstripping availability and a second course was constructed on the sandy peninsula of linksland adjacent to the town. There are now six courses within that area but the Old and New remain the most popular.

The 9th at the New Course, St Andrews – the holes are narrow on this course and demand a high degree of accuracy to avoid losing balls in the whins.

The New Course starts adjacent to the Old after which it turns away from the open arenas of the Old's 1st and 18th. The terrain that the two courses play over is therefore very similar in character with only strips of gorse and knobs of old dunes keeping them apart. If you have played the Old before the New, you will have been gratified by the size of the greens, many of them double, and, unless you strayed right, the comparative ease off the visitors' tees to keep the ball in play. This is not the case on the New Course, and most locals will tell you that the New is a tougher test from the visitors' tees as it is noticeably tighter and sterner. The greens are much smaller to aim at, though at the turn adjacent fairways offer sanctuary to off-target drives. The 3rd and 15th holes share their putting surface, the only double green on the course. The home stretch from the 15th can be especially tough when a hardy crosswind blows. The short 17th offers some respite.

St Andrews is also home to the Jubilee Course (1897, after Queen Victoria's Diamond Jubilee), the Eden, a milder but most enjoyable test, the Strathtyrum (1993), and the redesigned Balgove course ideal for juniors and new golfers.

14 Scotscraig

Scotscraig Golf Club, Golf Road, Tayport, Fife DD6 9DZ
TEL: 01382 552515 **FAX:** 01382 553130
EMAIL: scotscraig@scottishgolf.com
WWW: www.scottishgolf.com/scotscraig
LOCATION: 10 miles/16km north of St Andrews on the Tay Estuary and 5 miles/9km south and east of Dundee
STATISTICS: 18 holes, 6550yd/5987m, par 72, SSS 72
GREEN FEES: £££
FACILITIES: Changing rooms and showers, full catering, bar, pro shop, teaching pro, trolley hire
VISITORS: Welcome everyday though pre-booking is advised

From the 1st, you will find Scotscraig's fairways rolling and links-like, though the land does not border the sea shore. However, the course's character is not purely links but a combination of links, heathland and parkland. The present course was laid out by James Braid in the 1920s although there have been improvements especially on the back 9. Fairways are not over generous, but they are accommodating enough to the uncomplicated, straight strike. The rolling, lumpy nature of the majority of the holes can cause bewildering bounces, but generally you get what you play, and if you veer away from the middle that could spell serious trouble.

Scotscraig's rough is penal, mainly in the form of thick gorse or mature stands of pine trees. Any wild hit will not fair well, and therefore it is a course best enjoyed by experienced golfers rather than those that have yet to maintain steady and straight progress within the confines of the fairway. Indeed it has gained recognition as an Open qualifying venue for its resolute test.

The par-4 4th is a most formidable hole with a very well placed tee-shot needed to then allow the best approach onto a raised and sloping green. Many players sensibly choose a long iron or fairway wood off the tee to allow for the links-like run which could easily carry the ball into trouble. This should leave around 120 yd/110m onto the green.

Scotscraig is the 13th oldest golf club in existence and with this distinction the club emanates a strong sense of tradition, good golfing hospitality, and excellent catering.

15 *Drumoig*

The 9th at Drumoig threatens all golfers driving off the tee with a large expanse of water, 'East Loch', seen here in front of the 24-bedroomed hotel-clubhouse.

Drumoig Golf Club, Drumoig, St Andrews, Fife KY16 OBE
TEL: *01382 541800* **FAX:** *01382 542211*
EMAIL: *drumoig@sol.co.uk* **WWW:** *www.drumoigleisure.com*
LOCATION: *Take A91 from M90 motorway. From St Andrews take the A92 to Drumoig between St Michaels and Dundee*
COURSE: *18 holes, 7,006yd/6404m, par 72, SSS 74*
GREEN FEES: *££*
FACILITIES: *Changing rooms and showers, full catering, bar, golf academy, pro shop, teaching pro, trolley hire, buggy hire, club hire*
VISITORS: *Welcome everyday though pre-booking is advised*

Just five minutes' drive from the centre of Dundee are the recently created Drumoig Golf Club and the Scottish National Golf Centre. Although these facilities exist as single entities, they sit side-by-side. The Scottish National Golf Centre is the administrative base for the Scottish Golf Union and the Scottish Ladies Golfing Association. More to the point it offers one of the most comprehensive practice facilities in Europe, with a magnificent indoor pitching and putting room complete with sand bunkers and a winding burn. The driving range is the best of its kind and the outdoor practice facility includes five full holes that cover every aspect of on-course management.

Drumoig Golf Club and Hotel is therefore, despite its recent vintage, obliged to be of the highest standard and this is the case. It is long enough to warrant a championship event but it is still early days for the course. There are many good holes to be enjoyed, notably the 5th, a par 5, usually into the prevailing wind, which often requires two woods and at least a 5-iron to reach its quarry-surrounded green. On the other side of the quarry, the 13th can be reached with a drive and wedge, but the green remains a tiny target. The drives from both the 9th and 10th are threatened by wide stretches of water. This is a good course that will improve with time and is well worth a round when you are in this part of Fife.

REGIONAL DIRECTORY
Where to Stay
There are many good places to stay in and around St Andrews but the most prestigious must be the **Old Course Hotel Golf Resort & Spa** (01334 474371), which looks on to the St Andrews courses – the largest golf complex in Europe – and yet is only a short walk from the town's centre. Overlooking St Andrews Bay and only a short walk from the 1st tee on the Old Course is the **Hazelhead Bank Hotel** (01334 472466) a small but well-appointed facility well-used to catering for golfers. If you would like a more countrified setting then **Rufflets Country House Hotel** (01334 472594) is the place of choice, a small, luxury country house just outside St Andrews. Close to the Scottish National Golf Centre is **Sandford Country House Hotel** (01382 541802) with a fine restaurant and minstrel's gallery as well as its 16 en-suite bedrooms.

Not far from St Andrews the **Crusoe Hotel** (01333 320759) is an excellent example of modest accommodation though still full of character and creature comforts. Further along the coast is the **Old Manor House Hotel** (01333 320368) overlooking the Lundin Links golf course with Leven Links next door.

In the centre of the Kingdom near Glenrothes, **Balbirnie House** (01592 610066) is an exquisite Georgian mansion set in 400 acres of estate and country park encompassed by an 18-hole course. Close by Glenrothes itself is a **Holiday Inn** (01592 745509) with the adjoining **Fettykil Fox** family pub and restaurant, a most comfortable and affordable option in easy driving distance to many of Fife's courses. Handy for such courses as Ladybank is the **Fernie Castle Hotel** (01337 810381) a 16th-century castle whose bistro and wine bar was once the castle dungeon. Near Dunfermline, **Keavil House Hotel** (01383 736258) is next door to Dunfermline Golf Club.

Where to Eat
In St Andrews itself, the places to eat are **Rufflets Country House Hotel** (01334 472594) or the **Old Course Hotel** (01334 474371) where you will find the food both delectable and perfectly presented. The **St Andrews Links Clubhouse** (01334 466666) offers a pleasant restaurant overlooking the Old and New courses. For a simpler and indeed less costly meal try any of the dozens of good quality eateries throughout the town.

The imposing Dunfermline Cathedral dominates the town that was once Scotland's capital (until 1603). The 12th-century nave still survives, as does Robert the Bruce's links with this building.

Offering St Andrews bay lobster, inland, **Ostler's Close,** Bonnygate, Cupar (01334 655574) boasts 3-AA red rosettes and numerous other accolades. **The Peat Inn** (01334 840206) not far from Cupar has occupied top spot in Fife for a long time although there is now some serious competition such as the **Seafood Restaurant**, (01333 730327) in St Monans. Again for a lighter meal, on the pocket at least, the **Anstruther Fish Restaurant** overlooking the harbour has a strong following – judging by the queue.

What to Do

In St Andrews the **British Golf Museum** behind the R&A does an admirable job of presenting golf's misty history. The impressive ruins of **St Andrews Cathedral** at the top of North Street must be explored, especially to see Young Tom Morris's gravestone, while **St Andrews Castle** overlooking the sea offers a dramatic glimpse of the Kingdom's turbulent past.

One of the best excursions in Fife is simply to drive south along the coast from St Andrews visiting the fishing villages of the East Neuk. **Crail** is by far the most charming but each village offers a wonderful setting and native architecture. At Anstruther you will find the **Scottish Fisheries**

The cradle of golf – a view across the links fairways of St Andrews, where you can soak in the history just by visiting the site (and the nearby Museum of Golf).

Museum (01333 311073) while inland you could visit **Falkland Palace and Gardens** in the centre of the village, a rather impressive Stuart dynasty hunting lodge.

Under the prodigious spans of the **Forth Rail Bridge** in North Queensferry, Deep Sea World is essentially for children although everyone seems to enjoy it. Andrew Carnegie was born in Dunfermline before he emigrated to make his mark on American industry. **The Andrew Carnegie Birthplace Museum** is in Moodie Street, Dunfermline. Nearby **Dunfermline Abbey and Palace** are worth exploring. The town itself was once one of Scotland's foremost linen producers.

TOURIST INFORMATION OFFICES

St Andrews Tourist Information Centre, 70 Market Street, St Andrews, Fife, KY16 7NU, Tel : +44 (01334) 472021
Email : fife.tourism@kftb.ossian.net
Website : standrews.co.uk

Chapter 3

Angus, Dundee and Perthshire

From Dundee, in the south-east corner of Tayside, with its magnificent parkland course at Downfield, following the coast, with its host of superlative links including Carnoustie's three 18-hole courses, and then inland through Angus and into Perthshire, Tayside offers golf courses to suit the whole spectrum of handicaps.

But Tayside also offers a huge variety of scenery such as the expanses of the Angus Glens and its rolling farmland home to the famous beef cattle, and the Perthshire Highlands with its great lochs and glens.

Angus, Dundee and Perthshire between them can boast some of the most noted golf courses in Scotland, even the world. Mention Carnoustie and most golfers will recall the 1999 Open when Jean Van de Velde clutched defeat from the jaws of victory on the 18th hole. But of course the Championship course there

has long been recognised as perhaps the toughest in the world. Tayside is also home to Gleneagles' King's and Queen's courses – two first-class courses set by the 'Palace in the Hills', the Gleneagles hotel complex.

Aside from the cream courses, there are plenty of other less publicised courses equally worthy of a visit. Those in the know and looking for high-class golf will add Blairgowrie's Rosemount course or Montrose's Medal to their itineraries.

The Land of Lochs

Perth is recognised as the Gateway to the Highlands, and for centuries the area has been home to such famous whisky names as Bell's and Famous Grouse. Salmon and wool are also linked to the area and nearby Pitlochry has long been a favoured stopping place for purchasing a Scottish tartan, viewing the salmon leap up on their annual migration and savouring the local whiskies. Nearby Loch Tummel and Loch Rannoch offer fabulous scenic spectacles.

Left: Loch Tummel from the 'Queen's View' – quintessential Scottish scenery. Monroe climbing (above), Monroes are peaks over 3,000ft (2,742m) in Scotland.

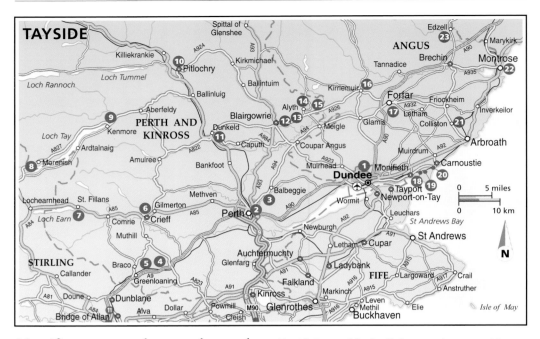

Magnificent man–made spectacles are also on view such as the red–sandstone outline of Glamis Castle, birthplace and ancestral home of HRH, the Queen Mother.

Even the port of Dundee has its

Threading through high ridges on the north and west sides of the Gleneagles Estate, the Queen's Course offers woodland mixed with moorland. This is the 18th.

Tayside is one of Scotland's largest regions, comprising Angus, Dundee and Perthshire. Dundee makes a good 'base camp' for many golfing excursions.

welcoming modern-day attractions including theatres, cinemas and fine restaurants. Dundee is the largest conurbation in Tayside and a noted university and medical research centre.

Planning an Itinerary

To plan your visit to this large and varied area, it is best to select a part of the region and cover its courses, or choose the courses you wish to play and set out each day from a central base. Dundee is good for its travel facilities, amenities and central location to all of Tayside. From Dundee you can travel west towards Perth and its many surrounding courses, including Gleneagles, then branch north to discover the delights of Highland Perthshire with beautiful settings around Pitlochry, Aberfeldy or Dunkeld. The A9 from Perth is the main route adjoining these areas as well as carrying on north into the Highlands.

Travelling east again, our course sequence takes you to Blairgowrie and the famous Rosemount course with its near neighbours at Alyth. You then cross into Angus again following the A926 onto Kirriemuir and Forfar Golf Clubs.

It is easy to pick up the coast either from Forfar following the A958 towards Carnoustie or from Dundee following the A92. Here are a string of notable courses all within striking distance of Carnoustie or Dundee.

The northern part of the region of Angus offers both coastal and inland courses of great merit. Again these are easily accessed from Dundee following the main Dundee-Aberdeen dual carriageway, the A90, and branching off for instance to Edzell's course or east towards Montrose.

From Sir Walter Scott to more recent surveys, Perth – set by the River Tay and recognised as the gateway to the Highlands – has long had its scenic praises sung.

SPECIAL PASSES

For a more economic golfing break, there are few better deals than the 'Perthshire Highland Golf Ticket'. With this you can play a day's golf on any of five participating 9-hole courses. There is also the good-value 'Perthshire Green Card' allowing five rounds on participating 18-hole courses.

For details on these special offers contact Perthshire Tourist Board's Activity Line on 01577 861186. For details of golf in Carnoustie Country telephone 01369 708004.

1 Downfield

Turnberry Avenue, Dundee, Angus DD2 3QP
TEL: *01382 825595* **FAX:** *01382 813111*
LOCATION: *North of Dundee city centre via A923, turn right at Camperdown roundabout, then 1st left and left again around housing estate*
COURSE: *18 holes, 6803yd/6218m, par 73, SSS 73*
GREEN FEES: *££*
FACILITIES: *Changing rooms and showers, full catering, bar, pro shop, teaching pro, trolley hire*
VISITORS: *Welcome weekdays between 9.30am and 12pm and 2.30 to 3.45pm. Weekends are not bookable*

Set in Dundee's northern boundary, at the gateway to Carnoustie Country, Downfield is undoubtedly one of the finest parkland courses in the area. Highly praised by touring professionals, this is a course without weakness offering an outstanding variety of holes in a splendid setting.

Having said that, don't be put off by the 1960s housing development at its entrance. In the 1920s James Braid laid out the original design mostly in the area now occupied by the housing development. In 1963, the present course was laid out further west with only the 10th, 11th and 12th still existing as original Braid holes.

Downfield's lush fairways wend through a long established country estate with mature specimen trees ornamenting each hole. Each hole also offers a different set of challenges that keeps a player thinking with little let up.

The 4th is a superb par 5 playing to the crest of a hill at around 250yd/228m then down over the Gellie Burn to the green. Big hitters can clear the ridge and roll to a position from which to reach the green in two, but there are thick woods on either side that will catch misdirected drives, and the burn will collect any short second shot. A par 5 of moderate length, the 11th hole requires an accurate draw off the tee to set up an attacking position for the green; but both strikes must be solid and exact as they need to cross a pond, as well as a concealed ditch, immediately in front of the green.

The 12th, a short hole across some water and surrounded by trees, has the added kudos of being considered one of the best par 3s in the world by legendary golfer Gary Player.

2 King James VI

King James VI Golf Club, Moncrieffe Island, Perth, Perthshire PH2 8NR
TEL: *01738 632460* **FAX:** *01738 445132*
LOCATION: *Set on an island on the River Tay in the town of Perth, the course is accessed by footbridge from Tay Street*
COURSE: *18 holes, 5664yd/5177m, par 70, SSS 69*
GREEN FEES: *£*
FACILITIES: *Changing rooms and showers, full catering, bar, pro shop, teaching pro, trolley hire*
VISITORS: *Welcome everyday although pre-booking is advised*

Home to Perth's oldest course, King James VI Golf Club was established in 1858 and laid out in a picturesque setting – on an island in the middle of the River Tay. Surrounding it are the Perthshire hills with Kinnoul Hill and its 18th-century folly being most prominent.

It is a pleasure to play golf here and to take in the gentle scenery. The only drawback is in reaching the clubhouse and 1st tee. Visitors have to carry their clubs some distance from the car park across the river, up a steep flight of stairs, along a footpath attached to a railway bridge, downstairs and at least another few minutes to the clubhouse.

Once the tranquil haven of Moncrieffe Island has been reached you are sure of a wonderfully relaxing round of golf. Being absolutely flat throughout, the course is not taxing on the legs but there is plenty to test in terms of length and precision.

The par-4 4th is 463yd/423m off the yellow tees and requires two sound strokes to reach the green (which adjoins the 1st to form a double green). Long putts are therefore often called for on this hole.

Two other stimulating holes are the par-4 11th, with trees tight along the left and a transverse mound built to keep out floodwaters and the par-3 13th. Both greens are built close to the river bank and it is easy to play too strongly and end up in the reeds or river.

The 18th is a long hole of 423yd/387m off the yellows, a fine finish but reasonably straightforward if you keep away from the trees on either side.

Moncrieffe Island on the River Tay is the setting for King James VI Golf Club.

3 *Murrayshall*

Murrayshall Scone, Perthshire, PH2 7PH
TEL: *01738 551171* **FAX:** *01738 552595*
LOCATION: *From Perth take the A93 north towards Scone for 2 miles/3km and the hotel and golf complex is signposted to the right just before entering Old Scone*
COURSE: *18 holes, 6441yd/5887m, par 73, SSS 72*
GREEN FEES: *££*
FACILITIES: *Changing rooms and showers, sauna and steam room, full catering, bar, pro shop, teaching pro, driving range, indoor practice facility, buggy hire, club hire, trolley hire*
VISITORS: *Welcome everyday but pre-booking is advised*

Overlooking the Vale of Strathmore to the mountains of Highland Perthshire, Murrayshall is a only few minutes drive from the historic capital of Perth. Set in 130 acres/53 hectares of beautifully wooded grounds and surrounding an imposing country house hotel it is an ideal retreat either for the day or for a short break.

On holes such as the 1st, 2nd and 12th it can be slightly hilly but hardly taxing. Lines are taken from or through the stands of tall mature trees that abound throughout the course. The fairways are generous and the rough fairly forgiving. The 7th is probably the best hole on the outward nine, named Dog's Grave after the rather eerie burial marker to two dogs at the back of this green. The hole is a tight dogleg right of 379yd/346m with a narrow approach to the green and well-guarded with a thicket of fully grown trees and a burn passing near the front of the green. The 10th is also a delightful, downhill hole where it is best to lay up short of the pond before tackling the green. A well positioned tee-shot is critical.

Overall the par 5s are accessible in two shots to the competent hitter and Murrayshall remains a very fine test of rolling parkland golf. After golf, the hotel restaurant has a menu with traditional Scottish ingredients. The clubhouse also serves lunch and snacks.

Gleneagles (King's)

Gleneagles (King's), Gleneagles, Auchterarder, Perthshire, PH3 1NF

TEL: *01764 694469* **FAX:** *01764 694383*

EMAIL: *visitor.golf@gleneagles.com* **WWW:** *gleneagles.com*

LOCATION: *On A9 Perth to Stirling dual-carriageway, turn north (well-signposted) on A823 to hotel entrance*

COURSE: *18 holes, 6125yd/5598m, par 68, SSS 71*

GREEN FEES: *££££££ +*

FACILITIES: *Changing rooms and showers, full catering, bar, pro shop, teaching pro, golf academy, full driving and practice facilities, trolley hire, club hire*

VISITORS: *Welcome anytime though pre-booking is advised. Twilight golf is available after 5pm at reduced costs May to September*

GLENEAGLES
KING'S COURSE

HOLE	YD	M	PAR	HOLE	YD	M	PAR
1	352	322	4	10	429	392	4
2	386	353	4	11	221	202	3
3	360	329	4	12	352	322	4
4	443	405	4	13	423	387	4
5	149	136	3	14	249	228	4
6	455	416	5	15	438	400	4
7	430	393	4	16	128	117	4
8	155	141	3	17	367	335	3
9	335	306	4	18	453	414	4
OUT	3065	2801	36	IN	3060	2797	34

6125 YD • 55987M • PAR 68

The man who dreamed up Gleneagles, Donald Matheson, would be surely be pleased if he saw his creation today. His vision for a 'Playground of the Gods' has been realised, and Gleneagles' basks in the reputation of being one of the world's leading golfing resorts.

At the turn of the 20th century, Matheson beheld 670 acres/271 hectares of desolate moorland in the Vale of Strathallan bordered by a railway line and road and envisaged one of the world's first major golfing and leisure developments.

Five-times Open winner James Braid was asked to design two golf courses – the King's and Queen's. At the time, no professional golfer had ever designed a course so once again Matheson had contrived to start a trend. As it turned out for Braid, these two courses were considered the best of his work. The famous King's course and its neighbours still form part of one of the most beautiful golf settings in the world, surrounded on three sides by hills, glens and mountains with peaks such as Ben Ledi and Ben Vorlich away to the western distance.

Playing on the King's course gives one the impression of playing the Perthshire glens and straths in miniature (and you are the giant). The first few holes climb and fall over a surging terrain surrounded by heather, gorse, bracken and indigenous pine and birch trees. There is some restraint after the 5th where carrying distance and precise aiming are needed. Perhaps more than any other championship course, the King's offers the ultimate three-dimensional golf.

Braid's favourite hole on the King's was the 13th, aptly named Braid's Brawest. From the blue tees it plays blind to an undulating

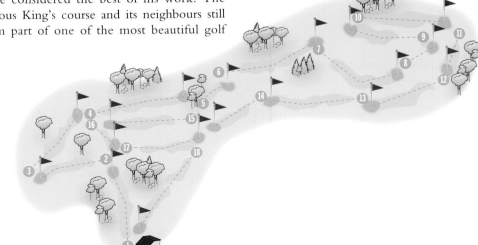

fairway. A sensible tee shot should avoid the large bunker on the left leaving a long second shot to a plateau green. Here the putting surface is beautifully framed by the scenery and slopes away from the fairway causing the ball to run away to the rear and beyond.

This course is not all hard work. There is plenty of fun to be found on holes such as the short par-4, 14th where a birdie or eagle is clearly possible. The finish is remembered for the saddle ridge that only the mightiest hitters will clear; then it is on to the green and home with all the comfort of the Dormie House.

Nature and golfing genius have conspired here to create one of the most unconstrained and aesthetically pure golf layouts. Wildlife abounds, and yellowhammers, oystercatchers, deer and grouse, are as much part of the course as are the daily golfers.

Looking back towards the Gleneagles Hotel from the 17th hole, the King's has a classic moorland setting with heather and coniferous trees and fast, large greens.

FROM MONARCH TO WEE

The Monarch's Course, the newest of Gleneagles' courses, is a bold and brassy test of over 7000yd/6400m, with roller-coaster cart paths and the hallmarks of an American course (or course designer at least) on furlough in Scotland. Laid out by golfing legend Jack Nicklaus, the course follows the natural contours of the landscape and has five tee positions per hole so novices can play a 5065yd/4629 as opposed to the tips which are too difficult for most mortals.

It is a course that was designed to accommodate the modern game and yet benefits from the wonderful Gleneagles setting. Unlike the King's and Queen's Courses, buggies are available for hire on the Monarch.

There is also at the Gleneagles complex a 9-hole, par-3, Wee Course which provides a more spontaneous test of your golf skills with two of the best par 3s on the estate: the 3rd and the 4th. It was part of the original 9 holes built in the 1920s. You will also find an excellent teaching and short practice area to help refine your game.

5 Gleneagles (Queen's)

Gleneagles (Queens), Auchterarder, Perthshire PH3 1NF
TEL: *01764 694469* **FAX:** *01764 694383*
EMAIL: *visitor.golf@gleneagles.com* **WWW:** *gleneagles.com*
LOCATION: *On A9 Perth to Stirling dual-carriageway,*
turn north (well-signposted) on A823 to hotel entrance
COURSE: *18 holes, 5660yd/5173m*
GREEN FEES: *££££££+*
FACILITIES: *Changing rooms and showers, full catering,*
bar, pro shop, teaching pro, golf academy, full driving and
practice facilities, trolley hire, club hire
VISITORS: *Welcome anytime though pre-booking is*
advised. Twilight golf available after 5pm (May-Sept)

Many visitors find the Queen's course at Gleneagles a gentler and more charming alternative to the King's. Maybe it does hide a more 'feminine' character. Certainly there are few more peaceful or attractive corners of golf to be walked through than those you encounter on this course. Stand along the 8th and 9th – the furthest point from the starter – on a fine summer's evening, and there is a temptation to simply set aside the clubs and drink in the tranquillity.

Unusually for a James Braid design, the Queen's tests from the outset with the 1st being one of the toughest holes on the course. At 409yd/374m from the visitors' tee, it doglegs left demanding an accurate tee shot to set up a reasonable crack at the green.

Teeing off from the 18th at the Queen's. You might consider hiring a caddie to help you round the course.

The 6th is a majestic hole that asks everything from your game: correct clubbing, length and accuracy with out-of-bounds to the right. Bunkers come into play off the tee as well as on the approach shots to the slightly elevated green. Locals say if you can hold your score together on the front 9 you should score well for the round.

The homeward stretch is a bit shorter with par 3s back-to-back at the 13th and 14th and water in play on both. At the 13th all the danger comes from a pond on the right, whereas the 14th has a two-tiered green raised high, and is guarded with deep bunkers with water on the right.

6 Crieff

Crieff Golf Club, Ferntower Course, Perth Road, Crieff
Perthshire PH7 3LR
TEL: *01764 652909* **FAX:** *01764 655096*
LOCATION: *On the east side of Crieff town, 17 miles*
/27km west of Perth on A85
COURSE: *18 holes, 6402yd/5851m, par 71, SSS 71*
GREEN FEES: *££*
FACILITIES: *Changing rooms and showers, full catering,*
bar, pro shop, teaching pro, buggy hire, trolley hire, club hire
VISITORS: *Welcome weekdays, and weekends except*
between 12am to 2pm and after 5pm; pre-booking is advised

A gently rising parkland course, Crieff combines a supremely groomed course, with a forgiving and generous design taking in sparse tree-lined avenues and uplifting views over the Strathearn Valley.

Accurate and long-distance tee shots are needed on this course. As most of its overall length is uphill, there is much work to be done to cover distances. There are three par 5s, all on the front 9 and all long, though reasonable, in that stray shots are not overly punished.

The 7th hole is a long par 4, usually playing into the wind and sloping right to left. The green is ample, allowing for the hole's 454yd/415m; most find it easier, indeed necessary, to lay up and attack the flag. Stop here to take in the views over the valley. The 12th is an even longer par 4 with a gentle dogleg right playing downwind and downhill to a tricky green. The adjacent Dornoch course makes an ideal 18-hole holiday outing.

7 St Fillans

St Fillans Golf Club, South Loch, Earn Road, St Fillans, Perthshire PH6 2NJ
TEL: *01764 685312* **FAX:** *01764 685312*
LOCATION: *12 miles/19km west of Crieff on the A85 route to Crianlarich*
COURSE: *9 holes, 5796yd/5298m, par 68, SSS 67*
GREEN FEES: £
FACILITIES: *Changing rooms and showers, full catering, trolley hire, club hire*
VISITORS: *Welcome weekdays except Saturday, although pre-booking is advised*

The long par-5 9th/18th hole at Killin Golf Club — possibly one of the most beautiful finishes in Scottish golf.

A taste of true holiday golf in beautiful surrounds with wild goats and deer close by awaits the visiting golfer at St Fillans. The course is a fairly easy layout set on the flat valley floor with only one slight elevation at the 3rd. Good golfers might find it a little short but it is ideal for trying out mid-iron play into small and sometimes undulating greens. The long 2nd hole, however, at 462yd/422m, is as tough as any par 4 in the area. The 3rd tee is elevated on the only hill on the course and this is barely a 20ft/6m climb. The unusual outcrop seen from here to the south is associated with the 6th-century Christian monk St Fillan.

The 7th is a long par 4, and to the left is a major burial ground associated with the Stewart family. Be warned, the village is a magnet for caravaners and vacationers and the course can get very busy in summer.

8 Killin

Killin Golf Club, Killin, Perthshire FK21 8TX
TEL: *01567 820312*
EMAIL: *djjenks@hotmail.com*
LOCATION: *A827 – west end of Loch Tay, east side of village of Killin*
COURSE: *9 holes, 5016yd/4585m, par 66, SSS 65*
GREEN FEES: £
FACILITIES: *Changing rooms and showers, full catering, bar, pro shop, trolley hire, buggy hire, club hire*
VISITORS: *Welcome weekdays and weekends apart from Medal competitions, although pre-booking is advised*

Killin Golf Club has, arguably, the most beautiful finishing hole in Scotland, the par-5, 9th/18th playing back down to the clubhouse framed by the dramatic but tranquil peaks of the Breadalbane Hills. The course itself is perched on the foothills of Ben Lawers just outside the charming Highland village of Killin, home to the Breadalbane Folklore Centre overlooking the Falls of Dochart.

This is a holiday course but one that most golfers would be delighted to play mainly because of its scenery and quirky holes. None of the holes are long, apart from the 9th, but there is plenty of appeal in each. The 4th offers a beguiling challenge for first-timers with a blind tee shot to a marker then a 2nd blind shot to the green. A nice touch is the old, hand-operated fire bell found half way up the fairway to warn the following group that you are clear. The 5th is a tiny par 3 that plays over a wall with the green tucked close behind calling for a high lob to clear it and still hold the small green. Once you have played the course you will appreciate a further round all the more knowing the ways of this tricky little gem.

9 Taymouth Castle

Taymouth Castle Golf Club, Kenmore, Perthshire PH15 2NT
TEL: *01887 830228* **FAX:** *01887 830765*
LOCATION: *6 miles / 10km west of Aberfeldy on the A827*
COURSE: *18 holes, 6066yd / 5544m, par 69, SSS 69*
GREEN FEES: *£*
FACILITIES: *Changing rooms and showers, full catering, bar, pro shop, teaching pro, trolley hire*
VISITORS: *Welcome everyday but pre-booking is advised*

It is hard to believe that the imposing Taymouth Castle is an ordinary golf club, open to members and the public with green fees that are quite cheap. Driving through the turreted gates and on to the Breadalbane Estate you might conjure up a magnificent Victorian hunting lodge or mansion at its centre, but the castle that comes into view surpasses all expectation.

The course that runs through its grounds appears so serene that the castle and the surrounding hills become, after a hole or two, a mere backdrop. Beautiful, mature broad-leafed trees stand sentinel over many of the holes and the wonderful view to the west of Ben Lawers and other peaks make an idyllic setting for golf. James Braid designed the course in the 1920s, and quickly tests any

As impressive as Gleneagles, but Taymouth Castle's fairly flat course is much easier to play.

golfer's metal with two short par 4s, a longer one, then a delightful par 3 over water at the 4th. Then there is a long and exacting par-5th. But overall the course plays fair with the rough kept down so players of every level will thoroughly enjoy this picturesque arena.

BARONIAL SCOTLAND

Not far north of Kenmore, at Blair Atholl, lies Blair Castle in Perthshire. This white-washed, turreted castle began as a tower in 1269 then went on to become the centre of the Atholl Dukedom held successively by the Stewart and Murray families. It was occupied by Cromwellian troops in 1652 and transformed into its present appearance in the 19th century. Over 30 rooms are open to the public and there are sumptuous paintings, furnishings, including a highly ornate four-poster bed, and tapestries to savour. The Ballroom typifies baronial Scotland with its timber roof and antlers on display. Outside you may encounter an Atholl Highlander piper playing the bagpipe – just to add to the atmosphere. On a more practical note, there is also a self-service restaurant indoors.

10 *Pitlochry*

Pitlochry Golf Club, Golf Course Road, Pitlochry,
Perthshire PH16 5QY
TEL: *01796 472792* FAX: *01796 473599*
LOCATION: *In Pitlochry, ½ mile/0.75km north from west
end of Main St, via Larchwood Road*
COURSE: *18 holes, 5811yd/5311m, par 69, SSS 69*
GREEN FEES: *££*
FACILITIES: *Changing rooms and showers, full catering,
bar, pro shop, teaching pro, trolley hire*
VISITORS: *Welcome weekdays and weekends although pre-
booking is advised. Play before 9.30am not allowed*

Looking back south over the Tummel
Valley from the 5th tee offers the golfer
one of Perthshire's most stirring panoramas.
The stiff climb at the first four holes of
Pitlochry is soon forgotten, though you may
still bear beads of sweat from the effort. Still,
after these early holes are scaled there is little
else to take your breath away except the
views.

On the tough climb of the opening holes
you also need to be able to pitch high on to
elevated greens. The 5th, whilst level, also
presents a high green with little to aim at as

*Pitlochry opens and closes on the side of a hill but
otherwise plays on largely undulating terrain.*

the rise continues on the right. After this it is
mainly downhill with an arresting array of
holes, especially the par-3, 16th densely
packed with pine trees. Pitlochry offers a
memorable round of golf and the chance to
enjoy the views and the fresh Highland air.

11 *Dunkeld and Birnam*

Dunkeld and Birnam Golf Club, (1892) Fungarth,
Dunkeld, Perthshire PH8 0HU
TEL: *01350 727524* FAX: *01350 728660*
LOCATION: *Northeast of the village of Dunkeld on the
Blairgowrie Road (A923)*
COURSE: *9 holes, 5322yd/4864m, par 70, SSS 67*
GREEN FEES: *£*
FACILITIES: *Changing rooms, catering, bar, trolley hire,
club hire*
VISITORS: *Welcome everyday except Saturday 10 to 11am
and between 1 to 2pm; pre-booking is advised*

Highland Perthshire is ideal for a few
casual rounds of golf in idyllic scenery
especially on the fine choice of 9-hole courses
known for their challenge as well as their
reasonable price. Dunkeld and Birnam is one
of the most popular, overlooking as it does
the Tay Valley and the Loch of Lowes. With
a new 9-hole section scheduled to open in
Spring 2001, playing close to the Loch, the
already agreeable layout will be extended into
what is anticipated to be an excellent 18
holes.

The original course offers some good tests
particularly at the 3rd hole which presents a
defensive rocky outcrop ahead of the green
and forces a lay-up and pitch over to a blind
green. For many, this long par 4 is best
played as a par 5. From the lofty outlook of
the 3rd green, the new section of the course
can be appreciated with the famous Loch of
Lowes as its background where Ospreys
breed each year.

Built on a pleasing, fertile piece of land,
the new section promises to add greatly to
the character of this already appealing course,
and make it one of Perthshire's most
entertaining layouts. But as it stands, there is
little wrong with the current configuration
for holiday golfers and low handicappers
alike to enjoy.

12 *Blairgowrie*

Rosemount Course (1889), Rosemount, Blairgowrie,
Perthshire PH10 6LG
TEL: *01250 872622* **FAX:** *01250 875451*
EMAIL: *admin@blairgowrie-golf.co.uk*
WWW: *blairgowrie-golf.co.uk*
LOCATION: *On A93, 15 miles/24km north-east of Perth,
signposted on west side of Blairgowrie*
COURSE: *18 holes, 6588yd/6021m, par 72, SSS 72*
GREEN FEES: *££££+*
FACILITIES: *Changing rooms and showers, full catering,
bar, pro shop, teaching pro, trolley hire, buggy hire, club hire
and caddies available if booked in advance*
VISITORS: *Welcome everyday, but pre-booking is advised*

*Yawning cross-bunkers await wayward shots at the 18th
green at Blairgowrie. This is a good driving hole with
most danger coming from the copse of trees on the right.*

Blairgowrie's Rosemount course enjoys a worldwide reputation for its long heather- and tree-lined fairways and immaculate greens. The greenkeeping here is second to none. The magnificent heathland layout will charm those that can hit straight and long, and frustrate the life out of those that stray. Long grass, heather, gorse and brambles carpet the avenues of pine and birch and a visit to either side of the fairway usually spells disaster.

This heathland course opens with a long par 4, slightly doglegged towards the green and guarded by typical Braid-designed bunkering. The 10th and 11th stand out as two back-to-back par 5s that dogleg in opposite directions. The most memorable holes are the closing three with the 16th being a mental test as much as anything. A stand of trees occupies the middle distance with out-of-bounds left and a loch also threatening. On the outer limits of a par 4, it needs a sure tee shot otherwise both distance and the narrowing fairway and bunkers ahead of the green will dismantle an attack. The 17th is a picturesque par 3 played from a raised tee over a wide gully with a fine, two-tiered green. Play long and, at worst, hope for assistance from the back-banking; play short and you'll get into all sorts of problems.

Rosemount's adjacent Lansdowne course is an equally tough test. Relocated, it would stand alone as a premier venue. The Wee course is the original course and has a charming par-4 2nd hole. This is by no means a par-3 course and calls for every club.

13 *Strathmore*

Strathmore Golf Centre, Leroch, Alyth, Perthshire PH11 8NZ
TEL: *01828 633322* **FAX:** *01828 633533*
EMAIL: *strathmore@golfcentre.freeserve.co.uk*
WWW: *uk-golf.com/clubs/strathmore*
LOCATION: *Near village of Alyth, just off the A926
Blairgowrie to Kirriemuir road south of Blackbird Inn*
COURSE: *18 holes, 6454yd/5899m, par 72, SSS 72*
GREEN FEES: *£*
FACILITIES: *Changing rooms and showers, full catering,
bar, pro shop, teaching pro, trolley hire, buggy hire, driving
range, practice bunkers and green; disabled facilities*
VISITORS: *Welcome everyday but pre-booking is advised*

As a pay-and-play facility Strathmore welcomes visitors with a most rewarding round combining challenge and a delightful setting overlooking the Vale of Strathmore. The Rannaleroch course's main defence on this fertile farmland tract is the rough bordering the wide fairways. However, it tends to be thin and wispy, so recovery is feasible. The 6th is a super short par 3 with a large pond at the green's edge.

Leitfie Links is an adjacent 9-hole, par-29 course, and Strathmore also has a floodlit driving range and all-purpose practice area.

14 Alyth

Alyth Golf Club, Pitcrocknie, Alyth, Perthshire PH11 8HF
TEL: *01828 632268 Fax: 01828 633491*
EMAIL: *mansec@alythgolf.freeserve.co.uk*
LOCATION: *16 miles/26km north of Dundee on A926 then one mile along B954 and well signposted*
COURSE: *18 holes, 6205yd/5671m, par 70, SSS 71*
GREEN FEES: *££*
FACILITIES: *Changing rooms and showers, full catering, bar, pro shop, teaching pro, buggy hire, trolley hire, club hire, practice area*
VISITORS: *Welcome anytime though pre-booking is advised*

Of the three 18-hole courses to be found near the village of Alyth, Alyth Golf Club is the original and some would still say the best. Laid out originally by Old Tom Morris and augmented and extended by James Braid it has all the character and challenge you would expect from a course of this heritage.

Though the fairways are tree-lined they are also generous so it is distance and accurate approaches into the greens that will yield points. There is the occasional oddity that you will find on any old Scottish course, such as blind tee shots or concealed greens but these are not frequent here and only add to the drama.

Of the front 9, the 5th is notable with a twisting burn creating a virtual island on which to lay up before attempting one of the hardest shots at Alyth. The green should only be 150yd/137m from your tee shot, but it stands high above with steep ramparts to roll a ball away and so is difficult to hit and hold. The back 9 produces a trio of holes that stand above the others, namely the 9th, 10th and 11th. These two long par 4s, followed by a par 5, pose a tight tee shot in every instance as well as narrow green approaches.

The long par-4 10th hole at Alyth.

15 Glenisla

Glenisla Golf Club, Pitrocknie Farm, Alyth, Perthshire PH11 8JJ
TEL: *01828 632445* **FAX:** *01828 633749*
EMAIL: *info@glenislagolf.com* **WWW:** *glenislagolf.com*
LOCATION: *16 miles/26km north of Dundee on A926 then one mile along B954 and well signposted*
COURSE: *18 holes, 6402yd/5851m, par 71, SSS 70*
GREEN FEES: *££*
FACILITIES: *Changing rooms and showers, full catering, bar, golf shop, buggy hire, trolley hire*
VISITORS: *Welcome anytime though pre-booking is advised. Tee times reserved for members before 9am and between 1 to 2pm*

For one of Scotland's newest courses, the Glenisla is already in excellent shape and set for a bright future. It is predominantly undulating with the design following the flow of the natural terrain, and there is ample challenge for the strongest players. The 2nd, aptly named The Whale, can cause your game to flounder at the opening stages if the wind is in your face. It is a 588yd/537m leviathan off the back tees and each firm blow will have to negotiate wind, well-positioned sand, and deep rough on both sides. There are two very large ponds on the course and the 4th and 5th incorporate the water to good effect. The back 9 is dominated by one hole, The Monster, a par 5 of 612yd/559m at full length

Monster par 5 holes are just some of the challenges presented by the Glenisla course near Alyth.

doglegging left. With trees still young the corner and its bunker can be flown, but too greedy an angle will end in snarling rough. The course concludes with two good tests, the 17th, a par 4 onto an elevated green, and the 18th, guarded by the Alyth Burn.

16 Kirriemuir

Kirriemuir Golf Club, Shielhill Road, Northmuir, Kirriemuir DD8 4LN
TEL: *01575 573317* **FAX:** *01575 574608*
LOCATION: *East side of Kirriemuir, taking the road from town centre and at crossroads of A926 and A928*
COURSE: *18 holes, 5510yd/5036m, par 68, SSS 67*
GREEN FEES: *£*
FACILITIES: *Changing rooms and showers, full catering, bar, pro shop, teaching pro, trolley hire, club hire*
VISITORS: *Welcome weekdays after 9.30am although pre-booking is advised. No visitors at weekends*

Above the charming town of Kirriemuir, Gateway to the Angus Glens, James Braid met the challenge of fitting 18 holes into just 77 acres/31 hectares: the result is an admirable and highly entertaining heathland/parkland course.

The front nine holes at Kirriemuir are reasonably straightforward although there are good tests at the 1st, 3rd and 6th. On the back nine beware the thicker vegetation along avenues of woods, gorse, and broom. The last two holes present difficulties: the 17th, a long par 3 of 180yd/165m is closed in by two majestic trees on either side of the green along with attendant bunkers. The par 4 388yd/ 355m 18th presents a long, uphill drive with a large oak tree blocking the right half of the fairway.

17 Forfar

Forfar Golf Club, Cunninghill, Arbroath Road, Forfar DD8 2RL
TEL: *01307 463773* FAX: *01307 468495*
LOCATION: *14 miles/22km north of Dundee. One mile from Forfar on A932 towards Arbroath*
COURSE: *18 holes, 6052yd/5532m, par 69, SSS 70*
GREEN FEES: *£*
FACILITIES: *Changing rooms and showers, full catering, bar, pro shop, teaching pro, driving range and putting green, trolley hire*
VISITORS: *Welcome everyday but on Saturday after 2.30pm, and pre-booking is advised*

Originally laid out by Old Tom Morris in 1871, this medley of links, parkland and heathland was upgraded by James Braid in 1926. The land was used in the 18th century to dry long rows of flax and the process established quite distinct rises and drops. The course is also carved through 80 acres/32 hectares of wooded estate making each hole feel enclosed.

A memorable test on the front 9 is the 5th hole, a par 3 of 200yd/183m through the trees. It is a long carry over rough, often into a wind to an awkward double-tiered green. The 12th is a rugged par 4 of 444 yd/406m where two excellent shots will be required to reach the green across the well-bunkered fairways.

The 15th, Braid's Best, is the signature hole, a long par-4 dogleg right, though not as drawn out as the 12th. A fade off the tee and fade for the second shot should put you onto the raised, sloping green, but par is still a respectable result.

18 Monifieth Medal

Monifieth Golf Links, The Links, Princes Street, Monifieth DD5 4AW
TEL: *01382 532767* FAX: *01382 535553*
LOCATION: *7 miles/11km east of Dundee off the A930 coast road*
COURSE: *18 holes, 6655yd/6083m, par 72, SSS 72*
GREEN FEES: *£££*
FACILITIES: *Changing rooms and showers, full catering and bar, pro shop, teaching pro, practice area, trolley hire, club hire*
VISITORS: *Welcome weekdays after 9.30am and weekends after 2pm Saturday and after 10am Sunday although pre-booking is advised*

The Medal Course is rather underrated or perhaps little known by visitors from outside the area. Amongst locals it has always been a popular links course and deservedly so. You tee off at the 1st hole next to the main East Coast railway line (the same one that passes many of the links courses on this coast). Any sign of a slice will arrive at the perimeter fence or onto the track itself.

Angling away from the railway line, the 4th is a notable par 4, a beautiful hole designed by nature which is quite difficult to reach in two because of its length. It is called the Feather Bed. The 5th and 6th return to the railway line and can be equally if not more daunting than the 1st. The 7th is one of the course's best holes playing over the burn – not unlike Carnoustie's famous 17th – where a winding burn narrows the driving area. A firm favourite though with many golfers is the little 14th, Sand Bed, perhaps the most enchanting hole on the course.

The 14th at Monifieth Medal – a qualifying course for the Open. The next-door Ashludie Course is less demanding.

19. *Carnoustie Championship Course*

Carnoustie Golf Links, Links Parade, Carnoustie, Angus DD7 7JE
TEL: *01241 853249* **FAX:** *01241 852720*
WWW: *carnoustie.co.uk*
LOCATION: *12 miles/19km north of Dundee following the A92 or coastal A930. In the centre of Carnoustie, follow signs for beaches and golf courses*
COURSE: *18 holes, 6941yd/6344m, par 72, SSS 75*
GREEN FEES: *££££+*
FACILITIES: *Changing rooms and showers, full catering, bar, pro shop, teaching pro, trolley hire*
VISITORS: *Welcome weekdays and weekends although pre-booking is advised. Handicap certificates must be shown to the starter prior to play and it is advisable to book well in advance*

CARNOUSTIE CHAMPIONSHIP COURSE

HOLE	YD	M	PAR	HOLE	YD	M	PAR
1	401	367	4	10	446	408	4
2	435	398	4	11	362	331	4
3	337	308	4	12	479	438	5
4	375	344	4	13	161	146	3
5	387	354	4	14	483	442	5
6	520	475	5	15	459	420	4
7	394	360	4	16	245	224	3
8	167	153	3	17	433	396	4
9	413	377	4	18	444	404	4
OUT	3429	3133	36	IN	3512	3211	36

6941 YD • 6344M • PAR 72

The Carnoustie Golf Club is one of the oldest in the world. Early records mention play in the Carnoustie area as far back as the 1520s, although, even by then, 'gowf' seems to have been well established.

The Open first came here in 1931 when Tommy Armour triumphed. Later, Henry Cotton, Ben Hogan, Gary Player and Tom Watson all took the trophy, and Paul Laurie from Aberdeen claimed the trophy in 1999. On its return to the Open championship circuit in that year, the course reinstated itself as perhaps the greatest test of golf in the world. In the first two days of the tournament the course was heavily criticised by some of the best-known golfers in the field, for its narrow fairways and unforgiving long rough.

As the 1999 Open progressed, it became evident that the course and the elements were contriving a battle royal and most, even the dissenters, conceded to the course's greatness and bowed to those who even came close to level par.

With a sandy sub-soil and open, rolling links terrain, this site is patently intended for the game. Allan Robertson laid out the first 10 holes on the current site in 1842 and 25 years later Old Tom Morris added a further eight. It was James Braid who designed the course as seen today although some of his holes were reckoned too weak for competitive play. The notorious final three were redesigned forming what is often

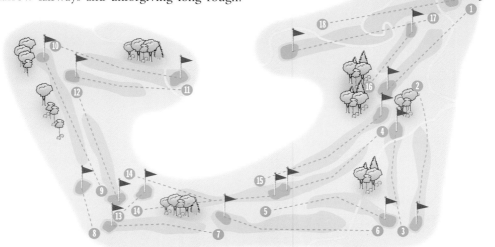

Barry Burn at the 10th (inset) and the 1st with Carnoustie town behind – two views of one of the greatest, most natural links in the world.

referred to as the sting-in-the-tail. The second is a significant test, a distinct links-like hole with the wind usually blowing from the right. It plays through an increasingly narrow valley and Braid's Bunker looms in the centre of the fairway at around 190yd/174m from the tee.

The 6th, Hogan's Alley, is one of the world's great par 5s. The tee shot is intimidating; out-of-bounds run left and two strong central bunkers force players to take the safer line to the right. In his one-and-only appearance in The Open in 1953, Ben Hogan took the more direct route between the fence and the bunkers in each of his four rounds on his way to victory, hence the name Hogan's Alley.

The 16th is set at the furthest distance allowed for a par 3. It is very well defended on the frontal approach with three deep, pot bunkers on the right side and one dominant bunker on the high ground of the left approach. Coupled with a tail wind, it is very difficult to reach and stay on the green in one.

The snaking Barry Burn dictates the landing area from the tee on the 17th or Island hole. It is foolhardy to try anything other than a safe landing on this narrow peninsula and even then, playing back into the wind, much can go wrong. The 18th – with its new tee box set back to maximise the hazards such as the Barry Burn, out-of-bounds to the left and rough to the right, completes this harrowing finale. The burn is where Frenchman Jean Van de Velde's hopes of winning the 1999 Open went out with the tidal waters.

There are two other excellent courses adjacent to the Championship course. The laudable Burnside course stands at 6020yd/5502m, par 69 and has its own intricacies and character not unlike its elder. The shorter Buddon Links, at 5420yd/4964m, par 66, is a scenic course, ideal for mid- to high-handicappers, although its greatly improved design and condition make it a fine and most enjoyable test for any player. Visiting golfers also have access to the new Carnoustie Golf Hotel and any of the six local clubs that play over this consumate linksland.

20 *Panmure*

Panmure Golf Club, Barry By Carnoustie, Angus DD7 7RT
TEL: *01241 853120* **FAX:** *01241 859737*
LOCATION: *On the A92 Dundee to Arbroath Road turn right at Signpost for Barry. Drive towards village and follow signs for course*
COURSE: *18 holes, 6317yd/5774m, par 70, SSS 71*
GREEN FEES: *£££*
FACILITIES: *Changing rooms and showers, full catering, bar, pro shop, teaching pro, trolley hire*
VISITORS: *Welcome weekdays. No visitors on Saturday and restrictions exist on Sunday; pre-booking is advised*

Full of Scottish links vigour, tradition (jackets and ties for the lounge), and distinction, Panmure is a testing neighbour to Carnoustie. At any time of the year it is challenging and if the wind and rough are high, it can be utterly demanding.

The course starts with an easy par 4 and 5, then becomes progressively more rigorous leading to the hardest hole on the course, the par-4 6th. At 387yd/354m, it leaves no room for error. Doglegging left amidst gorse and heather the target area from the raised and open tee is restricted, while the green is also raised and surrounded by gorse with the main East Coast railway line to its rear.

The majority of holes are more open and many, but not all, have a traditional links appearance. A serpentine burn defends the sloping 12th green while the 14th plays parallel to the railway with gorse on the left and some well positioned bunkers.

21 *Letham Grange Old*

Letham Grange, Old Course, Collision, Arbroath, Angus, DD11 4RL
TEL: *01241 890377* **FAX:** *01241 890725*
EMAIL: *lethamgrange@sol.co.uk*
WWW: *www.lethamgrange.co.uk*
LOCATION: *4 miles/6km north west of Arbroath on A993 and about 10 miles/16km northwest of Carnoustie*
COURSE: *18 holes, 6968yd/6369m, par 73, SSS 73*
GREEN FEES: *£££*
FACILITIES: *Changing rooms and showers, full catering, bar, pro shop, teaching pro, trolley hire, buggy hire*
VISITORS: *Welcome weekdays and weekends although pre-booking is advised. No visitors before 9.30am on weekends and before 10am on Tuesday*

The 'Augusta of the North' is what you'll often hear the Old Course at Letham Grange referred to. The parkland setting surrounds a mansion house hotel within a huge walled estate of mature woodland. The 1st hole starts in front of the hotel, an easy par 4 from an elevated tee – as long as you steer clear of the rough, which in the full-flush of growth is a serious hazard.

Designed with Augusta's Amen Corner in mind, Letham Grange's 8th to 10th holes are beautifully manicured and staged. The 8th plays over an ornamental lake, and calls for precise club selection and exact execution, otherwise water or woods surrounding the

The 8th at Letham marks the section of the course players might happily compare to Augusta National.

green will gather the ball. In late May and June, rhododendron bushes line the right side and with a little weir and pond it really is an outstanding setting. The 9th is a stretching par 5, doglegging left and asking for a draw from your second shot. If you make correct contact, you will be looking at the green. From its high tee the 10th offers a delightful view over a pond biting deep into the fairway from the right. There is a possible bail-out to the left but with various awkwardly placed trees and a slim landing surface it isn't much of an option. The Glen's Course is a 1000yd/914m shorter than the Old with none of the hazards. It's fun and testing with six par 3s.

22 Montrose

Montrose Medal Course, Traill Drive, Montrose, Angus DD10 8SW
TEL: 01674 672932 FAX: 01674 671800
LOCATION: Follow the A935 coastal route to Montrose and signs to golf courses
COURSE: 18 holes, 6495yd/5936m, par 71, SSS 72
GREEN FEES: ££
FACILITIES: Changing rooms and showers, full catering, bar, pro shop, teaching pro, trolley hire
VISITORS: Welcome everyday but pre-booking is advised

Of Angus's links courses there are none more linkslike than Montrose's Medal Course. Between the golf links and the beach there is little more than some raised, marram-grass-covered dunes. The wind, sand and sea spray all shake hands with a golfer encountering Montrose, especially on the front 9 which marches away from the clubhouse towards the water then turns left to flank the long, fine sandy beach.

The fairway undulations are relentless and pronounced on most holes, except for those that branch inland towards Montrose's second course, the Broomfield. Broom and gorse play a more significant roll in this section before the line turns back to the dunes at the 16th. This is a tough test into the wind and one that US golfing pro and historian Ben Crenshaw found especially intriguing when he visited. A par 3 of 235yd/215m, it presents a formidable tee

shot, wind or no wind. The green, should you avoid the bunkers and reach it in one, is heavily undulating and long, with the flag usually placed at the back.

The course remains rigorous to the end. The 17th is a fastidious par 4 at 418yd/382m onto a raised green with out-of-bounds up the right side. The 18th is open to south-westerly winds and has treacherously long grass to the right. Six bunkers surround the green and it is surprising how many make mistakes on this seemingly innocuous finish.

It is a little known fact that this singular and most challenging links is the fifth oldest course in the world, as golf has been played here since 1562. For serious links enthusiasts or golf historians Montrose is a must.

23 Edzell

Edzell Golf Club, High St, Edzell, Angus DD9 7TF
TEL: 01356 648462 FAX: 01356 648094
EMAIL: secretary@edzellgolfclub.demon.co.uk
LOCATION: Turn left onto B966 signposted to Edzell from main A90 dual carriageway just north of Brechin
COURSE: 18 holes, 6348yd/5802m, par 71, SSS 71
GREEN FEES: ££
FACILITIES: Changing rooms and showers, full catering, bar, pro shop, teaching pro, buggy hire, trolley hire, driving range, short game practice area
VISITORS: Welcome weekdays except between 4.45 to 6.15pm and weekends 7.30am to 10am and 12 to 2pm although pre-booking is advised

Edzell lies at the gateway to the Grampians in a delightful heathland setting. You begin the course on a gentle par 4, but on the 2nd tee, the fairway is unseen over a sudden rise with only a marker for guidance. At 436yd/399m from the visitors' tee and usually into the wind, the green is hard enough to reach in two yet it is also concealed from view below a wide, grassy bunker.

After this trial you can settle into a more relaxed trek through impressive groves of pine and larch with views north to the Grampian Mountains. Distance is required at several par 4s exceeding 400yd/365m but there is nothing overstrenuous. A particularly good par 3 is the uphill and well-protected 14th, Majuba (after a battle in the Boer War).

REGIONAL DIRECTORY

Where to Stay

Angus and Dundee Everyone wants to play Carnoustie's Championship course and now there is a splendid new hotel overlooking the links. The **Carnoustie Golf Hotel** (01241 411999) offers a wide range of facilities. Near Arbroath, **Letham Grange Resort Hotel** (01241 890373) has two fine golf courses. Dundee is the largest city in the area and the **Stakis Dundee** (01382 229271) is well situated for golf throughout Dundee, Angus and Fife, again with good leisure facilities. Somewhat classier is **South Kingennie House** (01382 350562) near Broughty Ferry, a converted farmhouse with an excellent restaurant. If you want to be near the action, **Fisherman's Tavern Hotel** (01382 775941) in Fort Street, Broughty Ferry, offers comfortable rooms with good food and excellent beer. On the other side of town is the larger **Swallow Hotel** (01382 641122) with a small leisure club.

Perthshire The regional centre of Perth is a good cultural base with plenty of golf close at hand. Just outside the city is the 4-star **Huntingtower Hotel** (01738 583771) with its excellent restaurant. **Murrayshall Country House Hotel** (01738 551171) is a very relaxing base with its own exceptional 18-hole parkland course.

Perthshire is well-endowed with excellent country house hotels tucked away in delightful scenery. Escaping into this wonderful hinterland, the **Lands of Loyal Hotel** (01828 633151) in Alyth is full of Victorian charms, while the nearby **Drumnacree House Hotel** (01828 632194) is a pleasant guest house. If you are playing at Rosemount, the **Moorfield House Hotel** (01828 627303) between Blairgowrie and Cupar Angus is worth considering. Also near Blairgowrie, **Kinloch House** (01250 884237) is supreme with 5 stars. **Dunkeld House Resort Hotel** on the banks of the Tay (01350 727777) offers good leisure facilities. Pitlochry is an ideal base for highland scenery, theatre and shopping with a host of courses nearby. Here, **Burnside Apartments** (01796 472203) offers upmarket studio accommodation with a delightful little bistro. Near Aberfeldy, **Farleyer House** (01887 820332) dates back to the 15th century and has an 'honesty bar' in the main lounge. It's surprising how honest you can be after a few of its fine malts.

To the west of the region, **Gleneagles Hotel** (01764 662231) reigns supreme with its King's and Queen's courses, as well as the newer Monarch's. The resort offers everything you could wish for but its two Braid courses are all most golfers need. Nearby **Auchterarder House** (01764 663646) offers 4-star comfort.

Where to Eat

Angus and Dundee For an exotic, delicious meal in Dundee, try the **Agacan Turkish Restaurant** (01382 644227). The **Royal Oak** (01382 229440) in Brook Street looks basic from outside but serves perhaps the best Indian cuisine in Scotland. Just outside Dundee is the more traditional **Old Mansion House** (01382 320366) near Auchterhouse offering haute cuisine. East of Dundee, **South Kingennie House** (01382 350562) has an excellent local reputation.

In Carnoustie the best restaurant is 11 Park Avenue, (01241 853336), a real hidden gem and most worthy of its one AA rosette. Travelling up the coast, the little **But'n'Ben** (01241 877223) in Auchmithie serves the tastiest local dishes such as a smoked haddock pancake or 'tatties, mince and skirly'. In the Angus interior, **Lochside Lodge** (01575 560340) is handy for Alyth or Kirriemuir courses with two AA rosettes.

Perthshire The two best eateries in Perth are the directly named establishments of **Let's Eat in Kinnoul Street** (01738 643377) and **Let's Eat Again in George Street** (01738 633771) which is slightly smaller with simpler fare. **The Lang Bar & Restaurant** (01738 472709) in the Perth Theatre is also worth considering.

Go out of your way for lunch at the **Ballathie House Hotel** (01250 883268) near Stanley, just north of Perth, and you will be entranced. Near the Birks of Aberfeldy, **Guinach House** (01887 820251) is run by international masterchef Bert MacKay and nearby **Farleyer House** (01887 820332) offers fine dining as well as a relaxed bistro. Dunkeld's **Stakis Dunkeld** (01350 727771) has a good restaurant. If you are playing at Crieff, call in at **Satchmo's Restaurant** (01764 656575) in the High Street.

What to Do

Angus and Dundee The city of **Dundee** appeals to those with a sweet tooth with its culinary delights such as Dundee Cake, marmalade (said to have been invented here in the 19th century by a local housewife) and old-fashioned sweets. These should not be hard to shop for. Journalism has also played a key role in the city's development and amongst the many titles that are produced in Dundee, are the famous 'Dandy' and 'Beano' comics. **RRS Discovery** and **Discovery Point** next to Olympia Leisure Centre and opposite the railway station is Dundee's main visitor attraction while **Verdant Works** in West Henderson's Wynd exposes the hardships of this industrial town's past. **Dundee Contemporary Arts** in the Nethergate hosts exhibitions of a topical nature. **Glamis Castle** is perhaps the top visitor attraction in Angus, birthplace of HRH the Queen Mother. North of Forfar on the B9134 is the famous **Aberlemno Sculptured Stones**, an amazing set of Pictish monoliths by the side of the road. Carry on to Brechin to discover the whole Pictish story at **Pictavia**. **Edzell Castle** is mainly ruined but the gardens are a delightful place to sit on a sunny day. More quirky is the **Glenesk Folk Museum**, 16 miles (26km) north-west of Brechin. Heading back towards Montrose, the **House of Dun** is on the A935 and is worth exploring. Towards Perthshire, the **Meigle Museum** contains some ancient specimens of Pictish stone carving.

Perthshire offers some fine lowland whisky and tours of Pitlochry's **Blair Atholl Distillery and Visitor Centre** and **Edradour Distillery,** 2 miles (3km) east of Pitlochry are enlightening. **Pitlochry Festival Theatre** on the west side of town and over the River Tummel is an excellent evening's diversion. The **Pass of Killiecrankie** is especially beautiful in Autumn, and the **Queen's View** of **Loch Tummel** takes some beating. A little further north on the A9, the **House of**

Bruar is a fantastic Scottish shopping emporium, probably the best in the country. Gifts range from clothing to food.

Travelling south again, near Kenmore the **Scottish Crannog Centre** at Croft-na-Caber is an interesting reminder of Celtic times. Nearer Perth, **Scone Palace** off the A93 is very popular while in Perth, the **Perth Theatre** puts on some excellent productions.

USEFUL INFORMATION
Angus & Dundee Tourist Information
Dundee, 7-21 Castle Street, Dundee DD1 3AA
Tel: 01382 527527 Fax: 01382 527550

Perthshire Tourist Information
Lower City Mills, West Mill Street, Perth, PH1 5QP Tel. 01738 627958

Aside from the King's and Queen's courses, both designed by James Braid, the five-star resort hotel of Gleneagles in Perthshire also boasts the 18-hole Monarch course designed by Jack Nicklaus, with five different tees at each hole.

Chapter 4
Aberdeen and Grampian

The broad shoulder of land at Scotland's north-east is known as Grampian – a mountainous region famous for malt whisky and archetypal Scottish castles. While there are indeed many such attractions to see and visit, as well as the spirit of the region to sample, few visitors realise the range of golf opportunities both within Grampian and outlying regions including the Isles of Orkney and Shetland. Grampian actually embodies some of the oldest and finest links courses in Scotland with Royal Aberdeen and Cruden Bay instantly springing to mind. There are many more excellent links courses all along the spectacular coastline, some well known and others nestling in sleepy coves and relished by locals. But the area is not confined to its coastal courses. Royal Deeside for instance has a half dozen of the finest parkland and heathland tracks

Left: Follow the castle trail – this is Craigievar Castle at Banchory in Aberdeenshire – or join as a spectator at the Braemar Gathering (above) in Deeside.

nestled in stunning scenery and commanding a high level of playing skill. The area was discovered by Queen Victoria and remains a hide-away for today's Royals yet it is equally welcoming to all of its visitors.

Aberdeen Golf

The city of Aberdeen itself has many admirable golf courses. Despite the Granite City's reputation as the oil capital of Europe, golf has never become expensive. The city's premier municipal course, Hazelhead No 1, was laid out by Dr Alister Mackenzie (the architect who forged Augusta National in Georgia), and the course can be played for little more than the cost of a golf glove. Other facilities such as King's Links Golf Centre can help fine-tune a player's swing with a host of modern teaching aids to prepare for the many challenges that can be reached all within a short drive of the city.

Newmachar Golf Club is the home course to the 1999 Open Champion, Paul Lawrie, and both of its 18-hole

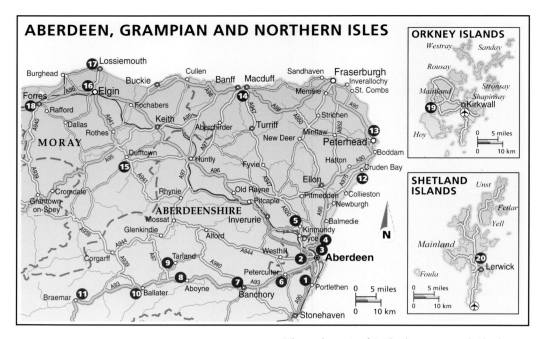

ABERDEEN, GRAMPIAN AND NORTHERN ISLES

ORKNEY ISLANDS

Westray   Sanday
Rousay
Mainland   Stronsay
                  Shapinsay
(19)   Kirkwall
Hoy   0   5 miles
             0   10 km

Lossiemouth
Burghead
Cullen   Banff Macduff   Sandhaven Fraserburgh
(17)
Buckie   Inverallochy
(16) Elgin   Memsie   St. Combs
Forres   Fochabers
(18) Rafford   Keith   Strichen
Dallas   Aberchirder Turriff
Rothes   New Deer
MORAY   Dufftown   Mintlaw   (13)
                                 Peterhead
(15)   Huntly   Fyvie   Boddam
Cromdale   Rhynie   Old Rayne Hatton   Cruden Bay
Grantown-   Ellon   (12)
on-Spey   Pitcaple Pitmedden Colliston
        ABERDEENSHIRE   Newburgh
Mossat   Inverurie   (5)
Glenkindie   Kinmundy   Balmedie
                Alford   Dyce (4)
Corgarff   Westhill (3)
          Tarland   (2)   Aberdeen
(9)   Peterculter
(8)   (7)   (6) (1)
Braemar (11) (10) Ballater Aboyne Banchory Portlethen 0 5 miles
                                              0 10 km
                                     Stonehaven

N

SHETLAND
ISLANDS   Unst
                      Fetlar
                      Yell
Mainland
                      (20)
Foula   Lerwick
           0 5 miles
           0 10 km

The northeast tip of Scotland centres around Aberdeen with Cruden Bay, Duff House Royal and some spectacular island courses awaiting.

The 18th on Old Moray is called appropriately Home. It is a par-4 of over 400yd/365m.

venues are well worth experiencing. Further north is a string of both parkland and seaside clubs stretching from Fraserburgh to Forres. These include in their ranks the excellent parkland course of Duff House Royal, another Mackenzie creation, renowned for the size and quality of its greens.

Inland towards the Grampian Mountains, the area is equally blessed with a multitude of attractive courses, but there is one hazard you might not have prepared for. This is malt whisky country and the bulk of Scotland's distillers are found throughout these misty glens. With a dram on offer at many of these establishments, driving of any description may best be abandoned.

Planning an Itinerary
The routing for a golf trip to Aberdeen and Grampian is again, a matter of choosing which courses you wish to play.

There are several segments that are worth considering on their own such as Aberdeen city and its surrounding courses, Royal Deeside, the north east coast with Cruden Bay and Peterhead, the interior area with Huntly and Inverurie, or the Moray Coast which has a fair number of courses including Duff House Royal and Old Moray to name just two exceptional clubs. Most of these are within striking distance of Aberdeen which offers good rail, air and road links.

The Northern Isles

The Northern Isles of Orkney and Shetland are best reached either via plane from Aberdeen airport or by ferry from Aberdeen harbour – although Orkney is also served by the shorter ferry crossing from Scrabster on the north coast of the Scottish mainland. Orkney is famed for its archaeology while Shetland may be most famous for its ornithology. Nevertheless both island areas offer golf of a very good standard, along with an exceptional welcome to players who take the time to visit these remote courses.

For further information on the Aberdeen and Grampian region *see pages 100-101*.

Surrounded by Duff House Royal golf club, the Georgian Baroque mansion of Duff House rises majestically.

⛳ *Portlethen*

Portlethen Golf Club, Badentoy Road, Porthlethen, Grampian AB12 4YA
TEL: *01224 781090* **FAX:** *01224 781090*
LOCATION: *Off A90, south of Aberdeen. Turn off at superstore and follow signs for Badentoy Park*
COURSE: *18 holes, 6670yd/6096m, par 72, SSS 72*
GREEN FEES: *£*
FACILITIES: *Changing rooms and showers, full catering, bar, pro shop, teaching pro, trolley hire, buggy hire, club hire, driving range, short game practice*
VISITORS: *Welcome everyday but pre-booking is advised*

From its impressive clubhouse, the relatively new golf course of Portlethen appears open to the elements and generally plays longer than its yardage suggests.

The course offers a good mixture of holes in its rolling parkland. There are several lengthy holes nicely balanced with delightful par 3s. The toughest hole on the course, the par-5 506yd/462m 18th, is a beast. If the wind is coming at you, a good-looking score could end up in the litter bin. The hole has out-of-bounds down the left, a burn crossing the middle of the fairway and a lot of distance to cover with every strike. This is a hole that throws everything at you.

Portlethen offers a charming hole at the 5th, a gorgeous little par 3 hole played across a pond with trees protecting the left side along with a stone bridge.

⛳ *Hazelhead*

Hazelhead No 1, Hazelhead Park, Aberdeen, Grampian, AB15 8BD
TEL: *01224 321830*
LOCATION: *In Hazelhead Park on the west side of Aberdeen off Westhill Road*
COURSE: *18 holes, 6204yd/5670m, par 70, SSS 7*
GREEN FEES: *£*
FACILITIES: *Pro shop, teaching pro, putting green*
VISITORS: *Welcome everyday but pre-booking is advised*

A real surprise awaits golfers who might not expect too much from a busy municipal facility. The course hass been much remodelled since Alister Mackenzie had a hand in it, and heavy use has taken some toll, but Hazelhead is well maintained by the greenkeepers.

The course plays through tree-lined avenues but also opens out to provide airy views across to Aberdeen. There are several fairly tight, tree-lined par 4s, such as the 2nd at just under 400yd/366m, and the 18th which is an excellent finishing hole, but it is the short holes which make the course. Both the 9th and the 12th are long par 3s with out-of-bounds and bunkers presenting a clear danger. The par-3 5th is deceptive with the woods behind it and a marked dip to the front, which is not appreciated from the tee. For first timers it is easy to select the wrong club. By contrast, the par 5s offer some hope.

The Whisky Trail

Scotland gave many things to the world but golf and whisky are two of the most appreciated. For many, a dram of good Scotch whisky, particularly of the single malt variety, goes as much with the post–game ceremonies as a handshake at the 18th and adjournment to the 19th hole.

The commercial production of Scotch whisky began more than 300 years ago when an Argyll farmer produced the drink in a simple device using a similar method to that of the monks who were distilling centuries earlier. In the late 17th century a landowner, Duncan Forbes, was granted the rights to produce whisky 'from any of the grain grown on his estate' without paying tax. When, in 1784, this 100-year-old monopoly was abolished, distilleries rapidly sprang up throughout central Scotland and began to export to England. The English war with France and high taxes forced these small lowland distilleries out of business, but the trade carried on by means of illicit stills.

Remote Highland glens provided the ideal setting to conceal the new cottage industry, and the peat fires and pure water of the glens, allied to more traditional methods, resulted in an even more palatable product.

Regional Variations

Scotland's whiskies vary from region to region. The distilleries below a line from Dundee to Greenock produce lowland malts which are lighter with a subtle flavour best suited as aperitifs. Whisky produced above the line is considered Highland. The east of Scotland from Dundee to Royal Lochnagar produces a whisky whose predominant flavour is malt, although much depends on how it is casked. To the west, from Speyside to Oban, the whisky is very well balanced. There are, however, distinct flavours to be found in the Islays.

Speyside is the modern heart of whisky production with over 30 per cent of Scotch malt whisky including Glenlivet, Glenfarclas, and Glenfiddich coming from this small area. This is where the illegal trade used to flourish. A Malt Whisky Trail is clearly signposted along some 70 miles/112km of winding roads.

Some Scottish Whiskies by Region

• **Speyside** Aberlour • Cardhu (Aberlour) • Cragganmore (Ballindalloch) • Dallas Dhu (Forres) • Glendronach (Huntly) • Glenfarclas (Ballindalloch) • Glenfiddich (Keith) • Glen Grant (Rothes) • Glen Keith (Keith) • Glenlivet (Ballindalloch) • Macallan (Aberlour) • Strathisla (Keith)

• **Northern Highlands** Clynelish (Brora) • Dalwhinnie Glenmorangie (Tain) • Glen Ord (Muir of Ord) • Tomatin
• **Eastern Highlands** Fettercairn Glencadam (Brechin) • Royal Lochnagar (Ballater)
• **Southern Highlands** Aberfeldy • Blair Atholl • Edradour (Pitlochry) • Glengoyne (Dumgoyne) • Glenturret (Crieff)
• **Western Highlands** Ben Nevis (Fort William) • Oban

• **Lowlands** Glenkinchie (Pentcaitland)

• **Islay** Bowmore Lagavulin (Port Ellen) • Laphroaig (Port Ellen)
• **Islands** Arran (Lochranza) • Highland Park (Kirkwall, Orkney) • Talisker (Carbost, Skye) • Tobermory

Glen Grant's distillery at Rothes, Speyside.

Royal Aberdeen

Royal Aberdeen Golf Club, Balgownie Links, Links Road, Bridge of Don, Aberdeen, AB23 8AT
TEL: *01224 702571* **FAX:** *01224 826591*
LOCATION: *2 miles/3km north of Aberdeen, off A92 at Bridge of Don. Turn right at Ellon Rd, and turn left into Links Road*
COURSE: *18 holes, 6372yd/5824m, par 70, SSS 71*
GREEN FEES: *££££££*
FACILITIES: *Changing rooms and showers, full catering, bar, pro shop, teaching pro, trolley hire, caddies and caddie cars by arrangement, club hire*
VISITORS: *Welcome weekdays between 10 to 11.30am and 2 to 3.30pm, and weekends after 3.30pm, although pre-booking is advised. Handicap certificates are required*

ROYAL ABERDEEN
BALGOWNIE LINKS

HOLE	YD	M	PAR	HOLE	YD	M	PAR
1	409	374	4	10	342	313	4
2	530	485	5	11	166	152	3
3	223	204	3	12	383	350	4
4	423	387	4	13	375	347	4
5	326	298	4	14	390	357	4
6	486	444	5	15	341	312	4
7	375	343	4	16	389	356	4
8	147	134	3	17	180	165	3
9	453	414	4	18	434	397	4
OUT	3372	3083	36	IN	3000	2743	34

6372 YD • 5824M • PAR 70

King Edward VII granted royal patronage to this club in 1903 – some 120 years after it was formed. Today the Balgownie Links remains a hidden gem of Scottish golf with a front nine of true Scottish links that is hard to beat. Interspersed with rich turf and tight, rolling fairways, no two holes are remotely similar, and each one gambols through a natural ecosystem that is both a delight to behold as well as to play.

Both Archie Simpson and James Braid had a hand in designing this course though the strong features of the terrain dictated their outcome. There have been few changes since.

Wind-driven sand from the dunes and beach frequently invades the first green as well as the high tees of the front nine perched along 50ft/15m hummocks. With a mix of heathland vegetation and long, hoary marram grass on the sea-side, as opposed to mainly gorse, heather and thick u n d e r g r o w t h l a n d w a r d,

there is little room for error with any shot.

The 1st appears to be an easy start but this proves not to be the case. A wide fairway plays downhill from the elevated tee and falls into a deep hollow just before the raised green. On a course not known for large greens the 1st offers the most difficult, leaning towards the fairway and also sloping away to the left.

The course then turns to play in the lee of the sand dunes mainly following a valley. This stretch is one of the most unaffected pieces of golf terrain that you are likely

to find and worthy of all the praise and rancour that is poured upon it in equal measures. The 2nd is a natural par 5 with a long carry over grassy hillocks. But again, as on any Balgownie hole, the wind remains relatively calm in the valley; therefore it is all too easy to be deceived as to the force of the gusts above dune level.

The 1st, 8th and 9th are the best of the outward stretch. The 8th is a delightful par 3 which can require a 3-iron one day and a

Large greens protected by fearsome bunkers with swales and hummocks, mark the Balgownie Championship Course as a classic links course. This is the lush 16th.

pitching wedge the next. The most favoured shot here is a low punch shot to the left of the green. There are no less than 10 bunkers surrounding the green. The 9th hole curves over the burn and along the last part of the dunes before the dunes carry on into the adjacent Murcar Golf Club's domain.

Turning towards the 10th the wind will most often be in your face. Less undulating than the front nine, the remaining holes use blind tee shots, hidden troughs and more difficult putting surfaces to defend themselves. The 12th to the 16th is a string of par 4s each with its own set of hazards aptly described by the name of the hole such as Blind, Dyke, Well and Hill. The 14th is a Stroke Index 1 which, on a normal day, is a wonderful hole requiring two perfectly struck shots. A dry ditch runs across the fairway at about 230yd/210m out which gathers more than its fair share of good tee shots. A long iron into the narrow right side of the fairway is the safer option, leaving a 190yd/174m second shot over an old dyke to a narrow, well-bunkered green.

The concluding three holes are an excellent 4-3-4 finish. The 16th sets up to put you over the top of the hill – blind off the tee, of course and two long accurate shots are essential – while the 17th is a fine example of the excellent short holes on this course. The 18th is reserved but defiant and could take advantage of the over confident or over tired.

Royal Aberdeen is not long on the card but tends to play longer because of wind conditions which change all the time. As Bernard Darwin, prolific golf writer (and relative of Charles), wrote: 'It represented a huge gap in my golfing education not to have played Balgownie until now, much more than a good golf course, a noble links.' For a less challenging, less wearing and less expensive round, try Royal Aberdeen's shorter 18-hole Siverburn Course.

🏌 *Murcar*

*Murcar Golf Club, Bridge of Don, Aberdeen, Grampian,
AB23 8BD*
TEL: *01224 704354* **FAX:** *01224 704354*
EMAIL: *murcar-golf-club@lineone.net* **WWW:** *murcar.co.uk*
LOCATION: *Off A90 at Murcar roundabout roughly 5
miles/8km from Aberdeen centre*
COURSE: *18 holes, 6287yd/5746m, par 71, SSS 71*
GREEN FEES: *£££*
FACILITIES: *Changing rooms and showers, full catering,
bar, pro shop, teaching pro, practice ground and driving
range, trolley hire, club hire, caddies by arrangement*
VISITORS: *Welcome except Tuesday before 12.30pm,
Wednesday after 12 noon, Saturday before 4pm and
Sundays before 12 noon, although pre-booking is advised. A
handicap certificate is also required*

The enduring response to a round at Murcar is that it is difficult, but will give way to those who are not over-ambitious with the driver and can adapt to the prevailing conditions. Murcar's course is no brute on length, but the main factor to face is how to play the ball into or against the wind.

Two easy par 4s open the course. The holes are straight, wide avenues lined with light rough and typical links bumps and dips. At the 3rd hole the links characteristics become exaggerated and the rough increases in ferocity, while the green is hidden in a natural bowl of dunes.

From a raised tee, and the sea to the right, the 7th at Murcar is an excellent challenge with two burns crossing the fairway although the second of these can threaten a good drive. If you land left you could block yourself out with the gorse and hill there, so this is a hole that will reward the straight drive. The green is protected by two distinct dunes and green-side bunkers. The 15th offers from its elevated tee superb views of most of the course towards Aberdeen as well as the sea. Next to it the 16th is a par 3 with carry most of the way on to a sloping, tricky green.

Keep in mind the enjoyable Strabathie course which is 5392yd/4928m and has two sets of tees offering an ideal outing for ladies or family groups. Whichever course you play you are sure to relish this tumbling stretch of challenging linksland.

*Teeing off from the 390yd/356m par-4 1st at
Newmachar's Hawkshill Course.*

🏌 *Newmachar*

*Newmachar Golf Club, Swailend, Newmachar,
Aberdeenshire AB21 7UU*
TEL: *01651 863002* **FAX:** *01651 863055*
LOCATION: *12 miles/19km north of Aberdeen and 2½
miles/4km north of Dyce on A947*
COURSE: *18 holes, 6623yd/6053m, par 72, SSS 74*
GREEN FEES: *£££*
FACILITIES: *Changing rooms and showers, full catering,
bar, pro shop, teaching pro, driving range and practice, trolley
hire, buggy hire, club hire*
VISITORS: *Welcome everyday but pre-booking is advised*

Combining an American flavour plus some of the best aspects of a Scottish heathland, the Hawkshill Course at Newmachar is a a championship–standard parkland course and a testing treat. There are two exceptional 18-hole layouts here as well as a magnificent clubhouse and one of the largest practice-teaching facilities in Scotland – making Newmachar one of the main golf complexes in the northeast.

Local Paul Lawrie's win in the 1999 British Open put Newmachar on the map but visitors who had played the courses before were already great fans. A regular host to the Scottish Seniors Open, parts of it are often likened to Rosemount or Gleneagles.

The new Swailend course is a broad, rolling parkland of 6300yd/5758m. It has been planted with over 15,000 still young trees, which present a considerable challenge.

Peterculter

Peterculter Golf Club, Oldtown, Burnside Road,
Peterculter, AB14 0LN
TEL: *01224 735245* **FAX:** *01224 735580*
LOCATION: *4 miles/6km from Aberdeen take North
Deeside Road (A93); turn left (signposted) on east side*
COURSE: *18 holes, 5924yd/5415m, par 68, SSS 69*
GREEN FEES: £
FACILITIES: *Changing rooms and showers, full catering,
bar, pro shop, teaching pro, trolley hire, buggy hire, club
hire, driving range, short game practice*
VISITORS: *Welcome everyday but pre-booking is advised*

Set on the banks of the River Dee,
Peterculter is a swanky Aberdeen suburb
with a golf club to match. You may wonder if
this is a private course for high-flying
members, but it could not be more easy-
going and welcoming to visitors.

It is relatively new and built on three
different levels with the River Dee forming
much of its southern boundary. It starts at its
highest point and meanders down towards and
along the riverside before working back again.
Some of the best holes are at river level
commencing with the tranquil 9th back-
dropped by the Dee and an old fishing lodge.
The following three holes zigzag back and
forth on the flat river basin and provide some
excellent golf with the 12th being the toughest
par 4 on the course.

Banchory

Banchory Golf Club, Kinneskie Road, Banchory,
Grampian, AB31 5TA
TEL: *01330 822365* **FAX:** *01330 822491*
LOCATION: *On the Royal Deeside route, the A93, 18
miles/28km south west of Aberdeen. From Stonehaven 13
miles/20km on A957*
COURSE: *18 holes, 5775yd/5278m, par 69, SSS 68*
GREEN FEES: ££
FACILITIES: *Changing rooms and showers, full catering,
bar, pro shop, teaching pro, practice area, trolley hire, buggy
hire, club hire*
VISITORS: *Welcome everyday but pre-booking is advised*

Banchory's golf course lies in the heart of
Royal Deeside and enjoys a delightful
riverside parkland setting next to the Dee. It
offers testing holes over burns or through
trees on a course that is split into two levels.

But its main quality is its picturesque
surroundings. There are many exciting holes
but it is not an over-strenuous course to play.

The 2nd is a good short hole of
224yd/205m. Most players take a driver or
wood but accuracy into the small green is as
important as distance. The 4th is an excellent
par 4 of 444yd/406m usually into a prevailing
wind making it a severe test. The par-4 8th is
one of the new holes on the course with a
wide but shallow green that is well-defended
by bunkers.

The 12th hole is regarded as one of the best
par-3s in the country. At 183yd/167m, the
green is surrounded by mature Scots pine, and
a narrow burn runs across its entrance. The
420yd/384m 13th is one of the most difficult
par 4s in the region: teeing off through a tree-
lined channel, the best strategy then is to lay-
up short of burn.

Out of this sequence of good holes the
16th is perhaps the most noteworthy: at only
88yd/80m the Doo'cot is one of Scotland's
shortest holes, almost as high as it is long, and
set next to the unusual structure that was used
to keep pigeons.

The par-5 514-yd/470-m 10th Oaks at Banchory.

Aboyne

Aboyne Golf Club, Formaston Park, Aboyne, Grampian, AB34 5HP
TEL: *01339 886328* **FAX:** *01339 887592*
LOCATION: *Follow the Royal Deeside road (A93) and signposted on the east side of village of Aboyne*
COURSE: *18 holes, 5944yd/5433m, par 68, SSS 69*
GREEN FEES: *££*
FACILITIES: *Changing rooms and showers, full catering, bar, pro shop, teaching pro, practice area, trolley hire, club hire*
VISITORS: *Welcome everyday but pre-booking is advised*

At Aboyne you almost feel that you are playing two separate courses. The front nine is a beautiful tree-lined parkland; the lush avenues have decorative cherry trees or short but maturing pines leading up to Aboyne Loch. But once you have played the 9th – a long dogleg that skirts Loch Aboyne – you appear to enter highland-mixed-with-heathland.

While the challenge up to now has been off the tees and placing the ball out of reach of the shrubbery, the test on this section is much tighter with little undulations making an even lie a rarity. The final holes are parkland again, but don't be lulled by the well-maintained decorative trees and ponds. Aboyne will give you a demanding run all the way back to the clubhouse.

Tarland

Tarland Golf Club, Aberdeen Road, Tarland, Aboyne, Aberdeenshire, AB34 4TB
TEL: *013398 81000* **FAX:** *013398 81000*
LOCATION: *From Aberdeen take the A944 then A974*
COURSE: *9 holes, 5816yd/5315m, par 67, SSS 68*
GREEN FEES: *£*
FACILITIES: *Changing rooms, catering, bar, trolley hire*
VISITORS: *Welcome everyday but pre-booking is advised*

One of the best golfing bargains in the region must surely be this 9-hole course a few minutes' drive north of Aboyne. The club is relaxed and very friendly. You rarely have to wait long for a tee time and the course is a gentle but exciting saunter through hilly Royal Deeside. A corner of the course comprising the 4th and 5th holes is the one to savour. The entrance to the 373yd/341m par-4 4th is safeguarded by a burn crossing about 20yd/18m in front of the green while trees and a pond beckon those not accurate with their second shot. The 5th is a long par 3 of 238yd/218m to a small, sloping green with trees on either side along the hole. The green is not easy to roll onto, but the distance could mean you have to hope for a kindly kick and some travel along the ground. The continuing holes journey back and forth on a more exposed stretch, but are just as testing.

The 9th at Tarland, a beautiful inland wooded course only some 45 minutes' drive from the centre of Aberdeen. The area is rich in wildlife and a pause on a fairway may be rewarded with the sight of soaring buzzards.

Ballater

*Ballater Golf Club, Victoria Road, Ballater, Grampian,
AB35 5QX*
TEL: *013397 55567* **FAX:** *013397 55057*
LOCATION: *42miles/68km west of Aberdeen on A93, and
on the west side of town.*
COURSE: *18 holes, 6112yd/5586m, par 70, SSS 69*
GREEN FEES: *£*
FACILITIES: *Changing rooms and showers, full catering,
bar, pro shop, teaching pro, practic area, trolley hire, buggy
hire, club hire*
VISITORS: *Welcome weekdays and weekends except
between 12 and 2pm although pre-booking is advised*

Framed by fir-covered mountains, Ballater
town has a splendid train station
sanctioned by Queen Victoria (she would not
have one nearer to Balmoral) and is famous
for its local spa water. It also has a welcoming
golf club just behind the centre of town. The
River Dee meanders alongside the course's
southern flank but rarely comes into play.

Ground conditions and the greenkeeping at
Ballater reflects its lofty status and combined
with the scenery, it produces an excellent
golfing escape. The fairways reveal subtle
undulations (not unlike a links course) that
can cause problems even to a well-hit ball or
lead to an awkward lie. The par-3 5th is one
of the finest in the area. It sports a formidable
bunker to the front right of the green, and a
10ft/3m drop along the left side. Many
visitors struggle with this hole trying to hit
and hold the green first time.

*Ballater is fairly flat, a mix of heathland and parkland,
and is surrounded by mountains. This is the par-5 11th.*

BRAEMAR GATHERING

Set over 1000ft/915m above sea level, Braemar is
an invigorating place and a fine setting for the
famous Highland Games. They are held each year
on the first Saturday of September. Dating back to
the 11th century, local clans would meet to pick
the strongest and bravest for battle in what is now
a worldwide event with tossing the caber (a
stripped pine nearly 20ft/6m long) being a
highlight. Since Queen Victoria's day the Royal
Family have attended so this traditional Scottish
gathering is doubly popular. Nearby Balmoral
Castle is open (just a few rooms and the grounds)
from May to July, Mondays to Saturdays.

Braemar

*Braemar Golf Club, Cluniebank Road, Braemar,
Grampian, AB35 5XX*
TEL: *01339 741618* **FAX:** *01224 704471*
LOCATION: *From centre of village follow signs and road
along west side of River Clunie about 1mile/1.6km from
village centre*
COURSE: *18 holes, 4916yd/4493m, par 64, SSS 64*
GREEN FEES: *£*
FACILITIES: *Changing rooms and showers, full catering,
bar, pro shop, trolley hire*
VISITORS: *Welcome everyday but pre-booking is advised*

Scotland's highest 18-hole golf course, set at
some some 2000ft/610m above sea level,
is nonetheless a short, easy-walking and
enjoyable course to play. Many holes run next
to the River Clunie. It is a holiday venue rich
in quality and challenge in one of the region's
most scenic spots.

The 2nd hole is one of the most exciting
par 4s in the Grampian region, for its raised
green, 25 ft/8m above the fairway, and the
amazing backdrop of Glenshee. Playing over
the valley of the River Clunie, the fairways
are flat with only one or two climbs from
green to tee or on to elevated greens.

Apart from the 2nd hole the river does not
come into play unless you are seriously errant,
and the main hazard is keeping your gaze
away from the views. Aside from the
refreshing golf, a visit to the delightful village
of Braemar makes a trip to this area most
rewarding.

Cruden Bay

Cruden Bay Golf Club, Aulton Road, Cruden Bay,
Peterhead, AB42 0NN
TEL: *01779 812285* **FAX:** *01779 812945*
LOCATION: *7 miles/11km south of Peterhead, 23 miles/
37km north east of Aberdeen off the A90 on the A975
signposted to Newburgh on Ythan*
COURSE: *18 holes, 6395yd/5841m, par 70, SSS 72*
GREEN FEES: *££££*
FACILITIES: *Changing rooms and showers, full catering,
bar, pro shop, teaching pro, driving range, practice facilities,
trolley hire, club hire, caddies available if booked well in
advance*
VISITORS: *Welcome weekdays and weekends although some
restrictions apply and pre-booking is advised*

CRUDEN BAY

HOLE	YD	M	PAR	HOLE	YD	M	PAR
1	416	380	4	10	385	351	4
2	339	310	4	11	149	136	3
3	286	261	4	12	320	292	4
4	193	176	3	13	550	502	5
5	454	415	4	14	397	363	4
6	529	484	5	15	239	218	3
7	392	358	4	16	182	166	3
8	258	236	4	17	428	391	4
9	462	422	4	18	416	380	4
OUT	3329	3042	36	IN	3066	2799	34

6395 YD • 5841M • PAR 70

Cruden Bay has risen steadily in stature to become one of the most favoured golf courses in Scotland, especially for players from other parts of the world. The traditional seaside links course is highly regarded and acknowledged to be a wonderful sight for those that behold it and play it for the first time. If you seek an outstanding example of natural links golf then look no further than the sandhills and deep, velvet valleys surrounding the Bay of Cruden – they are perhaps Scotland's finest.

Today, a magnificent new clubhouse overlooks the golf course but several decades ago a stately hotel and its ancillary buildings occupied the site. It was here, in 1899, that the Great North of Scotland Railway Company chose to build the 'Gleneagles of the North'. The complex that resulted was a grand site for its Victorian and Edwardian visitors, but the Great War and Depression years conspired to diminish its appeal. In the 1930s the hotel closed down. Fortunately, the golf course lived on to become part of golf

*The 3rd hole, Claypits, at Cruden Bay with Port Ellon
below: a unique landscape and excellent playing
conditions have placed this golf club, according to various
golf polls, in the world's top 100.*

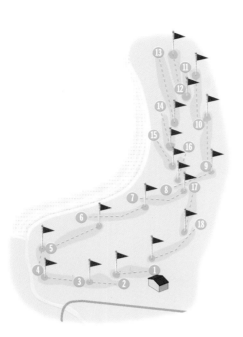

Peterhead

Peterhead Golf Club, Craigewan Links, Riverside Drive, Peterhead, Grampian, AB42 6LT
TEL: *01779 472149* FAX: *01779 480725*
LOCATION: *34 miles/55km north of Aberdeen, off Golf Road at north end of Peterhead at the mouth of River Ugie*
COURSE: *18 holes, 6173yd/5642m, par 70, SSS 71*
GREEN FEES: $£$
FACILITIES: *Changing rooms and showers, full catering and bar, trolley hire, buggy hire, club hire, practice area*
VISITORS: *Welcome weekdays and most Sundays, but not Saturdays. Check with the Clubhouse*

It is amazing that the thousands of visitors that take to Cruden Bay's splendid links each year have not yet discovered the considerably less expensive but nonetheless alluring challenges of Peterhead's Craigewan Links a mere 10 miles/16km up the road.

Sitting at the mouth of the River Ugie, there are lovely coastal views to be enjoyed from many parts of the course particularly up towards St Fergus. The Rattray Lighthouse away to the north can be seen on a clear day.

It was Willie Park Jr who laid out the original nine holes, and overall the 18 holes offer a fine blend of natural landscape assisted by human intervention: they are every bit as good as you will find on any top course in this area: testing the high handicap and scratch golfer alike with their naturally contoured handiwork.

To play a good round, you will find quite a bit of carry is required off many of the men's tees where rough or dips precede the fairway. The 11th, 12th and 13th demonstrate this amply. The 11th is a fine par 5 for the average player although good golfers should manage it without trouble. The 13th, played from a high tee to a high green, is a short par 3 with an especially testing carry over a large hollow as well as a burn. But as with any true links course, it is wind that is the predominant factor and rarely is there a day on this exposed north-east corner where the winds do not play their often treacherous role.

The clubhouse is newly built and offers the modern golfer and non-golfing visitor every comfort (and is most welcoming) as well as commanding views over the ever changing North Sea and its golden sands.

folklore. The marram-crested sand dunes are dramatic but it is the way the course is interlaced between them that is the true work of art – like a great painting it reveals more of itself on each subsequent visit yet still maintains a sense of mystery and power that comes from a course so integral with its natural surrounds.

The 1st tee takes its line off the distant silhouette of Slains Castle, inspiration and setting for Bram Stoker's 'Dracula'. The ruins form a useful reference for the first three holes before the course turns alongside Cruden Water and the village of Port Ellon. This, the 4th, is one of the great par 3s of Scottish golf calling for serious consideration of club selection. In varying weather conditions it is very difficult to judge correctly, despite its short length.

Once over the rise of the 5th what follows is a roller coaster of excellent holes, each as different and as cunning as you could hope for. Only nature could have arranged such a test with minimal contribution from man. There are one or two quirks that the more critical visitor would find objectionable, like blind tee shots followed by blind greens, but this only adds to its diversity and charm.

Duff House Royal

Duff House Royal Golf Club, The Barnyards, Banff,
Grampian, AB45 3SX
TEL: *01261 812062* **FAX:** *01261 812224*
EMAIL: *duff_house_royal@btinternet.com*
LOCATION: *Moray Firth coast east from Banff town centre*
COURSE: *18 holes, 6161yd/5631m, par 68, SSS 70*
GREEN FEES: *££*
FACILITIES: *Changing rooms and showers, full catering and bar, pro shop, teaching pro, practice facilities, trolley hire*
VISITORS: *Welcome weekdays after 10.30am and weekends pre-booking is advised due to competitions*

The premier course in the area, Duff House Royal is laid out on the plains of the River Deveron. It is renowned for its easy walking and, more importantly, some of the best greens in Scotland. They are the legacy of Scottish emigré Dr Alister Mackenzie, who designed Duff House in the 1920s and went on to create Augusta National under Bobby Jones's auspices. As a golf course designer Mackenzie gained a reputation for

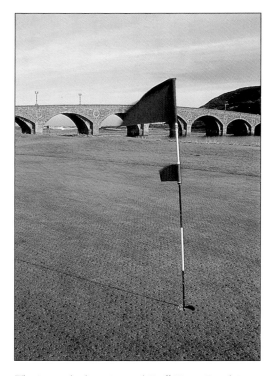

The immaculately maintained Duff House Royal is one of Scotland's hidden gems.

the precariousness of his putting surfaces, and the greens at Duff House are not only double-tiered but exceptionally large. They demand that you place your approach shot as close to, and on the same level as, the pin.

A seven-arched bridge announces your arrival to a course built around Duff House, a Georgian Baroque mansion recently refurbished and now opened as a country house art gallery. From the clubhouse, you see only the opening and closing holes with their lush fairways. But it is the greens, protected by some large bunkers, that are this course's rejoinder to those who think it appears easy. The 16th is a classic example, being a long par 3 (242yd/221m) where you may find it easier to play short and chip on using a 7-iron rather than risk a lengthy putt.

Dufftown

Dufftown Golf Club, Mether Cluny, Tomintoul Road,
Dufftown, Morayshire, AB55 4BS
TEL: *01340 820325* **FAX:** *01340 820325*
LOCATION: *1 mile/1.6km from Dufftown on the B9009 Tomintoul Road*
COURSE: *18 holes, 5308yd/4851m, par 67, SSS 67*
GREEN FEES: *£*
FACILITIES: *Changing rooms, catering by arrangement, bar, trolley hire, club hire*
VISITORS: *Welcome everyday but pre-booking is advised*

In Moray, a region dominated by links courses, Dufftown's lofty and scenic parkland is a rare and unusual round of golf. From the 1st tee, the course is undeniably a steep climb for the first two holes, but after this the inclines are not too noticeable. The overall experience is one of rolling fairways lined with heather and heath that make life difficult for the wayward hitter.

The 7th is one of the shortest holes in Scotland at 67yd/61m across a deep gully and very picturesque. The zenith of this lofty course occurs on the 9th fairway at 1294 ft/394m above sea level, while the absolutely stunning 10th tee stands at 1213 ft/370m. This is a dazzling downhill par 4 with a 340ft/103m vertical fall to the green. A bunker and area of rough stand to the left of

Dufftown was founded in 1896 and is exceptionally friendly, not least because of the famous malt whiskies that are distilled in the area.

the fairway where the wind will most often carry the ball. Without doubt Dufftown is as good a test of your game as you'll find – especially in a breeze.

Elgin

Elgin Golf Club, Hardhillock, Birnie Road, Elgin, Moray, IV30 8SX
TEL: *01343 542338* **FAX:** *01343 542341*
LOCATION: *½ mile/0.75km south of Elgin on the A941 via Birnie Road*
COURSE: *18 holes, 6411yd/5860m, par 69, SSS 71*
GREEN FEES: *££*
FACILITIES: *Changing rooms and showers, full catering, bar, pro shop, teaching pro, driving range and practice facilities, trolley hire, club hire*
VISITORS: *Welcome weekdays after 9.30am and weekends (limited) although pre-booking is advised*

The ground at Hardhillock was once described as 'a miserable piece of land' and not fitting for the farming methods of the day. But it was absolutely perfect for golf at

the turn of the century and remains resolutely so today much to the delight of the members and anyone else who has played the course.

Although an inland track it has many links characteristics such as a sandy subsoil, long, swelling fairways and raised undulating greens. It plays surprisingly long having 13 par 4s and only one par 5. The challenge commences at the 1st, a long deceptive opener if the wind comes from the south-west (as it regularly does). A similar test occurs at the 8th, The Beeches, another long, downhill par 4 of 453yd/414m with a large beech tree on the left side. The 10th plays towards the town to a high, raised green while The Spectacles, the 14th, includes the remains of an old boundary wall, largely covered with grass.

This is a course to try low-handicappers, but visitors can still enjoy it. After the round pop over the road to try out the complete driving and short game practice facility. Or you could settle down at the refurbished clubhouse with its large viewing windows onto the course, and fine bar and restaurant.

Old Moray

Moray Golf Club, Stotfield Road, Lossiemouth,
Morayshire, IV31 6QS
TEL: *01343 812018* **FAX:** *01343 815102*
LOCATION: *Next to the beach, 6 miles/9km north of Elgin*
in Lossiemouth
COURSE: *18 holes, 6643yd/6072m, par 71, SSS 73*
GREEN FEES: *£££*
FACILITIES: *Changing rooms and showers, full catering,*
bar, pro shop, teaching pro, trolley hire
VISITORS: *Welcome everyday but pre-booking is advised*

The wide expanse of gorse-encrusted linksland between the town of Lossiemouth and the Cove Sea lighthouse provides two of the best courses on the Moray coast – Moray Old and New Courses. Coupled with a micro-climate that results in more days of sunshine than in any other part of Britain, here is a year-round magnet for the holiday golfer.

The 1st and 18th of Moray Old are set next to the town, the front 9 progressing outwards before turning back for the remaining holes. The main task throughout this course is the nine par 4s of over 400yd/366m which call for frequent use of fairway woods. There are four on the front 9 and if played into a stiff breeze these will be arduous for any golfer. This remains the case even from the shorter visitors' tees. The 8th becomes an even more daunting prospect with thick heather and whins flanking the fairway. The prevailing wind comes from the

The 18th at Old Moray is regarded as one the finest finishing holes in golf as the surrounding banks make a natural amphitheatre from which to view the finish.

west into the face of outward-bound golfers again making progress difficult.

Moray Old provides perhaps the best finishing hole in Scotland, an impressive par 4 with out-of-bounds along the right in the form of houses and four large bunkers strategically positioned on the left. You need to hit a well-positioned drive to allow for the best approach on to the high plateau green, so it is wise to play to the steep-banked right of the green for some refuge.

The shorter New (1970s) course provides much of the panache of its older sibling with tight fairways and small greens. A 2-round day ticket for both courses is recommended, costing little more than one round on the Old.

Forres

Forres Golf Club, Muiryshade, Forres, Morayshire, IV36
2RD
TEL: *01309 672250* **FAX:** *01309 672250*
LOCATION: *1 mile/1.6km south of Forres and well*
signposted from town centre
COURSE: *18 holes, 6236yd/5700m, par 70, SSS 70*
GREEN FEES: *££*
FACILITIES: *Changing rooms and showers, full catering,*
bar, pro shop, teaching pro, practice facility, trolley hire,
buggy hire, club hire
VISITORS: *Welcome anytime though pre-booking is advised*

James Braid and later Willie Park helped establish the tree-lined fairways that identify much of this 100-year-old parkland course nestled between the Moray Firth to the north and the Farquhar Hills to the south.

The 1st looks deceptively easy from its high tee position but take it easy with the drive or you could blow the advantage. The 5th is a nice little hole on the front 9. Called Wee Birkie, it is not an easy putting prospect into an arena of trees. The course then hinders your progress with tree-lined holes before opening out again on the last holes. The most noteworthy test is the par 4 16th, aptly named Pond, where there are a number of hazards facing this raised tee. The safest line is over an island of gorse to the left of the fairway rather than risking the pond and the heavy vegetation of a hillock.

19 *Stromness*

Stromness Golf Club, Ness, Stromness, Orkney, KW16 3DU
TEL: *01856 850772* **FAX:** *01856 850255*
EMAIL: *orkneycyclehire@btinternet.com*
LOCATION: *16 miles/26km west of Kirkwall on the south side of Stromness off A965*
COURSE: *18 holes, 4762yd/4352m, par 65, SSS 63*
GREEN FEES: *£*
FACILITIES: *Changing rooms and showers, part-time catering, bar, trolley hire, club hire*
VISITORS: *Welcome weekdays and weekends. There is no pre booking system and generally no problem during the day*

The St Ola ferry from Scrabster on the Scottish mainland slips noiselessly past the Old Man of Hoy and Point of Ness with Stromness Golf Club sweeping into view. If you have not brought your golf clubs, at this point you may be kicking yourself as the course and its brand new clubhouse look so welcoming. But there is a remedy for the itchy golfer: simply call into the greenkeeper's house adjacent to the 1st tee and he'll have you suitably equipped and on your way. This is a casual style of golf that most will not be used to. Often the clubhouse is unmanned and an honesty box accepts the mere pittance they ask for a day's golf.

With Scapa Flow and the island of Hoy in the background the course is as picturesque from the ground as it was from the boat. For its rustic location there is a fair amount of style to the fairways with good definition and graded rough. It is tight but not too penal and every level of golfer can enjoy a good round. There are many good holes to find in this tiny parcel of land.

The 1st is a killer dogleg to the right that causes a lot of grief. The par-3 8th, The Bowl, at 99yd/90m is a fine hole. It is shaped like a dish that should collect the ball. However, a dyke, some serious humps and heavy rough, force many golfers to fly over the green into trouble, namely a bunker and heavy rough at the back.

Old war-time gun emplacements still exist and come into play at the 10th and 11th. The most interesting hole perhaps is the 15th at 199yd/182m across the road where another dyke stands at around 180yd/165m.

GOLF IN THE FAR NORTH

Across Orkney from Stromness, Kirkwall Golf Club overlooks the busy market town and harbour. But golf in the far north does not stop here. Moor Park Family Golf Centre in Lerwick and further north on the island of Whalsay, Whalsay Golf Club, is the most northerly course in Britain. It is quite different from the Shetland club as it is hewn out of the side of a moorland hill with no fairways as such and markers delineating the playing area. While the course may be a little rustic, the social life of the club is excellent.

Snow-bound golf in the very north of Scotland.

20 *Shetland*

Shetland Golf Club, Dale, Shetland, ZE2 9SB
TEL: *01595 840369* **FAX:** *01595 840369*
LOCATION: *4 miles/6km north of Lerwick on main A970*
COURSE: *18 holes, 5776yd/5279m, par 68, SSS 68*
GREEN FEES: *£*
FACILITIES: *Changing rooms, snacks and bar, trolley and club hire*
VISITORS: *Welcome weekdays and weekends except during competitions although pre-booking is advised*

Located at the head of one of Shetland's many voes (sea inlets), the course at Dale plays around the water with a burn coming into play on several holes. It is a hilly course, and can be a little damp early or late in the season. Still, it is a most welcoming place, rugged and generous in its views. The best way to approach the course is to pick your target and go for long carries − there is little run for the ball. But it's fun all the way with fairly generous fairways and welcoming greens. If you do stray off the path, the rough can be tough and usually hoary thick grass won't give up a ball easily.

The course sits in the middle of a valley in an area that is traditionally wet, so the greens are usually slow but you soon get used to the pace.

REGIONAL DIRECTORY

Where to Stay

There are two outstanding venues both to stay and to eat just outside Aberdeen. The 5-star **Marcliffe** at Pitfodels (01224 861000) on the North Deeside Road is truly luxurious in every way while **Ardoe House Hotel** (01224 867355) is a sumptuous Scottish baronial mansion on the South Deeside Road with traditional hospitality. If you wish to enjoy the city's many non-golfing diversions then the **Brentwood Hotel** (01224 595440) is near the centre of town just off Union Street. Near Aberdeen airport is the **Craighaar Hotel** (01224712275). North of Aberdeen en-route to the famous links of Cruden Bay is **Udny Arms Hotel** in Newburgh (01358 789444). This is a long-standing favourite with golfers mainly because of its comfortable yet economical environment and an exceptionally hearty menu. The **Red House Hotel** (01779 812215) overlooking Cruden Bay's links is also very popular with golfers.

The Moray Coast is outstanding for both golf and its scenery. In the secluded village of Fordyce, **Academy House** B&B (01261 842743) is an exceptional B&B at a reasonable price, small but salubrious. The little fishing village of MacDuff offers two modest and well appointed hotels at the **Seafield Arms Hotel** (01542 840791) and the **Bay View Hotel** (01542 841031). The **Knockomie Hotel** (01261 812947) in Forres is stylish and orientated to travelling golfers as is the nearby **Ramnee Hotel** (01309 672410).

Royal Deeside is another popular golfing area and the **Glen Lui Hotel** (01339 755402) is one of many good hostelries in this area. In Banchory **The Old West Manse** (01330 822202) is a 5-star B&B.

Where to Eat

If it's a simple meal you are after in Aberdeen, the **Ashvale Fish Restaurant** in Great Western Road constantly gains awards for its top-quality fish suppers; understandable as it is so close to Europe's busiest fish market. Both the **Marcliffe** at Pitfodels (01224 861000) and **Ardoe House Hotel** (01224 867355) serve exceptional food while one of the best eateries in the city is the **Courtyard Restaurant** (01224 213795) in Alford Lane.

Hazelhead No 1 course near Aberdeen is a scenic wooded course with superbly kept greens. Aberdeen, Grampian and the Northern Isles offer an excellent range of courses.

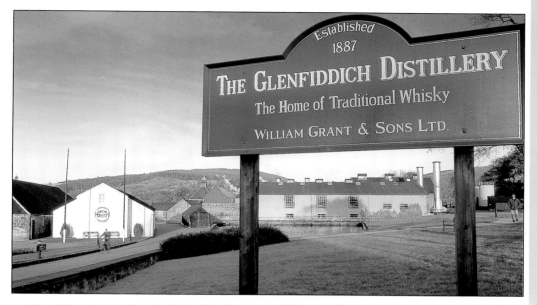

The **Udny Arms Hotel** (01358 789444) in Newburgh has an excellent menu but beware of the Sticky Toffee Pudding, it is highly addictive. On the Moray Coast both the **Seafield Arms Hotel** (01542 840791) and the **Bay View Hotel** (01542 841031) are recognised for fine seafood especially Cullen-Skink soup. The **Old Monastery Restaurant** (01542 832660) lovingly blends Scottish and French cuisine. The **Knockomie Hotel** (01261 812947) in Forres uses first-class local produce. Inland is Malt Whisky country and the **Craigellachie Hotel** (01340 881204) has the River Spey at the foot of the garden. More modest yet most charming is **A Taste of Speyside** (01340 820860) in Aberdeen and Grampian, a simple town restaurant offering wholesome Scottish fare.

The village of Ballater on Royal Deeside seems to have more award winning restaurants than in any other part of the UK. Try the **Green Inn** (01339 755701) or the **Glen Lui Hotel** (01339 755402).

What to Do

In Aberdeen, **His Majesty's Theatre** on the Rosemount Viaduct offers a great variety of entertainment. The history of the area is well presented at **Aberdeen Maritime Museum**, in **Provost Ross' House** near the harbour. Grampian, besides golf, is famous for its castles and its whisky. The **Castle Trail** brings together the best of these magnificent structures such as Balmoral, Castle Fraser and Gardens, Craigievar Castle and Drum Castle though there are many more while the **Malt Whisky Trail** around

Whisky distilling comes in close proximity to several Scottish courses: the world-famous Glenfiddich brand is just north of Dufftown.

Speyside offers seven world famous distilleries and a cooperage.

Other worthwhile attractions are **Duff House** near the golf course in Banff and **MacDuff's Marine Aquarium**. Near Fochabers is **Baxter's Visitor Centre**, based around the humble can of soup, and an entertaining stop. **Elgin Cathedral** offers a glimpse of the area's past as does the excellent little **Elgin Museum**. More spontaneous is an encounter with Moray's large number of dolphins frequently seen from the coastal courses. Grampian's coastline has many splendid, wild, natural beaches while the interior offers majestic mountains for rambling and skiing.

TOURIST INFORMATION

Aberdeen airport Tel 01224 722331

Car Hire at Aberdeen airport
Avis Tel 01224 722331,
Budget Tel 01224 725067
Europcar Tel 01224 725080
Hertz Tel 01224 722373

P&O Scottish Ferries
Tel 01224 572615

Aberdeen and Grampian Tourist Board
St Nicholas House, Broad Street, Aberdeen, AB10 1DE Tel: 01224 632727 Fax: 01224 620415
www.agtb.org

Chapter 5

Highlands and Islands

The Scottish Highlands and Islands are best known for their breathtaking scenery, superlative whiskies, drizzling glens or impressive castles overlooking great hunting estates. Golf then has immeasurable competition in this area but this is only a bonus to the thousands of golf visitors who travel into the Highlands and over to the Islands each year.

The Highlands
Taking the A9, known as the Great North Road, north from central Scotland, the portentous mountains of the Drumochter Pass stand like giant guards at the gateway of the Highland region. Beyond these dramatic mountains is the kind of scenery that most visitors associate with Scotland, startling upland vistas interspersed with purple glens and wild waters. Partly cut off from the rest of Scotland for many centuries the

Left: Eilean Donan Castle, near Kyle of Lochalsh and the road bridge to Skye. The windswept and hilly Kingussie golf course (above) offers dramatic viewpoints across to the Cairngorm Mountains.

Highlands and Islands developed their own character and culture that is still evident today. The lovely lilting accents of Inverness or the Isle of Skye are just one of the area's many endearing features. So is the hospitality that is innate to Highland culture.

Victorian Values
Golf came to the Highlands and Islands with the Victorian rush to join in the health-giving pursuits of upland Scotland made fashionable by Queen Victoria and her consort, Prince Albert. The resulting courses are considered some of Scotland's most desirable. Take Boat of Garten Golf Club, for instance, a long-time favourite of many established names in the game. Or Royal Dornoch, surely an Open venue if it lay further south, and the course where the great Donald Ross learned and perfected his craft before going on to become perhaps the most famous course designer in the USA. There are heathlands and moorlands throughout

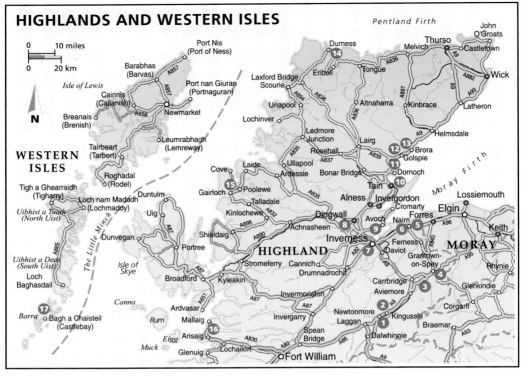

HIGHLANDS AND WESTERN ISLES

The highlands and western islands include Royal Dornoch golf course as well as the most northerly course on the British mainland, Durness.

the Highlands and Islands but there are also great seaside links such as Nairn and Brora. For an enjoyable, relaxing round with the family or friends, there are also wonderfully sporting holiday courses where golf is inexpensive and perfectly satisfying.

The town of Inverness is a good base for touring the area with Loch Ness, Urquhart Castle and many more attractions all within easy driving distance. East of Inverness, the holiday town of Nairn has two of the finest links courses in Scotland with the Nairn Golf Club hosting such prestigious events as the Walker Cup. Further north, following the Great North Road, John o' Groats beckons to those who wish to stand on the British mainland's dramatic northern perimeter. The west coast of the Highlands doesn't offer so much in the way of golf, just spectacular scenery. However, to add to the pleasure, it is

well worth seeking out Durness, the most northerly mainland course or Gairloch. Traigh, on the Road to the Isles, is also a good stop if you are approaching the Isle of Skye from the west coast town of Fort William.

Planning an Itinerary

The sequence of courses in this chapter starts in the south of the region and follows the A9, the main artery. There are several good Highland courses just off this road. Newtownmore, for example, is one good place to come off the A9 and savour both the Spey Valley at a more leisurely pace and take in the fine golf facilities.

A word of warning though. The A9 north of Perth is known for its many road

Urquhart Castle, once one of the largest castles in Scotland and a favourite place for Loch Ness Monster appearances.

traffic accidents. It is a busy route and narrows to two lanes at various points. The main problem is people speeding and overtaking in dangerous spots often caused by the long queues following caravans or tractors.

From Inverness the area branches out but the main courses are to be found by continuing up the A9 to Dornoch, Golspie, Brora − all of which are memorable − and finally John o' Groats.

The Isle of Skye and the Western Isles

The Isle of Skye and the Western Isles, along with miles of white sand beaches looking out to the Atlantic, are interspersed with fascinating courses, providing good sport and ideal if you are visiting these wild parts for their many natural attractions.

Some of the courses are still quite primitive but they make up in a lack of grooming by a most welcoming atmosphere and a feel of how the game of golf might have been played in the mists of time.

① *Kingussie*

Kingussie Golf Club, Gynack Road, Kingussie, Speyside PH21 1LR
TEL: *01540 661374* **FAX:** *01540 662066*
EMAIL: *kinggolf@globalnet.co.uk*
LOCATION: *Just off A9, turn at Duke of Gordon Hotel into Gynack Road and ½ mile/0.75km (signposted)*
COURSE: *18 holes, 5615yd/5132m, Par 67, SSS 68*
GREEN FEES: *£*
FACILITIES: *Changing rooms and showers, full catering and bar, pro shop, trolley hire, buggy hire, club hire*
VISITORS: *Welcome everyday but pre-booking is advised*

A drive up the A9 will confirm that this is one of the most magnificent parts of Scotland. The Drumochtar Pass acts as a gateway through the lofty, foreboding Grampian Mountains but then the scenery rapidly changes into the pastoral delights of Speyside. Kingussie is a major stopping point in this impressive valley and has been since Victorian times.

The Harry Vardon-designed moorland course situated behind the village, starts out on the flat then climbs the foothills of the Monadhliath Mountains with views east towards the Cairngorms. It is only hilly in parts and general plays over three different levels, each offering challenging but rewarding golf and stunning moorland scenery.

The course is not long but it is built for shot-makers and those who enjoy a hearty helping of Highland scenery with their golf. The 1st can be a vigourous opening, a par 3 of 230yd/210m with out-of-bounds on the left. The 4th was too difficult as a par 4 and, after recent alterations, is still a challenging par 5. The course crosses the River Gynack onto a flatter area for a few holes only.

The babbling River Gynack has to be taken into account on five of Kingussie's holes. The course is built on a craggy landscape with abundant heather and Scots pine.

② *Newtonmore*

Newtonmore Golf Club, Golf Course Road, Newtonmore, Speyside PH20 1AT
TEL: *01540 673378* **FAX:** *01540 673878*
LOCATION: *In the centre of village Golf Course Road look for signposts off Main Street*
COURSE: *18 holes, 6029yd/5510m, Par 70, SSS 69*
GREEN FEES: *£*
FACILITIES: *Changing rooms and showers, full catering and bar, pro shop and teaching pro, short game practice, trolley hire, buggy hire, club hire*
VISITORS: *Welcome everyday but pre-booking is advised*

P opular with groups and societies for its flat terrain – the Grampians, Cairngorms, and peaks of Lochaber merely make a stimulating backdrop – Newtonmore offers an easy amble. It is only the early and finishing holes that involve rolling land, while the rest of the course is based on the plain of the River Spey and therefore quite level.

The course does have a punishing rough on its earlier holes. Verdant islands of fescue grass and wild flowers as well as stands of tall pine divide the fairways. With an added element of wind blowing along the Spey Valley, most casual day trippers come off the course remarking how challenging it has been. Two such holes are the 3rd, which plays down to the plain from a high elevated tee with a swathe of rough as well as out-of-bounds on the right, and the 13th, which has a fairway very well protected by bunkers.

The club claims to have more left-handed golfers than any other club in the world. It also plays host to the Scottish Left Handed Championships, and Bob Charles, the only left-handed Open champion, opened the clubhouse extension.

Boat of Garten

Boat of Garten Golf Club, Boat of Garten, Speyside PH24 3BQ
TEL: *01479 831282* **FAX:** *01479 831523*
EMAIL: *boatgolf@enterprise.net*
LOCATION: *Off the A9 onto A95 north of Aviemore*
COURSE: *18 holes, 5866yd/5362m, Par 69, SSS 69*
GREEN FEES: *££*
FACILITIES: *Changing rooms and showers, full catering and bar, pro shop, short game practice, trolley hire, club hire*
VISITORS: *Welcome weekdays from 9.30am and weekends between 10am and 4pm although pre-booking is advised*

The fact that visitors, year after year, are queuing up to play at the Boat only confirms that this is one of the most attractive of the Highland's heathland courses. Some would say it is the lure of the scenery and it is surely magnificent.

With the Cairngorm Mountains towering to the south and other smaller ranges nearby as well as the River Spey fringing the course, there are few more delightful settings in Scotland. Heather and Silver Birch trees are abundant, along with broom bushes. But what could be said about the steam train that passes the 4th and 6th periodically throughout the day as if to outdo all the natural beauty the place offers?

James Braid arranged the Boat into an excellent test with all the demands of a championship course in a smaller parcel of land. The course opens with an easy par 3 (if you hit straight and putt true). The 2nd is more demanding especially behind the green, which slopes left and forward. The 3rd is another good par 3 and the 4th is where the distinctive rolls of the Boat's fairways begin. This is a beguiling par 5 where the luck of the bounce or the penalties of going off course can be severe with rough and the railway line on either side.

But it is the closing hole which is for many the toughest. The drive must be long and bisect the fairway to leave a reasonable shot into the green. Many choose to lay up their second shot on to the green (raised high on a pudding bowl mound) rather than risk rolling off the back or either side. Some brave souls will take a wood and hope the ball will roll up and on – a most dramatic finale whichever way you play it.

The 15th green at Boat of Garten – a course offering stunning scenery, and fairways mainly lined with birch.

4 *Grantown-on-Spey*

*Grantown-on-Spey Golf Club, The Clubhouse, Golf
Course Road, Grantown-on-Spey PH26 3HY*
TEL: *01479 872079* **FAX:** *01479 873725*
LOCATION: *Situated at north end of town, A9 to A95,
then turn right opposite the police station*
COURSE: *18 holes, 5710yd/5219m, Par 70, SSS 68*
GREEN FEES: *££ (Day Ticket only available)*
FACILITIES: *Changing rooms and showers, full catering and
bar, pro shop, practice ground, putting green, buggy hire,
club hire, trolley hire*
VISITORS: *Welcome everyday, but after 10am on
weekends, and pre-booking is advised*

Here is another airy Highland course,
especially scenic when heather and
broom come into flower. Some of the best
holes at Grantown play through attractive
woodland with occasional glimpses of the
Cromdale Hills to the east.

The first three holes are flat so the going is
easy. The holes play away from the clubhouse
across a road, over former farm pasture. At the
7th hole the course enters the wooded glades
with little room to avoid tangling with the
timber. The 9th is the course's signature hole,
a magnificent high tee outlook across the
valley below with the purple heathered
Cromdale Hills away in the background. The
11th is another long par 3. The little holiday
village of Grantown and the River Spey is as
popular with anglers as with golfers.

*At Nairn Dunbar, links and parkland combine in
different sections with the front 9 predominately sandy
and rolling: this is the 4th green with the town behind.*

5 *Nairn Dunbar*

*Nairn Dunbar Golf Club, Lochloy Road, Nairn,
Morayshire IV12 5AE*
TEL: *01667 452741* **FAX:** *01667 456897*
LOCATION: *Off A96 on the east side of town and turn
down Lochloy Road*
COURSE: *18 holes, 6720yd/6142m, Par 72, SSS 73*
GREEN FEES: *£££*
FACILITIES: *Changing rooms and showers, full catering and
bar, pro shop and teaching pro, short game practice, trolley
hire, buggy hire, club hire*
VISITORS: *Welcome weekdays except after 4.30pm and
weekends after 9.30am although pre-booking is advised*

Sitting a mile away from its illustrious
neighbour Nairn, the seaside course of
Nairn Dunbar with its gorse and whin-lined
fairways is easily overlooked. But at half the
price of a round at Nairn, and a course just as

challenging some would argue, you would be
misguided not to include Nairn Dunbar.

The course has been host to most of the
main Scottish tournaments, such as the
Northern Open, Scottish Ladies and Scottish
Boys, so not only is it prestigious, but it is also
an excellent test on a long and tight course.

The 414yd/378m 10th, a par 4 called
Westward Ho!, is easily the most challenging
hole. Here, thick gorse and trees line and
tighten the fairways with water occasionally
adding to the jeopardy. One of the new holes
on the course, a carry of 225yd/206m, often
into a headwind, is required to traverse a burn
with out-of-bounds and gorse bushes lining
the dog-legged fairway. At least a 3-iron will
often be required to have a chance of
reaching the raised green.

Scottish Golf Course Architects

While some of Scotland's oldest courses appear to be hewn out of what nature provided, a golden era of golf course construction began at the end of the 19th century and many noted players turned their talents to design, including Old Tom Morris, Willie Park Jr, Willie Fernie, Willie Auchterlonie, Archie Simpson, and Ben Sayers. Chances are that on a golfing visit to Scotland you will play on their courses (though often much modified) as well as those linked to such noted architects as Harry Colt, Hamilton Stutt, Dave Thomas, Donald Steel, Peter Alliss, Peter Thompson CBE and also Jack Nicklaus and Seve Ballesteros.

Alister Mackenzie

Old Tom Morris is responsible for many courses including Machrihanish, Carnoustie Championship, Royal Burgess, Nairn, Dunbar, King James VI and West Kilbride. He was 'Keeper of the Greens' at Prestwick where during his tenure the inaugural Open Championship was staged in 1860. In 1864, employed by the R&A as a golf pro, Old Tom set about revamping the Old Course employing two labourers, a wheelbarrow and a few basic implements. He continued well into his 80s as a course designer.

James Braid was the most prolific of golf course architects in the UK. His course total stands at over 200 for complete designs. Born in Earlsferry in Fife in 1870, he trained as a carpenter, reconditioning old clubs for his own use and developing an aggressive style of play out on the windy links. His parents had little time for the game but their farming background did help Braid to understand drainage and other elements of land use. The Triumvirate of Braid, Harry Vardon and JH Taylor dominated golf in the early 1900s and in 1910 Braid became the first player to win five Open championships. Much in demand as a designer, he is associated with many of the courses in this book, including Gleneagles, Carnoustie Championship and Rosemount.

Donald Ross spent much of his professional life in the USA and there, with a total of, some say, over 500 courses, became the most prolific golf course architect of the time. But he was born in Dornoch on the north-east coast of Scotland in 1872, and learned much of his skills on the great links of Royal Dornoch. As a young greenkeeper he worked with Old Tom Morris at St Andrews before returning to his native town. He emigrated to the USA and commenced his first course-building project at the Oakley Golf Club near Boston. His name is synonymous with Pinehurst No 2 which contains Dornoch-style features such as raised greens and is regarded as one of the finest courses in the world.

Like James Braid, Ross did not always visit the properties he created but often preferred to work in his office from topographical maps then send instructions to his construction crew. The system seemed to work admirably. His trademarks were compact layouts with no long walks between green and tee and links-like green approaches to allow bump-and-run shots.

Dr Alister Mackenzie was born in Yorkshire in 1870 and became the founder of the British School of Camouflage during the First World War. One of the greatest of golf course architects, his forte was his greens – Augusta National is living testament to that. He refrained from flattening natural undulations and contrived to create artificial undulations that were 'indistinguishable from nature'.

Nairn

Nairn Golf Club, Seabank Road, Nairn, Morayshire IV12 4HB
TEL: *01667 453208 fax: 01667 456328*
EMAIL: *bookings@nairngolfclub.prestel.co.uk*
LOCATION: *In the town of Nairn, 16 miles/26km east of Inverness on A96 take Seabank Road towards the shore*
COURSE: *18 holes, 6722yd/6145m, Par 72, SSS 74*
GREEN FEES: £££££+
FACILITIES: *Changing rooms and showers, full catering and bar, pro shop and teaching pro, practice ground, trolley hire, club hire*
VISITORS: *Welcome weekdays after 9.30am and weekends between 11 to 12 am and 2.30 to 6.00pm although pre-booking is advised. Handicap certificate must be shown*

NAIRN

HOLE	YD	M	PAR	HOLE	YD	M	PAR
1	400	366	4	10	540	494	5
2	499	456	5	11	161	147	3
3	400	366	4	12	445	407	4
4	145	133	3	13	435	398	4
5	378	345	4	14	221	202	3
6	183	167	3	15	309	282	4
7	551	504	5	16	422	386	4
8	359	328	4	17	361	330	4
9	359	328	4	18	554	506	5
OUT	3274	2993	36	IN	3448	3152	36

6722 YD • 6145M • PAR 72

Host to the 1999 Walker Cup, Nairn is a very challenging links championship course. So do not be fooled by the vision that greets your arrival of wide-open fairways and a welcoming beach next to Moray Firth. To be blunt, this is a tough golfing test for the best of players and unless you are capable of keeping the ball on target along narrow fairways you may be better advised to play somewhere less exacting.

The original course was laid out for a mere £36, and in 1890 Old Tom Morris expanded the course for the princely sum of £6.50. Another famous player and course architect James Braid extended the course in the early 1900s.

Today Nairn is undoubtedly one of the finest links courses in Scotland. The fairways are defined by curving, thick rough, and it is very easy to spend your time despairingly hacking a ball along the fringes rather than enjoying crisp strikes following the mown turf.

Along with the terrain, the wind blows by the Moray Firth and toys with all those fastidious golfers starting out with high intentions. If the rough does not get them then the beach could well. Many an admirable drive will rise only to be caught in the wind's clutches and diverted systematically onto the sand. As if the journey from tee to green was not difficult enough, the putting surfaces are usually lightening-fast and true.

There is no prescribed way to play the course except to keep the ball on the fairway. If you are a medium hitter but able to guide a ball straight then you could outgun your long-hitting companions here as they will often find the rough.

The layout at Nairn is almost typically links with 9 holes playing away from the clubhouse before turning back. There are a few variations on this, such as the 13th and 14th. But every hole is memorable and there is no weakness at all on the course. The 5th is a heavily-bunkered and testing par 4 usually straight into the wind. The course turns at the 8th but to's and fro's for the following holes with rough always being the adversity.

The 13th is a narrow passageway that rises towards the green and two good shots are necessary to reach it. The 14th turns downhill again, a long par 3 that rises slightly with three great bunkers covering the entrance. The 17th offers an unusual green sloping towards the Firth so if you reach in regulation it is all down to putting.

Like Carnoustie or the other great links courses, there is much to be considered with each stroke on every hole. Those that stand up and hope for the best will find it a long slog.

Once the examination is over – and a round here will examine every element of a players game – golfers are delighted to retreat to the comforts of the sumptuous clubhouse. Quality abounds at Nairn Golf Club, from the service to the level of catering and it is just as well that such worldly comfort is made available to help ease the distress that some might have experienced out on the links.

Purple heather fringing the fairways at Nairn (this is the 14th above) remind golfers that this is a course to hit straight and true. If the rough doesn't get you, the bunkers may well such as at the 16th (below).

7 *Inverness*

Inverness Golf Club, The Clubhouse, Culcabock Road,
Inverness IV2 3XQ
TEL: *01463 233422* **FAX:** *01463 239882*
LOCATION: *Off the A9 approaching Inverness, take the
first exit marked Inverness on to Culcabock Road and club
house is on left otherwise 1 mile/1.6km south of town centre*
COURSE: *18 holes, 6226yd/5691m, Par 69, SSS 70*
GREEN FEES: *££*
FACILITIES: *Changing rooms and showers, full catering and
bar, pro shop and teaching pro, practice ground, trolley hire,
buggy hire, club hire*
VISITORS: *Welcome weekdays and weekends although pre-
booking is advised. A handicap certificate is required*

A lush, parkland course within 15 minutes
of the bus and rail stations, Inverness
plays on two separate levels with the course
intersected by the main road. There is also the
Mill Burn, which comes into play on several
holes, depending on the tee used.

Inverness offers two par 5s (both reachable
in two for big hitters), five par 3s and 11 par-
4s. It is the latter that offer the greatest tests —
the 475yd/434m 14th being the classic hole. A
dogleg right, with the Mill Burn running all
the way up the right-hand side and high
banking on the left covered in gorse bushes
and trees, demands precision shots. The 11th
green and 12th tee have outstanding views
over Inverness to the Kessock Bridge and the
Black Isle.

*A classic Highland panorama makes Strathpeffer Spa a
must-play course: it is short but testing. There are only
three bunkers but many other natural hazards await you
including burns, lochans, whins and, of course, trees.*

8 *Strathpeffer Spa*

Strathpeffer Spa Golf Club, Golf Course Road,
Strathpeffer, Ross-shire IV14 9AS
TEL: *01997 421219* **FAX:** *01997 421011*
LOCATION: *5miles/8km west of Dingwall, ¼ mile/0.5km
north of Strathpeffer Square (signposted), 20 minutes north
of Inverness by A9*
COURSE: *18 holes, 4794yd/4382m, Par 65, SSS 64*
GREEN FEES: *£*
FACILITIES: *Changing rooms and shower, full catering and
bar, pro shop, short game practice, trolley hire, club hire*
VISITORS: *Welcome everyday but pre-booking is advised*

L ooking at the yardage of Strathpeffer Spa
might give one the impression that this is
a pygmy layout verging on a par-3 course;
but don't be mislead. This is a mighty
challenge, albeit a short one, and a course
you are liable to remember as one of the
most interesting. There are seven par 3s and
quite a few short par 4s but it is not their
distance that these holes rely upon to defend
themselves. Nor is it sand as there are only
three bunkers on the entire course. What
you are up against are the slopes. Strathpeffer
is hilly.

From the 1st tee you travel downhill
before zig-zagging back up again. The holes
are designed in a way that lessens the climb
but from the 2nd to the 11th there is a
gradual ascent before reaching the summit.
From here the views looking back down the
Cromarty Firth and Dingwall are what really
make this moorland course worth including
on any Highland itinerary.

9 Fortrose & Rosemarkie

Fortrose & Rosemarkie Golf Course, Ness Road, East Fortrose, Ross-shire IV10 8SE
TEL: *01381 620529* **FAX:** *01381 620529*
LOCATION: *From Inverness, A9 north to A832 east for 9 miles/14km*
COURSE: *18 holes, 5858yd/5354m, Par 71, SSS 69*
GREEN FEES: *£*
FACILITIES: *Changing rooms and showers, full catering and bar, pro shop and teaching pro, driving range, short game practice, trolley hire, buggy hire, club hire*
VISITORS: *Welcome weekdays apart from 9am to 10.15am and 1pm to 2.15pm then 4.45pm to 6.30pm and weekends although pre-booking is advised*

Here is an easy, undulating walk over a thin wizened finger of land stretching out into the Moray Firth. From this links course you can see the tawny walls of Fort George across the narrow stretch of water and may be lucky enough to catch a glimpse of the famous Moray Firth dolphins.

The course is encompassed by beach and water, but these do not often come into play. However the road that bisects the peninsula does. You play the ball as it lies on this hazard or lift and drop for a penalty stroke. It is a rare day that the wind doesn't blow and this can create problems on such an exposed piece of land. There are only two holes that go with or against it, the 9th and the 5th, while the rest are crossed by the prevailing south-westerlies.

10 Tain

Tain Golf Club, Chapel Road, Tain, Ross-shire IV19 1PA
TEL: *01862 892314* **FAX:** *01862 892099*
EMAIL: *tgc@cali.co.uk*
LOCATION: *Off A9, 33 miles/53km north of Inverness. Travelling north, turn right in middle of High Street, the Golf Club is 1 mile/1.6km*
COURSE: *18 holes, 6404yd/5853m, Par 70, SSS 71*
GREEN FEES: *££*
FACILITIES: *Changing rooms and showers, full catering and bar, pro shop and teaching pro, short game practice, trolley hire, buggy hire, club hire*
VISITORS: *Welcome anytime though pre-booking is advised*

Where the River Aldie merges with the sands of the Dornoch Firth lies 'Old Tom Morris's Northern Jewel' and an ideal proposition for a golf course. Unlike the friendly folk of this area, Tain's principal characteristic is that it is tight. Thick forests of gorse and broom line most fairways and the bunkers are strategically positioned for maximum damage. There is a run of good holes at the 2nd, 3rd and 4th. The 11th presents the Alps, a par 4 of only 380yd/347m with a concealed green behind two 30ft/9m mounds. Follow the burn and you'll find the famous Glenmorangie malt whisky distillery and Visitor Centre.

The par-3 16th at Tain designed by Old Tom Morris— with the burn which can get tide-swollen.

11 Royal Dornoch

*Royal Dornoch Golf Club, Golf Road, Dornoch,
Sutherland IV25 3LW*
TEL: *01862 810219* **FAX:** *01862 810792*
EMAIL: *rdgc@royaldornoch.com* **WWW:** *royaldornoch.com*
LOCATION: *45 miles/72km north of Inverness off the A9*
COURSE: *18 holes, 6514yd/5946m, Par 70, SSS 73*
GREEN FEES: *£££££+*
FACILITIES: *Changing rooms and showers, full catering and
bar, pro shop and teaching pro, practice ground and short
game, trolley hire, club hire*
VISITORS: *Welcome weekdays and Saturday after 3pm
weekends although pre-booking is advised. Handicap
required for Championship Course*

ROYAL DORNOCH
CHAMPIONSHIP COURSE

HOLE	YD	M	PAR	HOLE	YD	M	PAR
1	331	303	4	10	147	134	3
2	177	162	3	11	446	408	4
3	414	378	4	12	507	463	5
4	427	390	4	13	166	152	3
5	354	324	4	14	445	407	4
6	163	149	3	15	319	292	4
7	463	423	4	16	402	367	4
8	396	362	4	17	405	370	4
9	496	453	5	18	456	417	4
OUT	3221	2944	35	IN	3293	3002	35

6514 YD • 5946M • PAR 70

Despite its northerly latitude – nearly 200 miles/321km from Edinburgh – Royal Dornoch is still one of the most popular golf courses in Scotland. So well regarded is it that golf magazine polls across the world regularly have it in their Top 20.

The tiny town of Dornoch is unexpectedly sophisticated with a genteel air and a magnificent if somewhat diminutive 13th-century cathedral. The two courses of the town, the Struie and the Championship Course, are found only a short walk from the town centre and there are many good hotels and B&Bs in the immediate area as you will no doubt find if you come this far to play golf. It is worth noting that there is a significant discount on green fees for each night you stay in local accommodation.

Surrounding the area is some splendid Highland and coastal scenery so you should plan ahead to take a few days off and enjoy the region. Also in town is the home of Donald Ross. It was here that the architect of Pinehurst No 2 – as

well as many other fine American courses – lived and learned his trade and went on to spread the Dornoch influence to many other courses.

Golf has been played here since at least 1616 when the Earl of Sutherland ordered 'cleeks and balls' to take up the game that had become so popular in St Andrews. This makes Royal Dornoch the third oldest golf club in Scotland. As with other famous Scottish courses, a wide stretch of linksland lay adjacent to the community, used for light grazing, archery and breeding rabbits. It was Old Tom Morris who, in the 1880s, laid out the first 9 holes with a further 9 being added

If Royal Dornoch was any further south and somewhat longer it would be on the Open circuit. This is the 1st.

shortly afterwards.

For a venue of such stature, the course is surprisingly short, but the degree of difficulty is noticeable on many holes, with their bumps, dense gorse and bunkers, which halt the flow of wayward balls.

It is a classic links layout with the first eight holes following the natural slants and humps of the old dune embankments while the rest flank the sandy beaches of Dornoch Bay. Raised or sloping greens are characteristic as well as elevated tees so the target is usually well presented although rarely easy to reach. Dornoch perhaps more than most is a thinking golfer's course where it is not enough to simply keep the ball on the fairway. A position has to be sought on most holes where the green can be accessed to advantage.

The 6th, Whinny Brae, has to be one of the most fearsome par 3s, with no let up for those that go left into the gorse or right down a steep bank from where double-bogies are routine. The front 9 continues over a long, narrow headland before dropping down to the beach and the homeward 9. The 10th is an extraordinary par 3 that usually plays into or across a stiff breeze found at the tip of the headland. The options are the beach on one side and gorse on the other, but you may find yourself aiming at the beach in order to find home.

Harry Vardon deemed the very long par-4 14th as 'the most natural hole in golf'. With no bunkers, there is a succession of hillocks running up to the green on the right and it is imperative though most difficult to play left then onto the raised green. After the 15th where putting is the great challenge, another headland takes the course on to the level of the clubhouse with views up the Dornoch Firth to the prominent hill called the Struie.

. Dornoch town reflects its illustrious heritage and golfers, no matter how great, are welcomed as part of the community. The town does enjoy patronage from a wide range of personalities such as Tom Watson and Ben Crenshaw who both hold the course and its vicinity in great esteem, as well as Greg Norman and Michael Jordan.

12 Golspie

Golspie Golf Club, Ferry Road, Golspie, Sutherland KW10 6ST
TEL: *01408 633266* **FAX:** *01408 633393*
EMAIL: *golspie-golf-club.co.uk*
WWW: *golspie-golf-club.co.uk*
LOCATION: *10 miles/16km north of Dornoch on A9*
COURSE: *18 holes, 5890yd/5383m, Par 68, SSS 68*
GREEN FEES: *££*
FACILITIES: *Changing rooms and showers, full catering and bar, golf shop, driving range, short game practice, trolley hire, club hire*
VISITORS: *Welcome weekdays and weekends although pre-booking is advised*

The James Braid designed course of Golspie, north of Dornoch, is unusual in that it offers three different types of golfing terrain on one course. The opening holes start out over flat, lush and fairly forgiving meadowland. The 3rd hole takes the course along the beach where the conditions turn far more links-like for the remainder of the front 9. These are excellent holes with large mounds of duneland and firm greens.

The par-5 4th plays along the beach and can be troublesome in a stiff wind but otherwise presents a birdie opportunity. Then, as if you might tire of such seaside antics, the course turns back towards the clubhouse at the 11th into rich avenues of heath with heather, silver birch and pines marking the way. There are several lengthy par 4s over 400yd/365m especially the 14th which reaches to 454yd/415m.

13 Brora

Brora Golf Club, Golf Road, Brora, Sutherland KW9 6QS
TEL: *01408 621417* **FAX** *01408 622157*
LOCATION: *Approximately 54miles/87km north of Inverness and 16 miles/26km north of Dornoch on the A9*
COURSE: *18 holes, 6110yd/5585m, par 69, SSS 69*
GREEN FEES: *££*
FACILITIES: *Changing rooms and showers, full catering and bar, pro shop, short game practice, trolley hire, club hire*
VISITORS: *Welcome everyday but pre-booking is advised*

James Braid worked wonders on the natural blend of bent grass and dunes at Brora in 1923, and today the course has attained a certain mystic quality that overcomes its distance from the more populated and well-trodden pathways of Scottish golf. A half-hour's drive further north than the hallowed links of Royal Dornoch, Brora has the standing of a truly natural links.

In supreme condition due to recent warmer summers, the rough has risen higher defining the fairways, but there is one factor that keeps the fairways reasonable unlike some of its southern counterparts – grazing animals. Brora's linksland is still common grazing for a few of the crofters whose cottages look over the course. Cows and sheep are let out to forage and little electric fences stand between them and the pristine greens. Indeed the greens here are legendary and have been described to be 'as the glaciers left them'. The 9th green lies right next to the sea.

A memorable hole is the 17th which uses the lighthouse as a line from the elevated tee to drive off. The 13th is also quite beautiful. Nearby Dunrobin Castle, the northernmost of Scotland's grand houses (open from May-through October), is well worth a visit as is Clynelish Whisky Distillery and Hunter's Woollen Mill.

Pure putting pleasure in between the grass and dunes at Brora.

Teeing off at Durness's fantastic 110yd/100m 9th hole which plays over a wide, rocky cove.

14 *Durness*

Durness Golf Club, Balnakeil, Durness, Sutherland IV27 4PN
TEL: *01971 511364*
LOCATION: *On A838, 57miles/92km north-west of Lairg.*
COURSE: *18 holes, 5555 yd/5077m, par 70, SSS 69*
GREEN FEES: *£*
FACILITIES: *Changing rooms, snacks, trolley hire, club hire*
VISITORS: *Welcome weekdays and weekends except Sunday mornings. Please note the course is closed for lambing between 20th April and 15th May approximately*

The most northerly course on the British mainland, Durness lies in a remote and starkly beautiful setting – especially if the sun shines. Part links and part moorland, the course offers spectacular views over the sandy reaches of Balnakeil Bay and out over the Atlantic. This is the land of puffins, guillimots and shags and very occasionally a Harrier jump jet roaring up from Lossiemouth to test its bombing accuracy on a tiny island a couple of miles out to sea.

The course, opened in 1988, is quite remarkable for this remote corner of the country at Cape Wrath. Nine holes become 18 because they are played from markedly different tees – the 9th/18th being a notable example.

The par-5 6th/15th plays around Loch Lanlish (a lateral water hazard) and receives a lot of compliments but all the holes are varied and have their own personalities. Ronan Rafferty who visited here was most delighted with the course. Of note are the wild flowers found on and around the course: not only are they very beautiful but they are also of European importance and protected by Scottish National Heritage.

15 *Gairloch*

Gairloch Golf Club, Gairloch, West Highlands IV21 2BE
TEL: *01445 712407*
LOCATION: *One mile/1.6km south on A832*
COURSE: *9 holes, 4562yd/4170m, par 62, SSS 64*
GREEN FEES: *£*
FACILITIES: *Changing rooms, catering and bar, trolley hire, buggy hire, club hire*
VISITORS: *Welcome everyday though pre-booking is advised*

There are very few golf courses on mainland Scotland's north-west coast mainly due to visitors' preoccupation with the wealth of remarkable scenery. But for some who make the trek north, all the mountains and lochs become secondary to a good game of golf and Gairloch Golf Club supplies this most adequately.

Playing the 9-holes twice does not present a test in length, but it makes up for its short stature in delightful intricacies. The premier hole is the 526yd/480m par-5 8th/17th, a fantastic challenge to hold the narrow hog's back of a fairway. With the beach encroaching so close to the left side, it is a psychological challenge from the tee. A second shot if well struck, could take you over the crest of the hill and down into the bowl below, but it pays to lay up and attack the green from this lofted vantage-point. While this is most certainly holiday golf, a round or two at Gairloch will make you glad you brought your clubs.

16 Traigh

Traigh Golf Course, Road to the Isles, Arisaig, Inverness-shire PH39 4NT
TEL: *01687 450337*
LOCATION: *6 miles/10km south of Mallaig on the A830 Ft William/Mallaig Road*
COURSE: *9 holes, 4912yd/4490m, par 68, SSS 65*
GREEN FEES: *£*
FACILITIES: *Changing rooms and showers, full catering and bar, pro shop and teaching pro, driving range, short game practice, trolley hire, buggy hire, club hire*
VISITORS: *Welcome everyday but pre-booking is advised*

Traigh (pronounced *try* meaning beach) has one of the most spectacular Scottish settings. Perched on the dunes and headland looking towards the Hebridean islands of Skye, Eigg, Rum and Muck, the course was redesigned in 1995. Opening with an uphill par 3 of some merit, it then plays along a ridge with a 170yd/155m carry called for by the tee shot at Spion Kop. The 3rd aims

Sand, sea and . . . golf at Traigh. Not far from here lies the beach which was used in the film, Local Hero.

straight at the stunning islands followed by a short, testing par 4 where an accurate, short drive is essential.

THE ROAD TO THE ISLES

From Fort William to Mallaig is one of Scotland's most romantic and scenic routes with many small islands to the west and the Cuillins of Skye on the horizon. The Western Isles might not be as renowned as California as a golfing destination, but the coastal setting has similarities, and for a taste of golf in its purest ancestral guise they are well worth adventuring to. There are little golf course gems to savour from Lewis and Harris in the north to Barra – the most southerly course on the islands, and nearest Scottish golf club to America!

17 Barra

Barra Golf Club, Cleat, Isle of Barra HS9 5XX
TEL: *01871 890266* **FAX:** *01871 890266*
EMAIL: *isleofbarra.com/golf/html*
WWW: *golf@isleof barra.com*
LOCATION: *On the Isle of Barra, from Castlebay,*
approximately 5 miles/8km down west side and signposted
COURSE: *9 holes, 4792yd/4380m, par 68, SSS 64*
GREEN FEES: *£* **FACILITIES:** *None*
VISITORS: *Visitors most welcome anytime*

Some wags compare the 4th at Barra to the 7th at Pebble Beach, California. But Pebble Beach does not have cows gathering around the sturdily-fenced green. Nor does it have a shed for a clubhouse/greenkeepers quarters. But it's all part of the added value of playing at Barra. The views over Traigh Eais Bay and the wide Atlantic Ocean are also simply stunning.

The most westerly of Scottish courses opens with two par 3s playing downhill and around the Black Ben with a testing par 5 at the 3rd squeezed between the hillside and beach. Rocky outcrops strewn over the roughly defined fairway add to the incidental nature of the course. The 3rd and 4th greens are extraordinary with refreshing Atlantic spray breaking over the rocks. The 5th tee offers a fantastic view back to Seal Bay, but here the course turns and climbs straight uphill. The highest point, the 7th tee, offers commanding views of the entire course.

Grazing animals are a moveable hazard at Barra.

SCOTLAND'S FILM LOCATIONS

Scotland is renowned for its dramatic scenery, which has been employed by the film and television industry as inspiring backdrops and settings. Here is a small selection of the better known productions and locations

• *Braveheart* starring Mel Gibson. Fortress scene shot in Glen Nevis near Fort William.

• *Dr Finlay's Casebook* starring Andrew Cruikshank and Bill Simpson. The original TV series was filmed in Callander in the heart of the Trossachs.

• *Gregory's Girl* starring John Gordon Sinclair and Clair Grogan. This quirky love story and some of its sequel (1999) was set in Cumbernauld near Glasgow and featured Abronhill High School.

• *Greystoke, The Legend of Tarzan* starring Christopher Lambert, Ralph Richardson and Andie McDowell. Filmed in part at the magnificent Floors Castle near Kelso in the Scottish Borders.

• *Hamish MacBeth* starring Robert Carlyle. This popular TV series was filmed around the delightful village of Plockton in the north west just north of Kyle of Lochalsh.

• *Hamlet*, directed by Franco Zeffirelli and starring Mel Gibson. This was filmed at Dunnottar Castle, near Stonehaven just south of Aberdeen, as well as at Blackness Castle east of Edinburgh.

• *Highlander* starring Sean Connery and Christopher Lambert. The dramatic setting featured the Cuillins of Skye and Eilean Donan Castle on Loch Duich on the road to Skye.

• *Local Hero* starring Burt Lancaster, Dennis Lawson and Fulton Mackay. The seashore sequences were shot on the beaches of the Sands of Morar on the Road to the Isles near Fort William. The fishing village scenes were captured in the coastal village of Pennan north of Aberdeen on the Moray Firth.

• *Mrs Brown* starring Dame Judi Dench and Billy Connolly. Filmed in the Scottish Borders at Duns Castle just west of Berwick upon Tweed.

• *Rob Roy* starring Liam Neeson, Jessica Lange, John Hurt and Tim Roth. This was filmed in Glen Nevis, Morar and Drummond Castle in Perthshire as well as several other minor locations.

REGIONAL DIRECTORY

Where to Stay

If you start your Highland tour in Speyside to the south of the region, *Kingussie* offers attractive accommodation as well as food at **The Cross** (01540 661166) on Tweed Mill Brae. Alternatively there is the nearby **Osprey Hotel** (01540 661510). The Boat of Garten certainly should be visited for its golf and scenery and the best options here are the **Boat Hotel** (01479 831258) overlooking the railway and golf course or the well-appointed 4-star B&B at Chapelton House (01479 831327). The Victorian ambience at **Heathbank Hotel** (01479 831234) is also worth considering.

Grantown on Spey is a great base both for countryside and golf. The **Ardconnel** (01479 872104) is a carefully restored guest-house offering excellent value for money. On the outskirts of town is **Culdearn House** (01479 872106) and a little further on is **Muckrach Lodge Hotel & Restaurant** (01479 851257).

Nairn is a nodal point on most golfers' itineraries and the place to stay is the **Golf View Hotel & Leisure Club** (01667 452301) with its fitness centre and conservatory overlooking the Moray Firth. The **Newton Hotel** (01667 453144) is also very popular as is the **Claymore House Hotel** (01667 453731), all accustomed to meeting golfers' needs.

In the Highland capital of *Inverness*, a good base for touring the entire area, the **Culloden House Hotel** (01463 790461) is an upmarket, slightly formal country house but still very comfortable. In the centre of Inverness just below the castle and overlooking the River Ness is the family run **Glen Mhor Hotel** (01463 234308).

North of Inverness, the A9 leads to *Dornoch* and its world-famous links. The accommodation providers are very used to looking after golfers here. The **Royal Golf Hotel** (01862 810283) could not be better located overlooking the 1st tee and fairway of the Royal Dornoch course. The **Dornoch Castle Hotel** (01862 810216) opposite the cathedral is full of character, a little jaded perhaps although it dates, in part, back to the 1550s. **Burghfield House Hotel** (01862 810212) is an imposing turreted country house a few minutes walk from the village centre.

Golspie and *Brora* are great holiday golfing destinations and the **Links & Royal Marine Hotels** (01408 621225) in Brora overlook this excellent, natural links. There are also luxury apartments available attached to the hotel. On Golf Road, again overlooking the links, are three good B&Bs: **Tigh Fada** (01408 621332),

Lynwood (01408 621226) and **Glenaveron** (01408 621601).

To the west, *Fort William* is not a major golfing centre but a good base for West Highland sightseeing. The **Crolinnhe** (01397 702709) is a deluxe (5-star) B&B — very comfortable and breakfast is highly commendable. Head up the Road to the Isles for stunning views to Rhum, Eigg and the Cuillins on Skye.

If you want a great train ride you could catch a train from Fort William to Mallaig and back again. On the Road to the Isles **Arisaig House** (01687 450622) is very comfortable with the delightful Traigh Golf Club nearby.

Where to Eat

The south of the area is well provided for with *Aviemore* (Scotland's skiing centre in winter) being a popular tourist base. The **Old Bridge Inn** in Dalfaber Road (01479 811137) serves up an innovative menu with plenty choice on the malt shelf. **The Tipsy Laird**, in *Kingussie's* High Street (01540 661334), is a traditional family run bistro style restaurant and bar. The **Scotshouse Hotel**, also in Kingussie (01540 661351), offers a cosy bar with fine malt whisky, a good wine list and hearty bar meals.

Culloden House Hotel (01463 790461) in *Inverness* is the place to dine in Palladian opulence. The **Riverhouse Restaurant** in Creig Street (01463 222033) also in Inverness is recommended as is the 4-star **Dunain Park Hotel** (01463 230512) or the **Kingsmills Hotel** in Culcabock Road, (01463 237166) overlooking Inverness golf course.

In *Cawdor,* the **Cawdor Tavern** (01667 404777), in The Lane, is a traditional country pub and restaurant serving good Scottish fayre. Further north in *Tain* is the **Mansfield House Hotel** (01862 892052,) a family-run affair to a good Scottish standard. **Morangie House Hotel** (01862 892281), also has an excellent reputation for food.

The community of *Dornoch* is both sophisticated and simple at the same time. Try the **Quail Restaurant** in Castle Street (01862 811811), a traditional Highland townhouse. In *Brora*, both the **Royal Marine Hotel** and its sister **Links Hotel** (01408 621252) offer excellent cuisine. There is a casual bistro overlooking the pool in the Marine while the Links commands an excellent view of the 1st and 18th.

On the west coast the **Old Library Lodge Restaurant** (01687 450651) in *Arisaig* is charming. *Fort William* has the very popular **Crannog Seafood Restaurant**. Finally Spean Bridge is a quiet crossroads where both the **Coach**

House Restaurant (01397 712680) and the **Old Station Restaurant** (01397 712535) provide an excellent service.

What to Do

The Highlands are really all about one thing – the scenery – and there are miles of it that seems to get better every time you turn a corner. The east is perhaps not so dramatic but west Highland terrain is simply staggering, probably the best views in all of Europe.

At a more mundane level, in Newtonmore, the **Highland Folk Museum** is a fascinating reconstructed 1700s Highland township. You cannot miss the **Strathspey Steam Railway** which chugs through the Highland scenery from Aviemore to Boat of Garten and back. The **Rothiemurchus Estate Visitor Centre**, one mile/2km east from Aviemore, offers a host of off-road and rambling activities. In nearby Carrbridge is the **Landmark Visitor Centre** mostly targeted at children. Inverness is a shopping and entertainment hub for the Highlands and the **Eden Court Theatre** in Bishop Road (Tel 01463 239841) often hosts acclaimed productions.

Four miles (6km) to the east of Inverness on the B9006 is the **Battlefield of Culloden Visitor Centre**, run by the National Trust. The incidents leading up to, during and following this tragic battle fought between Bonnie Prince Charlie and his Red Coat opponents are brilliantly recaptured. It was the last major battle to be fought on British soil, and outside various plaques identify the clans and their positions as well as their graves. Fenced trails lead around the moor and battle site. A restored thatched cottage, **Old Leanach**, still stands, the only building to survive the battle and where 300 Highlanders were burnt alive. It was inhabited until the beginning of the 20th century and is now a folk museum.

Continuing along the B9006 for several miles, you will arrive at Cawdor village and **Cawdor Castle and Gardens**, locally pronounced 'Cawdir', one of the most romantic and best presented of Scotland's stately homes. Still lived in by the Cawdor family, it maintains an air of domesticity, making it more of a home than a chilly keep. The main tower is 600 years old with several quixotic additions that flourish around it. One of its most pleasant aspects is the walled garden, not so stately and formal as some but more congenial for its simple arrangements.

Loch Ness is a great attraction in itself with the hope of spying the great aquatic monster. Near Drumnadrochit is **Urquhart Castle** where many sightings have taken place along with the **Loch Ness Exhibition Centre**.

Further north on the A9 is the township of Tain and the very popular **Glenmorangie Distillery and Visitor Centre**. On the north side of Golspie, **Dunrobin Castle** is a most impressive fortification. The new **Clanland** and **Sealpoint**, at Foulis Ferry Point, Evanton, is an exciting and educational exhibition. For a thrilling aerial excursion check out **Trading Post Airboats**, near Bonar Bridge. The **Caledonian Canal Heritage Centre** in Fort Augustus gives a unique history of the canal, its uses and renovation.

TOURIST INFORMATION

Inverness Airport Tel 01667 462280

The Highlands of Scotland Tourist Board – Information Centre, Grampian Road, Aviemore, Inverness-shire, PH22 1PP, Tel : +44 (01479) 810363 Email : aviemore@host.co.uk Website : www.host.co.uk

Some 60 miles/100km west of Dingwall lies the 9-hole course at Gairloch. This is the 7th hole.

Chapter 6

Central Scotland

If you are looking for a combination of good golf, excellent scenery and a very warm welcome, then any part of Argyll, the Isles, Loch Lomond, Stirling and the Trossachs (otherwise known as the Central Region of Scotland) will fit the bill.

Access to the area is relatively easy with good road and rail connections from Glasgow, Perth and Edinburgh. However, in the summer months some of the minor roads can get congested as daytrippers head out of the big cities. Just a short drive from Edinburgh, the 'Wee County' of Clackmannanshire is one gateway to the region offering a host of courses where moorland mingles with parkland. The views down the Forth Valley and over the subtle splendour of the Ochil Hills are an added bonus. The narrow central lowlands are cut into by the Forth

and Clyde rivers leaving a narrow passage of land at one point barely 50 miles/ 80km across: and strategically placed to meet this bottleneck is the historic city and castle of Stirling.

Historic Stirling

If you enjoy history with your golf then Stirling is the place to go. This is one of Scotland's great cultural centres and well worth taking a day to explore, particularly the famous Stirling Castle and Old Town. Set below the castle's parapets is the excellent 18-hole course of Stirling Golf Club while, within a short drive, there are many welcoming parkland courses such as Dunblane New and Callander.

The nearby Falkirk area is a distinctive golfing region in itself and offers a variety of venues. The best course in the area is undoubtedly Glenbervie, scene of several amateur championships, very much a fine, parkland offering, secluded with lots of trees and a tendency to undulation. Northwest from Stirling, the A84 route leads across the Highland Boundary and

Left: Beautiful beaches and fine coastal views are among the many outstanding attractions in the Argyll and the Isles areas of the Central Region. Robert the Bruce stands guard at Bannockburn in Stirling (above). Bruce defeated the English under Edward II here in a famous battle in 1314.

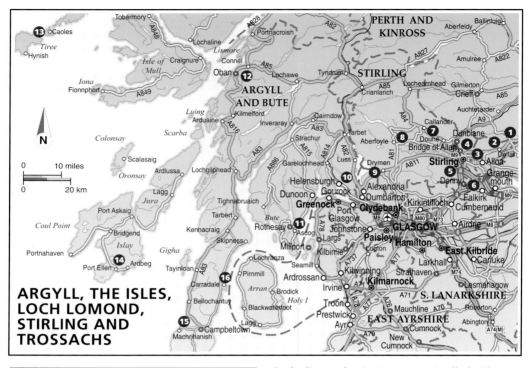

ARGYLL, THE ISLES,
LOCH LOMOND,
STIRLING AND
TROSSACHS

*The 6th at Aberfoyle, called Ditches, a difficult par-3
with views over the village of Aberfoyle and Ben
Lomond. Aberfoyle is just one of many friendly courses
within striking distance of Glasgow.*

*Scotland's central region incorporates Argyll, the Isles,
Loch Lomond, Stirling and the Trossachs, and is home
to Machrihanish and the Machrie golf clubs, to name just
two unique courses.*

into one of the most impressive parts of the country, the Trossachs and Breadalbane – Rob Roy Country. With courses such as Callander, Aberfoyle and Killin, this area has gained a much-deserved reputation for golf set in the finest scenic splendour.

A short drive north of Glasgow provides several splendid golf courses such as Cardross, Helensburgh and Dumbarton, overlooking the River Clyde. While nearly all of the courses in the area welcome visitors, a notable exception is Loch Lomond Golf Club. On the banks of one of Scotland's most celebrated beauty spots, the Loch Lomond course – although relatively new – has become known the world over through televised events for its quality and visual splendour. Unfortunately, it is closed to the public.

The areas surrounding the Firth of Clyde are ideal for holiday escapes and it is here that you find fine courses on the beautiful Cowal Peninsula such as the Cowal and Innellan clubs near Dunoon. Venturing further north and west the port of Oban and historic Inverary are attractive tourist destinations.

The town of Oban itself boasts a James Braid designed course at Glencruitten. From Oban, access is gained via the Caledonian MacBrayne ferry services to some of Scotland's western islands such as Iona, Mull, Jura, Colonsay, Tiree and Islay. Most of these have golf courses and while they are strictly holiday venues, they do make it worth taking your clubs with you.

The route south on the Kintyre Peninsula leads to one of Scotland's most dramatic courses, Machrihanish. Visitors come from every part of the world to test its rolling links but few are prepared to negotiate the first tee, played over the beach and usually into a very stiff wind, a fitting start to one of the finest links courses in the world.

The Isle of Islay

Another Scottish golf course to savour, and one which caught Nick Faldo's interest, is the Machrie course only a few miles from Port Ellen on the Isle of Islay. Although it takes time to reach, unless you fly direct from Glasgow airport, Machrie is a special golfing experience, more so if you are a keen imbiber of malt whiskies for which Islay is famous.

If you have time, take the alternative route by car and ferry. The region is reachable in three hours from Glasgow and a drive would take in Loch Lomond, Loch Long and Loch Fyne plus stunning mountain scenery. When it comes to choosing an area for golf in Scotland, the central region certainly offers diversity (*see pages 138-139*).

An idyllic setting close to Oban, the Isle of Eriska is one of many central locations offering excellent holiday golf.

From Dollar's 1st green, you can see the 15th-century fortress Castle Campbell, once called Castle Gloom.

① *Dollar*

Dollar Golf Club, Brewlands House, Dollar, Clackmannanshire FK14 7EA
TEL: *01259 742400* **FAX:** *01259 743497*
EMAIL: *dollargc@brewlandshousefreeserve.co.uk*
LOCATION: *Off the A91 in Dollar. Turn left at clock into West Burnside and signposted*
COURSE: *18 holes, 5242yd/4791m, Par 69, SSS 66*
GREEN FEES: *£*
FACILITIES: *Changing rooms and showers, full catering and bar, club hire*
VISITORS: *Welcome everyday but pre-booking is advised*

Designed by Ben Sayers in 1906, Dollar Golf Club is rather hilly but very enjoyable, perhaps because there are no bunkers. This multi-level golf course stretches out across the lower reaches of King's Seat Hill where snow can often settle in the winter months. The wooded ravines of the Burn of Care and the Burn of Sorrow run down either side of Castle Campbell and the 1st green – but don't let that put you off. The 2nd hole, called the Brae, is only 80yd/73m, but feels as high as it is long. You are faced with a 50ft/15m high bank to clear to get onto the hillside green, a par 3 calling for a

pitching wedge. Once onto this level, Dollar's course is not as hilly as it appears. It plays out over a wide, sloping expanse with views over Dollar's chimney-pots and the Devon Valley.

② *Muckhart*

Muckhart Golf Club, Drumburn Road, By Dollar, Clackmannanshire, FK14 7JH
TEL: *01259 781423* **Fax:** *01259 781544*
LOCATION: *Off A91, south of the village of Muckhart, 3 miles/5km east of Dollar*
COURSE: *18 holes, 6034yd/5515m, par 71, SSS 70*
GREEN FEES: *£*
FACILITIES: *Changing rooms and showers, full catering and bar, pro shop and teaching pro, practice area, trolley hire*
VISITORS: *Welcome everyday but pre-booking is essential*

Muckhart Golf Club sits neatly at the gateway to the Ochil Hills – a moorland setting with some parkland sections especially around the clubhouse. With the opening of a new 9-hole section, Muckhart now offers 27 excellent holes, and members and guests alike can wander the fairways with no pressure despite the course's popularity.

The original heathland front nine does require a slight hike at one or two points but it is remarkable how little you feel you

Teeing off from the 10th at Muckhart, with the Ochil Hills forming a constant scenic backdrop.

are playing around a hill. The course's highest hole, the 5th, Top of the World, offers magnificent views along the Forth Valley.

The 6th is called Lonesome Pine and looks west along the line of the Ochils. You can see Wallace's Monument down towards Stirling. The hole is around 190yd/174m, and often plays straight into the wind. On some days a driver might not be enough. However, the course's premier hole is the 18th, a magnificent par 5 playing from an elevated tee from which you can see marsh and burn dogging the fairway. As you approach the green, watch out for the burn which turns and crosses in front of it.

But it is the new holes that are most impressive. The layout is open and true to the curves of the land. There are several swampy areas that need to be carried or circumnavigated with judicious shots. All in all this is a lengthy stretch but a rewarding addition to an already good heathland layout.

3 *Alloa (Schawpark)*

Alloa Golf Club (Schawpark), Golf Course, Schawpark Sauchie, Alloa FK10 3AX
TEL: *01259 724476* FAX: *01259 724476*
LOCATION: *North of Alloa on the A908*
COURSE: *18 holes, 6229yd/5693m, par 70, SSS 71*
GREEN FEES: *££*
FACILITIES: *Changing rooms, showers, full catering, bar, pro shop, teaching pro, practice area, trolley hire, club hire*
VISITORS: *Welcome everyday but pre-booking is essential*

Alloa's Schawpark Course might appear hilly from the high 1st tee overlooking the broad backs of the Ochil Hills, but this is more parkland than moorland, more rolling than hilly. The tree-lined avenues allow a pleasant degree of privacy as the course winds through 150 acres/60 hectares of picturesque estate and will suit any level of golfer.

Of several notable holes, the 2nd is a long par 4 of 448yd/409m bending to the left with trees either side. A demanding par 3, the 173yd/158m 15th heads over a burn to an elevated green with four large bunkers beckoning. The 18th offers another short challenge usually into the prevailing wind with 191yd/175m of carry. This is as tough as finishing holes get.

4 *Dunblane New*

Dunblane New Golf Club, Perth Road, Dunblane, Perthshire FK15 0LJ
TEL: *01786 821521* **FAX:** *01786 821522*
LOCATION: *1 mile/1.6km off motorway (A9) main road and well signposted*
COURSE: *18 holes, 5930yd/5420m, par 69, SSS 69*
GREEN FEES: *££*
FACILITIES: *Changing rooms and showers, full catering and bar, pro shop and teaching pro, short game practice, trolley hire, club hire*
VISITORS: *Welcome weekdays from 9.30am to 12.30pm and 2.30pm to 4pm and restricted at weekends although pre-booking is advised*

Dunblane's supreme parkland condition, the views and the magnificent variety of trees make this a course worth savouring. The fairways are reputed to be the finest in Perthshire, gradually climbing from the clubhouse with lots of fringing trees and lush turf that is a treat to play off. There are a couple of quirky holes leaving awkward stances but these do not detract from the fine nature of a round here.

It is not what you would call a rigorous hike but a pleasant and panoramic stroll with views over to Stirling and the Trossachs. The 2nd, a slight dogleg-left par 4, calls for a precise drive and a pin-sharp pitch into the green and is undoubtedly the toughest hole. The 16th hole is a par-3, 190yd/174m in length onto a steep bank with a plateau green falling away to one side.

There are five short holes at Dunblane and each one is an excellent test to achieve par. The 9th is another but sharper dogleg to an elevated green and makes a good par 4.

5 *Stirling*

Stirling Golf Club, Queen's Road, Stirling FK8 3AA
TEL: *01786 464098* **FAX:** *01786 450748*
LOCATION: *1 mile/1.6km from Stirling town centre*
COURSE: *18 holes, 6409yd/5884m, par 72, SSS 71*
GREEN FEES: *££*
FACILITIES: *Changing rooms and showers, full catering and bar, pro shop and teaching pro, short game practice, trolley hire, buggy hire, club hire*
VISITORS: *Welcome everyday although pre-booking is advised. Midweek tee times available from 9am to 4.30pm. At weekends tee times may be reserved on day of play*

The area surrounding Stirling Castle was once marshland until, some centuries ago, hundreds of Highlanders were employed to drain it. It was this boggy mire that was Edward II's undoing when he stationed his heavy cavalry there the night before the historic Battle of Bannockburn. Robert the Bruce wasted no time in grasping the advantage early the next morning and the rest is history.

Today the course of Stirling Golf Club is a dry and delightful parkland lying close to the foot of the castle on rolling, open ground, with the Trossachs filling much of the views. The course was once the royal deer park. It is a comprehensive test of most parts of the game, perhaps a bit longer and more open than its nearest neighbours and made all the more interesting if there's a fresh breeze blowing. The 15th is a difficult dogleg uphill with no shortcut available. From the second shot it is all carry onto the green across rough (with no intervening fairway) placing even more emphasis on a sound and well-positioned drive.

Echoes of William Wallace, Robert the Bruce and Mary Queen of Scots reverberate a stone's throw or two away from Stirling's golf course.

🏌 Glenbervie

Glenbervie Golf Club, Stirling Road, Larbert FK5 4SJ
TEL: *01324 562605* FAX: *01324 551054*
LOCATION: *1 mile/1.6km north of Larbert on A9 Falkirk to Stirling road*
COURSE: *18 holes, 6423yd/5870m, par 71, SSS 70*
GREEN FEES: *£££*
FACILITIES: *Changing rooms, showers, full catering and bar, pro shop and teaching pro, practice area, trolley hire*
VISITORS: *Welcome weekdays before 4pm; booking allowed 24 hours in advance only*

The only hill of any consequence you will find at Glenbervie is the one upon which the clubhouse is built – and from which you tee off. After this the course plays across the wide Forth Valley working its way gently over rises and dips, before climbing again at the 18th where it returns to the upper level. The most remarkable feature of the course, from the 1st tee lookout at least, might be the backdrop of the Ochil Hills away in the distance.

The parkland course is sprinkled with impressive, centuries-old trees. Doglegs are a prevalent feature, as is the occasional blind summit as the course capers though this well-

Home to the Scottish branch of the Professional Golfers Association, Glenbervie's only hill supports the clubhouse.

groomed estate. The 2nd is an interesting if long par 5 with ancient trees adding to its character. The short par-4 5th can be troublesome, again with the danger of being blocked out by large trees. There is a run of tests from the 12th, a blind tee shot if you can hit long enough to the par-3 13th green, which has two big trees either side, and long, punishing rough beyond them. The 9th is Stroke Index 1, although many would consider the 14th the tougher hole, a long par 4 usually into the wind and tight off the tee with trees threatening to the left.

Glenbervie is one of the more established courses in central Scotland (a James Braid design), and, as with the majority of Scottish clubs it is always welcoming to weekday visitors who will enjoy its prestigious character. Speaking of characters, one of the club's most famous golfers is former Ryder Cup player John Panton who was Glenbervie's club professional for 33 years and who still plays this noteworthy course.

Callander

Callander Golf Club, Aveland Road, Callander, Perthshire
FK17 8EN
TEL: *01877 330090* **FAX:** *01877 330062*
LOCATION: *A84, 11 miles / 18km north of Dunblane,*
course is on the south side of village
COURSE: *18 holes, 5151yd / 4708m, par 66, SSS 66*
GREEN FEES: *£*
FACILITIES: *Changing rooms and showers, full catering and*
bar, pro shop and teaching pro, short game practice, trolley
hire, club hire
VISITORS: *Welcome everyday although pre-booking is*
advised

Surrounded by hills and overlooked by Ben Ledi, Callander Golf Club has a picture-perfect setting. It certainly made a fine filming location when the village was turned into the Tannochbrae of *Dr Findlay's Casebook* in the 1960s TV series.

The course remains a fine example of a mildly-climbing, parkland trail laid out by Tom Morris in 1913 and extended by Willie Fernie to 18 holes in 1913–14. It makes good use of the natural swells and tree-lined bowls to give variety, as well as offering more open, straight holes.

The backdrop is as uplifting as the course is diverse, and it is a pleasure to see your ball scorching towards its target against such scenery. The 6th is called the Dell and is claimed to be one of the finest examples of the work of Old Tom Morris still in existence. As it measures 372yd/ 340m, a good second shot is important to clear the bunker that stands guards to the approach of the green. This can be a daunting prospect. Another memorable hole is the 15th at only

Callander town can be viewed in the distance from the golf course. The town is the capital of the Trossachs, one of Scotland's most beautiful areas, and has a surfeit of mill shops and shortbread vendors. This is also Rob Roy country.

135yd/123m, called the Avenue which plays between a row of oak trees to the narrow portal of the green: very picturesque but don't underestimate the challenge. Indeed this remains the case for the entire Callander course. While it might appear short and simple there are few golfers who come off feeling that they have beaten the course.

Aberfoyle

Aberfoyle Golf Club, Braeval, Aberfoyle, Stirlingshire FK8
3UY
TEL: *01877 382493*
LOCATION: *A81 Callander to Glasgow road*
COURSE: *18 holes, 5218yd / 4769m, par 66, SSS 66*
GREEN FEES: *£*
FACILITIES: *Changing rooms and showers, full catering and*
bar, short game practice, trolley hire
VISITORS: *Welcome weekdays and weekends although pre-*
booking is advised. Visitors may tee off after 10.30am
Saturday and Sunday

Aberfoyle is one of the friendlier courses with a large contingent of Glasgow members who always make visitors feel welcome with that admirable quality of west coast humour. The heathland course itself is rather hilly but the burden brings beauty with prospects south over the fields and most impressively west with fantastic views over to Ben Lomond.

The 4th hole in particular is the one best remembered, whether it is for the climb to reach this, the highest point on the course, or the degrees of difficulty encountered in playing a short par 4 that is all uphill. You can see Stirling Castle from the green away to the east. The 12th, a short par 3 of

The 4th hole at Aberfoyle looking north towards the Trossachs.

168yd/154m, is also a little tough. Watch out also for the hazards of embedded rock on this course. Aberfoyle is a classic upland course offering pleasing views and good sport.

9 *Buchanan Castle*

Buchanan Castle Golf Club, Buchanan Estate, Drymen, Glasgow G63 0HY
TEL: *01360 660307* **FAX:** *01360 870382*
EMAIL: *buchanancastle@sol.co.uk*
LOCATION: *North of Glasgow, off the A811 and just south of Drymen village*
COURSE: *18 holes, 6059yd/5538m, par 70, SSS 69*
GREEN FEES: *£££*
FACILITIES: *Changing rooms and showers, full catering and bar, pro shop and teaching pro, short game practice, trolley hire, club hire*
VISITORS: *Visitors welcome Monday to Sunday except Tuesday and Saturday morning. Pre-booking is advised*

Less than a mile from Loch Lomond, Buchanan Castle is set by the banks of the River Endrick with the Campsie Hills in sight and is an easy-walking, flat parkland course designed by James Braid in 1935. Three holes on the front 9 and one on the back run by the river but this does not come into play. The 8th is a memorable par 3 that crosses water at Duncan Cameron's Lochan. James Braid was known to be keen on doglegs and Buchanan Castle offers 12 of them. A nice touch is the regular feature of two tall trees marking out the turn of the dogleg.

The ruins of the Scottish Baronial castle, once the centre of the estate, can still be seen but the hub now is the ancient and impressive clubhouse where a feeling of calm and tradition abides.

BUCHANAN'S BARONIAL CASTLE

Scenic splendour and Scottish history combine to offer visiting golfers something special at Buchanan Castle. On the ridge of the Buchanan Castle Estate lie the ruins of a Scottish baronial castle replete with turrets and steeped gables. The Graham Family, the Dukes of Montrose, bought the estate in the 17th century and have held it since. The Montroses bred and trained raced horses and the ground was once used as a racetrack and for gallop training. In 1879 their horse Sefton won the Derby. This victory is commemorated in the name of the 18th hole and in a huge oil painting of horse and jockey in the clubhouse. The Montrose family look over the elegant dining room in various oil portraits.

10 *Helensburgh*

Helensburgh Golf Club, 25 East Abercromby St,
Helensburgh G84 9HZ
TEL: *01436 674173* FAX: *01436 671170*
LOCATION: *A82 from Dumbarton, off Sinclair Street and*
signposted Abercromby Street
COURSE: *18 holes, 6104yd/5579m, par 69, SSS 70*
GREEN FEES: *££*
FACILITIES: *Changing rooms, showers, full catering, bar,*
pro shop, teaching pro, putting area, trolley hire, club hire
VISITORS: *Welcome weekdays but not weekends*

Overlooking the Clyde, this is one of the most demanding courses in the area because of its exposed moorland setting and the fact that there are few days when the wind does not affect play. The layout was approved by Old Tom Morris (paid £1 for the day) and later James Braid.

The course climbs to survey a busy part of the Clyde – Greenock and Gourock are on the opposite bank. Then it rolls down from the open moors to catch the heavy breezes. No two holes are the same and each is challenging. There are gullies, gorse and heather with several steep green approaches.

The 6th has fine views of Loch Lomond and a dogleg left with threatening out-of-bounds, although for the better player there is the chance to carry the corner of this 412yd/376m par 4. The 10th is a long downhill scamper towards the Clyde, while the 210yd/192m par-3 11th offers great views. The 18th finishes with a slight left-hand kink just before the green. The corner is fairly easy to clear but you are left with a noticeable dip unless you deliver the ball squarely on the green.

11 *Rothesay*

Rothesay Golf Club, Canada Hill, Rothesay, Isle of Bute
PA20 9HN
TEL: *01700 503554* FAX: *01700 503554*
LOCATION: *Reached via Wymess Bay and a 6-mile/10-*
km ferry crossing. The course is reached via the High Street
directly opposite the pier and from there is well signposted
COURSE: *18 holes, 5395yd/4931m, par 69, SSS 66*
GREEN FEES: *£*
FACILITIES: *Changing rooms and showers, full catering and*
bar, pro shop and teaching pro, short game practice, trolley
hire, power trolley hire, club hire
VISITORS: *Welcome weekdays and weekends although pre-*
booking is advised and essential at weekends

Rothesay, on the Isle of Bute, has long been a traditional holiday town for Scots seeking escape from city life. It is perhaps past its heyday but still has a dilapidated charm with Italian cafés and a wide promenade to

The 12th at Rothesay with views of the Firth of Clyde.

The rocky outcrops of Glencruitten add a mental as well as a physical challenge to play. Players who can relax and deliver the shots required will come off singing its praises, while those who are bothered by its quirkiness might feel frustrated.

12 Glencruitten

Glencruitten Golf Club, Glencruitten Road, Oban PA34 4PU

TEL: *01631 562868*
LOCATION: *1 mile/1.6km from centre of Oban and up Glencruitten Road.*
COURSE: *18 holes, 4452yd/4069m, par 61, SSS 63*
GREEN FEES: *£*
FACILITIES: *Changing rooms and showers, full catering and bar, pro shop and teaching pro, short game practice area, trolley hire, club hire*
VISITORS: *Welcome everyday but pre-booking is advised*

Oban is the starting off point for many sea journeys out to Scotland's armada of islands. From here you can ferry to the Isles of Tiree, Colonsay, Mull, Islay and others. However, few people realise there is such an excellent 18-hole course just at the back of town.

Glencruitten is a James Braid design and, apart from it being rather hilly with some tricky blind holes, it is a really delightful parkland test in top condition. From the 1st you get an idea of the terrain although you only see the first two hills – there are at least seven of them, albeit little ones, with fairways and greens laced engagingly in between.

The blind par 3s can be most troublesome for first time visitors to the course and there is danger of losing balls in the thick rough. If you do manage a second or third round you will have a better idea where to place the ball.

Glencruitten is a most unusual layout, playing to high-perched greens then down again into the lush valleys. The 16th is a good par 4 over the burn where you must judge the tee shot well. The 17th is a great hole, a long par 3 to a green 50ft/15m higher than the tee.

stroll along. The town is squeezed between the Clyde Estuary and Canada Hill with the entrance to Rothesay Golf Club situated not far from the town centre.

Just one look will tell you that there will be a degree of climbing, especially on the 1st hole. But then be prepared for probably the best prospect from any course in Scotland. The course reaches its zenith at the par-4 12th where an almost 360° panorama can be relished. From here you can behold the Firth of Clyde, Rothesay Bay below and the magnificent Kyles of Bute.

Rothesay's moorland is a welcome addition to any Scottish golf itinerary, offering fine views and challenges in equal measure on every hole, especially the 7th, 11th and 12th.

THE ISLE OF BUTE

If you are travelling to the Isle of Bute to play at Rothesay, you should also explore the rest of this small but popular holiday island. Rothesay is the only town and has long been a resort. It lies in a wide, sweeping bay backed by green hills, and has a traditional seaside promenade and a Winter Gardens set in pagoda-style. The moated ruins of Rothesay Castle are well worth exploring.

13 Vaul

Vaul Golf Club, Scarinish, Isle of Tiree, Argyll PA77 6XH
TEL: *01879 220562*
LOCATION: *On the Isle of Tiree, 2 miles / 3km from Scarinish and ½ mile / 0.75km from Lodge Hotel, ferry from Oban four hours and plane from Glasgow 45 minutes.*
COURSE: *9 holes, 5674yd / 5186m, par 72, SSS 68*
GREEN FEES: *£*
FACILITIES: *Changing rooms and showers*
VISITORS: *Visitors welcome Monday to Saturdays although pre-booking is advised. No golf on Sunday*

Visitors go to the Isles off Scotland's west coast for a host of different activities – bird-watching, wind-surfing and fishing to name a few. Golf isn't really a principal activity here. However, if you choose to pack your clubs, you will play on courses that evoke how the game of golf may have started out. These are simple, even primitive courses but for those very reasons they are all the more enjoyable.

The ferry from Oban takes about four hours to reach Tiree, the most westerly of the Inner Hebridean Islands. It is relatively flat with no trees and a population of only 800. Here, Vaul Golf Club is a rare gem if you are prepared to experience golf in its original form. The fairways are carpeted with buttercups and daisies and the best way of knowing where your ball has landed is by watching the grazing sheep scatter.

The greens are fenced like boxing rings to keep the sheep off and the bunkers are formed by wind, rain and sheltering animals, just as nature intended. The surrounding views over enchanting sandy bays and soft, flowing mounds hark back to a time when golf courses were more sensitively laid out over existing land features.

There is nothing overly demanding in playing Vaul's 9 holes (played twice) but the experience of the crisp light, blue sea, tawny bay and the random white cottages are all quite intoxicating. From the magnificent 4th tee you can just make out the islands of Muck, Rhum and Eigg to the north; possibly the more distant Outer Hebrides. This is golf at is most simple and a unique experience that only Scotland could offer.

Dining Out in Scotland

It is probably safe to say that the culinary arts in Scotland have, in the past, lagged well behind the rest of the world. Through the best part of the 20th century, a traditional Scots diet of red meat, bleached flour, excessive sugar and little fresh fruit and vegetables has lead to one of the highest incidences of heart disease in the world followed by an equally abysmal dental record.

Moreover you will still encounter unenlightened kitchens serving cheap, frozen, processed meals garnished with stale salad which remain under the illusion that they can charge inflated prices. If this is your experience, then complain wholeheartedly if you are not satisfied in any way with the food or service that you receive. It is only in this way that the message will eventually get through and standards will rise.

But on a much cheerier note, things have improved considerably over the past two decades in the catering business, and the number of quality food outlets in Scotland increases each year. Golf clubhouses are surprisingly good at offering a reasonable level of food. Again, some are exceptional while others get by on pre-packed, microwave

But'n'Ben in Auchmithie, Angus, has tasty seafood.

menus. Pubs offering lunches and dinners have also become common and the food in these establishments is often both satisfying and inexpensive.

A new wave of Scottish cuisine is happening and the chefs that are leading the way back to a more healthy, satisfying level of catering are making excellent use of the freshest local produce.

Some of that fresh product is still justifiably highly regarded. A prime example is Aberdeen Angus beef (cleared of all BSE beef-scare associations). Menus will tell you whether your steak is Aberdeen Angus or not. Given the number of red deer in Scotland, it is perhaps not surprising that venison is also on offer in many establishments and, in fact, it is low in cholesterol. Grouse is also available if you like game and this has a strong taste. But the quintessential Scottish dish is haggis, made from a sheep's stomach bag and stuffed with spiced liver, offal, oatmeal and onion. It is normally eaten with mashed neep (turnips) and mashed potatoes. Scots broth, porridge, fresh fish and various oatmeal dishes are also well worth sampling.

To find recommended restaurants, bistros, bars and other establishments offering food, see each regional directory at the end of each chapter. Another most useful publication to locate the best of Scottish cooking is *A Taste of Scotland*. The organization behind this publication only list those establishments who have successfully passed a rigorous inspection process, and achieved the highest standards of cooking, as well as showing a commitment to fresh Scottish produce in hospitable surroundings.

'Taste of Scotland', 33 Melville Street, Edinburgh EH3 7JF, Scotland
Tel: 0131 220 1900 Fax: 0131 220 6102
Email: info@taste-of-scotland.com

Typical Scottish hospitality: the Jigger Inn where Margaret Burton has pulled pints for 20 years.

14 The Machrie

The Machrie Hotel and Golf Links, Port Ellen, Isle of Islay
PA42 7AN
TEL: *01496 302310* **FAX:** *01496 302404*
EMAIL: *machrie@machrie.com* **WWW:** *machrie.com*
LOCATION: *On the Isle of Islay, adjacent to the airport (40 minutes from Glasgow by plane); ferries from Kennacraig daily (2 hours)*
COURSE: *18 holes, 6226yd/5690m, par 71, SSS 70*
GREEN FEES: *££*
FACILITIES: *At the hotel – full catering and bar, trolley hire, club hire*
VISITORS: *Welcome everyday but pre-booking is advised*

There are a few golfing encounters in Scotland that are absolutely unique and quite unmissable. The Machrie on the Isle of Islay is most certainly one of them. This enchanted island is famed for its brawny malt whiskies but the reputation of its golf course has also spread worldwide. Through the decades, golf's greats have taken the magical mystery tour either by air from Glasgow over the lochs and hills of Argyll or by boat from the Kintyre Peninsula to the Inner Hebridean haven.

On reaching the flat expanse of peat bog between mountain and sea, they might wonder why they came or where this fabled

Follow in the footsteps of Vardon, Taylor and Braid on the natural links of the Machrie. This is the par-4 308yd/282m 1st with the beach in the background.

course could be. But as you step onto the 1st tee, you will sense why it is so special and why it was worth the effort to come here to play.

The Machrie is a marvellous piece of links set on Laggan Bay. Man appears to have had little to do with its creation other than to stake out a few tees and greens where they naturally occurred. Indeed, it was the opinion of the course's architect, Willie Campbell, that it would 'make for very little money one of the best courses in Scotland as it will need very little more than cutting the puttin' greens and making a bridge here and there.'

One of the most imposing holes is the 7th, Scots Maiden, with a large dune immediately in front of the tee. Scenic views of the shoreline are also found at the 2nd, 8th and 9th looking over the 7 mile/11km stretch of beach known as the Strand. Few will come to the Isle of Islay or The Machrie only for one day, but the stay will give you an unrivalled sense of being totally away from it all.

15 Machrihanish

Machrihanish Golf Club, Machrihanish, Campbeltown, Kintyre PA28 6PT
TEL: *01586 810213* **FAX:** *01586 810221*
LOCATION: *On the Kintyre Peninsula, 135 miles/217km from Glasgow and 5 miles/8km west of Campbeltown on the B843. There are two daily flights (Mon-Fri) from Glasgow airport direct to Machrihanish*
COURSE: *18 holes, 6225yd/5690m, par 70, SSS 71*
GREEN FEES: *££*
FACILITIES: *Changing rooms, showers, full catering, bar, pro shop an teaching pro, trolley hire, buggy hire, club hire*
VISITORS: *Welcome everyday but pre-booking is advised*

Set on the west shores of the Kintyre Peninsula, this remote course is backed by low lying hills and faces the unbroken expanse of the Atlantic Ocean. It is not a pretty site but it's a bracing one; the wind blows up from the south west racing over the unprotected links.

Machrihanish plays out into the dunes over weaving fairways that pitch and roll as much as the sea behind. The 3rd flows towards the beach with the blond tips of marram grass close by but still leaving space. The par–3 4th is a Troon–style postage stamp to an island green fringed with twisting grass. In sum, as Old Tom Morris remarked, 'the area was designed by the Almighty for playing golf'.

16 Carradale

Carradale Golf Club, Carradale, Argyll, East Kintyre PA28 6QT
TEL: *01583 431643*
LOCATION: *On the Kintyre Peninsula, 135 miles/217km from Glasgow and 5 miles/8km west of Campbeltown on the B843; a few miles from Machrihanish; daily flight there from Glasgow airport*
COURSE: *9 holes, 2314yd/2115m, par 65, SSS 64*
GREEN FEES: *£*
FACILITIES: *Changing rooms, bar, trolley hire. Catering available at one of the two hotels near the starting box*
VISITORS: *Welcome everyday but pre-booking is advised*

Those who make it to Machrihanish, should also check out the less celebrated Carradale, overlooking the Kilbrannan Sound to the northern peaks of the island of Arran. This short, bunkerless course is one of Kintyre's best kept secrets. Rocky outcrops and wild goats are just two of the more notable hazards; but you may be treated to the sight of seals and dolphins as you make your way over the seaside holes.

The rough between the fairways is kept well cut, but the course can be an exciting test despite the lack of bunkers. The most memorable holes, especially for their views, are the 2nd, 5th, 6th and 7th.

SCOTLAND'S PREMIER OPENING HOLE?

Stand on the 1st at Machrihanish, a dogleg par 4 called Battery, and you are forced to confront how much Atlantic and beach you dare play over. The three-hour drive from Glasgow is nothing compared to the 200yd/183m drive that now faces you. Not unreasonably, this has been described at the premier opening hole in Scotland. While the wind may assist you in your endeavours at the 1st, do not rely on it to be at your back on other holes here, as it will turn with the tide or just at its own whim.

REGIONAL DIRECTORY
Where to Stay

Cameron House Hotel (01389 755565), overlooking Loch Lomond near Alexandria, is truly excellent in all ways with full facilities including a 'Wee Monster' 9-hole course. It is next door to Loch Lomond Golf Club but has no sway in getting you a game on this exclusive course. Nearby is the lovely village of Drymen and the **Buchanan Arms Hotel** (01360 660588), useful if you wish to golf and enjoy the peace of the countryside. In the village of Kinbuck just beyond Dunblane is **Cromlix House Hotel** (01786 822125), a 5-star Baronial country house hotel, which is one of Scotland's best with a relaxed and opulent ambience. In Stirling itself is the **Stirling Highland Hotel** (01786 475444) in the centre of town, close to the castle and well-placed for enjoying this historic hub.

If you cross over to the Isle of Tiree, the **Glassary** (01879 220684) in Sandaig is exceptional. Iain Macarthur is the proprietor/chef cooking an extensive a la carte menu using mostly local produce. It is also a very comfortable B&B. **Isle of Eriska Hotel** (01631 720371) on the tiny Isle of Eriska just north of Oban is a great retreat with its own golf course. One of the best experiences is to stay and play at the **Machrie Hotel and Golf Links** (01496 302310) on the Isle of Islay. For excursions to Machrihanish there is the **Ardell House** (01586 810235) a guest house overlooking the golf course and Machrihanish Bay. Most hotels are found in and around nearby Campbeltown such as **The** **Craigard** (01586 554242), or the **Seafield Hotel** (01586 552741) overlooking Campbeltown Loch. Glasgow airport is only 20 minutes away, and under £100 to get there.

Where to Eat

In Stirling, the **Scholars Restaurant** within Stirling Highland Hotel (01786 475444) offers an elegant, wood panelled dining room with a choice of a la carte or table d'hote menus, and an excellent wine list. In nearby Falkirk is **Quennelles Restaurant** (01324 877411), a family run restaurant situated in a 100-year-old cottage serving contemporary Scottish food. Dunblane's top eating spot is **Cromlix House Hotel** (01786 822125) with its restaurant earning two AA rosettes – this is probably about as good as it gets. The **Inverard Hotel** (01877 382229) in Aberfoyle is a family run Victorian hunting lodge, set amidst spectacular scenery and serving an unusual combination of Scottish and Filipino menus. The **Lade Inn** (01877 330152) in Callander is a country pub par excellence as recommended by Egon Ronay, the AA, Britain's Best Pubs guide and just about every other good food and beer guide. The **Georgian Room** at Cameron House Hotel (01389 755565) overlooking Loch Lomond is rather formal but well worth the extra effort to dine there. Before setting off for the islands dine at the **Manor House Hotel** (Tel: 01631 562087) in Oban

Visitors to Rob Roy country taking a cruise aboard the Sir Walter Scott *on Loch Katrine.*

Oban Harbour is the starting off point for sea trips to many Scottish islands. Glencruitten is the nearest golf course.

overlooking the bay with its 2-AA Red rosettes. On the Isle of Mull try the **Back Brae Restaurant** (01688 302422) in Tobermory, the island's oldest restaurant serving delicious home made food with an excellent wine list. On Islay the **Machrie Hotel** (01496 302310), is the place to play and stay. It offers reasonable food but it is the after-dinner drams that make it memorable.

What to Do

Queen Elizabeth Forest Park north of Aberfoyle is recommended for walking. Nearby, a sail on Loch Katrine with the *Sir Walter Scott* steam ship is very relaxing unless it is crowded. This is **Rob Roy** country and the story of this kindly villain is fondly told at the town of in Callander. There are castles of note at Dollar and Doune but **Stirling Castle** is the pinnacle of a historic tour as is the climb to **William Wallace's Monument** near Stirling. In the Old Town of Stirling near the castle is **Stirling Old Town Jail**, and a rather alarming recounting of grisly old days complete with live actors. **Bannockburn Heritage Centre,** south of Stirling helps to bring

to life this momentous battle for Scottish Independence, following the efforts of (*Braveheart*) William Wallace and Robert the Bruce. **Doune Motor Museum** just north of the town of Doune on the A84 is interesting.

Check out the **Dunmore Pineapple**, north of Airth between Falkirk and Stirling for a slice of unusual architecture. Fans of the great Scottish architect, Charles Rennie Mackintosh will enjoy **Hill House** in Helensburgh. If you want to take to the hills try hiking on **Ben Lawers** just outside the village of Killin where you will also find the **Breadalane Folklore Centre**. On the road to Oban and the Isles, **Inverary Castle and Gardens** just outside Inverary and **Inverary Jail** in town are both worthy of your time. On the Isle of Islay the whisky distilleries, including **Bowmore**, **Laphroaig**, **Ardbeg** and **Laggavullan**, offer tours and a nip of the malt.

Tourist Information Offices

Argyll, the Isles, Loch Lomond, Stirling & Trossachs Tourist Board – Information Centre, 7 Alexandra Parade, Dunoon, Argyle, PA23 8AB, Tel : +44 (01369) 703785 Fax: 01369 706085 Email *info@scottish.heartlands.org* www: *scottish.heartlands.org*

Chapter 7

Glasgow, Ayrshire and Arran

Glasgow has always been a city of contrasting impressions – the European City of Culture, bargain hunting in the Barras, a boisterous nightlife, rare antiquities at the Burrell Collection. The city has at once its serious and its jocular side. Glasgow people are industrious but also have a very comic disposition, quick with a joke and funny in the warmest way.

Glasgow Golf

According to the local tourist board there are over 80 parkland, heathland and moorland courses in the area, and yet it is not well known for its golf. This is good news for those seeking an unfettered round of the highest standards. Haggs Castle is the nearest course to the city just a few minutes over the Kingston Bridge on the M8 motorway. The other two notable clubs close to town are Pollok Golf Club and Glasgow Golf Club itself.

Pollok enjoys an air of tradition in a setting that is idyllic considering it is only minutes from the busy motorway or town centre of Glasgow. Pollok's overall length makes it a comfortable and pleasurable outing. The gently rolling fairways are not taxing and it is a delightful walk through this beautiful estate. The magnificent oaks and chestnut trees define the holes and along with the many well-placed bunkers provide the course's defence while the greens are usually wide and receptive. A round or day ticket affords full access to the facilities of the traditional clubhouse making it a special day out. The Glasgow Golf Club at Killermont is private with admission only if accompanied by a member.

It is a mere half-hour's drive from the city centre's clamour to discover numerous hidden golfing gems. Glasgow's network of motorways can have you in the countryside or down to the coast and golfing in a comfortable period. Lanark, Renfrew, Cumbernauld, Dumbarton, East

Left: The famous Brig o' Doon bridge at Alloway as featured in Robert Burns's poem Tam o'Shanter. Glasgow at night (above) is a vibrant place.

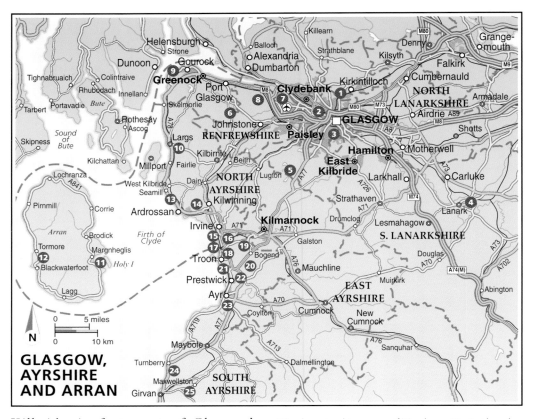

GLASGOW, AYRSHIRE AND ARRAN

Kilbride, in fact most of Glasgow's surrounding communities support excellent golf venues.

Planning an itinerary

A regular holiday retreat for Glaswegians in the city's industrial heyday was a trip 'doon the watter' creating a demand for golf courses therefore all along the Firth of Clyde: and there are notable courses there.

The main routes for this area all emanate out of Glasgow, Scotland's largest city. With its own international airport (also the hub for domestic flights from London and to other Scottish regions), Glasgow is a very strategic travel point.

The Glasgow city motorway system is well developed but always busy so be aware of the peak times when it becomes congested. The main route south of

The championship courses of Turnberry, Prestwick and Royal Troon are all reachable from Glasgow as are some 80 other courses in the Glasgow area.

Glasgow is the M77/A77 which can have you on the Ayrshire coast in half an hour. To access this from Glasgow airport turn towards the city and it is well signposted before entering Glasgow itself. On the Ayrshire coast, Prestwick airport is becoming increasingly active with both internal and international flights giving excellent access to Ayrshire's famous links.

Ayrshire

The Glasgow and Clyde Valley area merges seamlessly with Ayrshire and here exists another of Scotland's most famous golfing stretches. Although the game of golf took root on the east coast of Scotland, it quickly migrated west to the coastal fringe of Ayrshire. The first Open championship was held here at Old

Prestwick in 1860. Now there are three venues which have hosted the Open championship including Royal Troon and Turnberry's Ailsa Course.

But Ayrshire also has many less prominent courses to be discovered. Western Gailes and Troon's Kilmarnock Barassie course are firm favourites on the golfing trail. There are also some excellent public courses such as Ayr's Belleisle and Troon's Lochgreen.

Glasgow by design

One non-golfing name linked with a visit to Glasgow must be Charles Rennie Mackintosh, one of the most adventurous architects of the turn of the century. He developed a style which blended together elements of Gothic and Art Nouveau with Scottish Baronial. Good examples of his work still exists at the Willow Tea Rooms at 217 Sauchiehall Street, the Glasgow School of Art in Renfrew Street and, a short walk away, Queen's Cross Church. This is the best example, both inside and out, of Mackintosh's work. Beside Glasgow there are other architectural examples of his work in Helensburgh, not far from the golf course. See *pages 160-161* for more details.

The marina at Largs, viewed from Largs Golf Club. The isle of Cumbrae is visible in the distance and this forms a constant backdrop to any view from the course.

🏌 *Cawder*

Cawder Golf Club, Cadder Road, Bishopbriggs, Glasgow
G64 3QD
TEL: *0141 772 7101* **FAX:** *0141 772 4463*
LOCATION: *A803 north of city, then behind Bishopbriggs
Retail Park (Strathkelvin)*
COURSE: *18 holes, 6295yd/5754, par 70, SSS 71*
GREEN FEES: *£££*
FACILITIES: *Changing rooms and showers, full catering and
bar, pro shop and teaching pro, driving range, short game
practice, trolley hire, buggy hire, club hire*
VISITORS: *Welcome everyday but pre-booking is advised*

You'll find a most rewarding day's golf on the two parkland courses at Cawder Golf Club in Bishopbriggs, just north east of Glasgow. If you decide to spend the day here play the par 70 Cawder first, as it is a little more physically demanding. Then try the Kier. The Cawder offers a fair challenge often needing a reasonable carry off the tee. The layout gets progressively harder demanding your concentration especially at the testing holes 13 to 16, where you can easily drop shots. The par-3 18th is 200yd/183m of downhill carry to a green ringed by bunkers – and pet peacocks.

The Kier course is an easier amble but deceptive. You need to drive the ball well to set up for the small, well-bunkered greens. A bonus here is that there are rarely any lost balls as the rough is kept short and manageable.

Cawder's varied terrain keeps golfers thinking about every shot.

The conclusion to Haggs Castle, a very much upgraded layout close to Glasgow's centre.

🏌 *Haggs Castle*

Haggs Castle Golf Club, 70 Dumbreck Rd, Dumbreck,
Glasgow G41 4SN
TEL: *0141 427 3355* **FAX:** *0141 427 3355*
LOCATION: *2½ miles/4km southwest of Glasgow city
centre exiting at Junction 1 off M77 with clubhouse entrance
via filter lane immediately on the right*
COURSE: *18 holes, 6419yd/5867m, par 72, SSS 71*
GREEN FEES: *£££*
FACILITIES: *Changing rooms and showers, full catering and
bar, pro shop and teaching pro, short game practice, trolley
hire, buggy hire, club hire*
VISITORS: *Welcome weekdays only; pre-booking is advised*

The nearest course to the city centre of Glasgow, Haggs Castle is just a few minutes over the Kingston Bridge and just off the M8 motorway, yet its leafy fairways could not seem more calm and countrified.

The course has changed quite radically of late with a new section of six holes opened in May 1999. Dave Thomson was responsible for this new section from the 4th to the 9th, and he has introduced more modern elements that have refreshed the challenge of this one-time venue for the Bell's Scottish Open. The 496yd/453m par-5 4th can be relatively easy or difficult depending on the wind. The old 6th hole is now the 10th, a par 4 that calls for two big shots into a wind.

Haggs has a good mixture of holes carved through pleasant parkland, not too heavy with trees but narrow and lengthy enough to warrant its position as a fine venue for professional events. Generally the demand is off the tees with trees, out-of-bounds and doglegs prevailing. Another feature is the relatively small yet well-defended greens.

Pollok

Pollok Golf Club, 90 Barrhead Road, Glasgow, G43 1BG
TEL: *0141 632 4351* **FAX:** *0141 649 1398*
LOCATION: *From Glasgow city centre take M8/M77 to Junction 2 and go left , follow A736 to Barrhead Road*
COURSE: *18 holes, 6295yd/5754m, par 71, SSS 70*
GREEN FEES: *£££*
FACILITIES: *Changing rooms and showers, full catering and bar, short game practice, trolleys and club hire*
VISITORS: *Welcome weekdays; pre-booking is advised. No ladies unless on Sunday after 2pm with a member. Play at weekends only with member. Contact in advance for bookings*

Quiet, leafy Pollok Golf Club enjoys an air of tradition in an idyllic setting only minutes from the hustle and bustle of Glasgow. Tributes to its character have come from none less than Gene Sarazen and Sandy Lyle. Set on a beautiful parkland estate, magnificent oaks and chestnut trees define the holes and along with the many well-placed bunkers provide the course's defence, while the greens are wide, receptive and true.

Watch out for several demanding holes like the 14th with its drive over the bend of White Cart Water. The wide river is very much in play and if you choose to play away from it this leaves a very long shot into the green. The 18th, about 400yd/365m, leaves a tricky second shot uphill on to the plateau green.

Lanark

Lanark Golf Club, The Moor, Whitelees Road, Lanark, Strathclyde ML11 7RX
TEL: *01555 663219* **FAX:** *01555 663219*
LOCATION: *East side of Lanark town centre just off A73*
COURSE: *18 holes, 6423yd/5870m, par 70, SSS 71*
GREEN FEES: *££*
FACILITIES: *Changing rooms, showers, full catering, bar, shop, teaching pro, short game practice, trolley and buggy hire*
VISITORS: *Welcome everyday but pre-booking is advised*

Over the past 25 years Lanark has been a regular Scottish regional qualifier for the Open Championship and as such has gained a wide and well-deserved reputation. The singing of Lanark's praises continues, mainly by word of mouth, and golfers from around the globe find their way to the Lanark Moo as the land was once known.

The 18th green and clubhouse at Lanark – one of the most intimidating finishes of any Scottish golf course.

In 1897 Old Tom Morris was hired for three days to upgrade an existing tract to an 18-hole layout. Ben Sayers later offered his services and, in the 1920s, James Braid added length and bunkers. While it is most definitely an inland course surrounded by moors, Lanark plays very like a links course with a sandy based subsoil and, if the summer conditions are right, the thin, firm fairways encourage the ball to roll on.

The Moor was purchased from the people of Lanark in the mid 1990s by the golf club and, like St Andrews, locals still have preferential rates of play. And it is an excellent test of golf. There are three par 4s over 450yd/410m and two of these play into the prevailing wind. The 15th is 470yd/430m from the back tees, usually into the south-westerly. There are no short par 4s off the medal tees, and little in length between visitors and medal tees. The 8th is a 530yd/484m par 5 that offers little opposition to well-placed balls unlike some of the many demanding par 4s on the course.

In contrast, the 10th is a 152yd/139m short hole through an avenue of trees to an elevated green defended by three large bunkers. The hole considered the ultimate challenge here is the last, a 216yd/197m par-3. The green is set directly beneath the clubhouse window under the gaze of observers dining behind reinforced-glass.

5. *East Renfrewshire*

East Renfrewshire Golf Club, Pilmuir, Newton Mearns, Strathclyde G77 6RT
TEL: *0141 333 9989* **FAX:** *01355 500206*
LOCATION: *8 miles/13km south west of Glasgow on M77 towards Prestwick*
COURSE: *18 holes, 6097yd/5572m, par 70, SSS 70*
GREEN FEES: *£££*
FACILITIES: *Changing rooms and showers, full catering and bar, pro shop and teaching pro, short game practice, trolley hire, club hire*
VISITORS: *Welcome weekdays up to 3.30pm although pre-booking is advised*

To the south of Glasgow city and easily accessible via the new M77 motorway connection is the Gleneagles of Glasgow: East Renfrewshire Golf Club. A typical James Braid rolling heathland layout, it has plenty of sudden inclines and dips though it's never very hilly. Raised greens and small stands of short pine trees also characterise the course.

The 9th is an amazing hole from a high plateau tee with an ominous out-of-bounds fence to the right tightening the fairway. From there it is on to a narrow front green. This is where many scores have been destroyed but it is an exciting way to drop shots. The 18th is a good driving hole from a raised tee with the prevailing wind behind. The burn at 270 yd/247m can easily come into play if you hit a wind-assisted drive.

6. *Ranfurly Castle*

Ranfurly Castle Golf Club, Golf Road, Bridge of Weir, Strathclyde PA11 3HN
TEL: *01505 612609* **FAX:** *01505 612609*
LOCATION: *Exit 29 off M8 – 5 miles/8km north-west of Johnstone. Clubhouse is via Prieston Road which is the first exit off main road*
COURSE: *18 holes, 6284yd/5744m, par 70, SSS 71*
GREEN FEES: *£££*
FACILITIES: *Changing rooms and showers, full catering and bar, pro shop and teaching pro, short game practice, trolley hire*
VISITORS: *Welcome everyday but pre-booking is advised*

Ranfurly Castle Golf Club in Bridge of Weir is a classy heathland/moorland layout, probably the best of its nature in the area and well worth seeking out. The course offers a variety of gorse and trees as natural hazards in a hillside setting with views over to Glasgow and the surrounding hills.

The most challenging hole on the course is no doubt the 8th, a very long par 4 playing off a slightly elevated tee then moving into a valley. This presents a particularly tough tee shot as the driving area for good golfers narrows down to only 15-20 yd/13-18m in width. The 2nd shot is equally long but this time uphill into a two-tiered green. To succeed here requires two precise and uncompromising golf shots. Most club golfers play the hole as a par 5.

Visitors delight in East Renfrewshire's inland, undulating and tree-lined course.

Another testing par 4 comes at the 11th again played from an elevated tee and sweeping down to the left. At 441yd/403m, a good drive will favour a draw leaving another long iron across a hogs back and into a well-bunkered green. This hole overlooks the city of Glasgow as well as the Kilpatrick Hills and Ben Lomond.

Renfrew

Renfrew Golf Club, Blythswood Estate, Inchinnan Road, Renfrew, Strathclyde PA4 9EG
TEL: *0141 886 6692* **FAX:** *0141 886 1808*
LOCATION: *From Glasgow, follow the M8 west exit Junction 26 proceed along Glasgow Road to Normandy Hotel and course is signposted*
COURSE: *18 holes, 6818yd/6232m, par 72, SSS 73*
GREEN FEES: *££*
FACILITIES: *Changing rooms and showers, full catering and bar, pro shop and teaching pro, short game practice, trolley hire*
VISITORS: *Welcome Monday, Tuesday, Thursday; pre-booking is advised*

Renfrew represents an excellent round at Championship level. Its fine local reputation has yet to pass over to the wider world although this may be set to change as it is now a Scottish regional qualifying course for the Open championship. Having been laid out relatively recently, in 1973, the course may not be as mature as the many that usually host such prestigious events, but in every other way it is demanding and worthy, and has already twice been the venue for the Scottish Amateur Championship.

This hitherto unsung parkland plays down to the Rivers Cart and Clyde with the 7th green looking directly over the water to the old George Brown's shipyard where the *QE2* and many of the famous liners of the day were constructed. The Blythswood Estate's earlier history includes visits by nobility of the period including Queen Victoria, Queen Mary and Sir Walter Scott.

The course's near proximity to the water means there can be brief, early spring flooding, but this drains well and the affected fairways have the advantage of being carpeted in a lush loam for the rest of the year. At the 6th and 7th water is easily reached and tightens both these holes considerably. The rivers also come into play at the 8th and 11th. But the course's sternest test comes at the 4th, a par 4 of 455yd/416m from the back tees and 438yd/400m for visitors. The hole is tightly tree-lined with several well-placed bunkers to ensnare the ball: distance is imperative off the tee.

Another good hole is the 178yd/163m par-3 10th played over a charming combination of decorative water and lovely specimen trees of some 29 varieties that abound throughout the estate. Nearby Braehead has a leisure centre with curling and skating rinks.

Gleddoch

Gleddoch Golf Club, Langbank, Strathclyde PA14 6YE
TEL: *01475 540304* **FAX:** *01475 540201*
LOCATION: *From Glasgow, follow the M8 west past Glasgow Airport to Langbank roundabout, exit left and follow signs for 1½ miles/2km*
COURSE: *18 holes, 6238yd/5702m, par 71, SSS 71*
GREEN FEES: *£££*
FACILITIES: *Changing rooms and showers, full catering and bar, pro shop and teaching pro, short game practice, trolley hire, buggy hire, club hire*
VISITORS: *Welcome anytime though pre-booking is advised*

On a clear day with Dumbarton Rock and its castle reflecting off the River Clyde, Gleddoch promises evocative golf. It is a well-kept course, slightly hilly at times, but rarely tiring.

Of particular note are the three par 3s. The 7th can take some effort to cross over a small, decorative pond, and the hole plays longer than it appears. Club selection is difficult and calls for anything from a mid-iron to 4-iron into a head wind. The 12th is probably the best par 3 on the course, a nervy test through an avenue of trees. The 14th is a difficult uphill par 3 with a sea of gorse to the right, a potentially disastrous landing area. The views from this highest tee or at the adjacent 15th tee take in a sweeping panorama of the River Clyde and Glasgow. The course's ultimate challenge occurs at the 17th, a demanding dogleg from a high tee, so scenic yet so dangerous at the same time.

Gourock

Gourock Golf Club, Cowal View, Gourock, Strathcylde PA19 1HD
TEL: *01475 631001* **FAX:** *01475 631001*
LOCATION: *Southwest side of town off A770*
COURSE: *18 holes, 6512yd/5952m, par 73, SSS 73*
GREEN FEES: *££*
FACILITIES: *Changing rooms and showers, full catering and bar, pro shop and teaching pro, trolley hire*
VISITORS: *Welcome weekdays and weekends (Saturday after 3.30pm) although pre-booking is advised*

For breathtaking views, there are few to beat those from this fine course overlooking the Clyde Estuary to the Cowal Peninsula of Argyll. But for any beauty there is a beast, and that beast is the uphill ascent, especially on the 1st and 10th holes.

The course overall is surprisingly level considering its commanding position. It is also a well laid out venue, James Braid and Henry Cotton having helped to nudge nature towards perfection. The exposed and rugged moorland holes are mainly on the front 9. Then there are some lovely parkland touches on the closing holes but thick gorse lines the banks. The 9th is a great downward drive and the 18th is similar except it doglegs and is generally considered the better hole. Wind

The 16th at Gourock with sailboats on the Clyde Estuary. The course rises at the 1st and 10th and drops down at the 9th and 18th with many fine viewpoints.

can really add to the course's challenge. Its position tends to accommodate every south-westerly breeze, adding to the trials of the front 9 yet offering little advantage on the return.

Largs

Largs Golf Club, Irvine Road, Largs, Ayrshire KA30 8EU,
TEL: *01475 673594* **FAX:** *01475 673594*
LOCATION: *On the A78 to the south side of Largs*
COURSE: *18 holes, 6115yd/5589m, par 70, SSS 71*
GREEN FEES: *££*
FACILITIES: *Changing rooms and showers, full catering and bar, pro shop and teaching pro, trolley hire*
VISITORS: *Welcome weekdays and weekends after 3pm although pre-booking is advised*

Playing over a lovely stretch of gently sloping parkland between Kelburn Estate and the main coast road south through Ayrshire, Largs Golf Club weaves its way through a variety of large trees with stirring views over the marina to the isles of Cumbrae and Arran. It is not a long course but you have to be in the right place to negotiate some difficult doglegs or play into the greens. There are many difficulties to tackle from the 8th to 12th holes, especially from the tight, tree-lined doglegs. The 18th travels up a steep bank, but the drive over a burn is exhilarating as is the next shot over gorse bushes and bunkers at a two-tiered green.

11 Lamlash

Lamlash Golf Club, Lamlash, Isle of Arran KA27 8JU
TEL: *01770 600296* **FAX:** *01770 600296*
LOCATION: *On the Isle of Arran, 3 miles/5km south of Brodick on the A841*
COURSE: *18 holes, 4640yd/4241m, par 64, SSS 64*
GREEN FEES: *££*
FACILITIES: *Changing rooms and showers, full catering and bar, shop, trolley hire, buggy hire, club hire*
VISITORS: *Welcome everyday but pre-booking is advised*

On the Isle of Arran, Lamlash is a slightly undulating heathland course with invigorating views of Holy Island and the Firth of Clyde. This is only one of seven fine holiday courses on this much-favoured island. Each is quite different yet all offer relaxing golf in the sedate rhythm of a peaceful island.

Looking at the scorecard, it might appear short but there are many testing holes here, particularly the long par 3s. The 1st is a good

Holy Island framed by trees at the 1st hole at Lamlash: the club's facilities have benefitted from a lottery grant.

opening par 4 best played as a slight dogleg right, although it appears straight from tee to green. The 5th, with its tee sited beside the road, lets you see all of the green, which is in a hollow with rough and a burn to carry. The best hole of the back 9 is perhaps the 16th, a par 3 of only 97yd/87m, so simple that it can become difficult.

12 Shiskine

Shiskine Golf and Tennis Club, Blackwaterfoot, Shiskine, Arran KA27 8HA
TEL: *01770 860226* **FAX:** *01770 860205*
LOCATION: *On the Isle of Arran, off B880 at Blackwaterfoot*
COURSE: *12 holes, 2823yd/2580m, par 42, SSS 41*
GREEN FEES: *£*
FACILITIES: *Changing rooms and gents shower, Easter to October catering, golf shop, trolley hire, buggy hire, club hire*
VISITORS: *Welcome everyday although pre-booking is essential*

Are 12 holes the ideal number for holiday golf? The answer is an emphatic yes for those who play this curious little 12-hole course that has risen into the UK's top tiers. So popular is it in the summer months that visitors are restricted to two rounds a day (24 holes) and bookings are taken only one day in advance.

The course at Blackwaterfoot is short and tight with minuscule greens so the golfer who is accurate with a mid-iron usually comes away from here with a smile. The opening holes are very linkslike, open to the elements with views over to the Kintyre Peninsula. The 3rd hole, aptly named Crows Nest, is only 117yd/107m long but at least 80ft/24m in elevation. This is a tricky proposition and generally plays blind.

The 4th heads back down almost to sea level again with a stunning backdrop of the cliffs. It was here in a small cave that Robert the Bruce forged that famous golfing adage 'if at first you don't succeed, try, try, try, again'.

The Himalayas is another testing short hole, virtually 161yd/147m of hill from tee to green. But the sweetest point on the course surely comes standing on the 5th tee with the marvellous views up the Kilbrannan Sound.

13 West Kilbride

West Kilbride Golf Club, 33-35 Fullerton Drive, West Kilbride, Ayrshire KA23 9HT
TEL: *01294 823911* **FAX:** *01294 823911*
LOCATION: *On A78 Greenock to Ayr Road, signposted in Seamill*
COURSE: *18 holes, 6452yd/5897m, par 71, SSS 71*
GREEN FEES: *££*
FACILITIES: *Changing rooms and showers, full catering and bar, pro shop and teaching pro, short game practice, trolley hire, buggy hire, club hire*
VISITORS: *Welcome everyday but pre-booking is advised*

Set on the coast, West Kilbride is a traditional, flat seaside links that catches all the best efforts of wind and weather. But this makes it all the more challenging. Old Tom Morris designed this layout and apart from some changes in the 1930s it is still pretty much as he had intended.

There is a variety of hazards to keep you thinking about your shots, such as a burn that comes into play on the 1st, 16th and marginally at the 18th. Depending on the strength and direction of the wind, other tricky holes are found at the 10th and 13th. Out-of-bounds dogs both these holes and can make for a demanding tee shot. West Kilbride plays host to events such as the Scottish Boys Championships and, in the right conditions, is a course that good golfers will not find easy.

Between the stonewall and the sea – the 316yd/288m par-4 14th green at West Kilbride.

14 Ardeer

Ardeer Golf Club, Greenhead, Stevenston, Ayrshire KA20 4JX
TEL: *01294 464542* **FAX:** *01294 465316*
LOCATION: *From Stevenston take the country road north off A78 for about ½ mile/0.75km*
COURSE: *18 holes, 6401yd/5850m, par 72, SSS 71*
GREEN FEES: *££*
FACILITIES: *Changing rooms and showers, full catering and bar, golf shop, short game practice, trolley hire*
VISITORS: *Welcome weekdays and Sunday although pre-booking is advised for Sunday*

A very well presented parkland course only a few miles from the main A78 Ayrshire coast route, Ardeer manages to remain secluded and peaceful. Though every hole is attractively arranged, there is an edge or danger to each that calls for caution. It is also more hilly than one might first expect as many of the holes play over rolling avenues.

The 9th and 11th greens have recently been improved and are both exceptional holes played across a burn. The 9th is easily reachable with the second shot but the challenge is all on the green. The 11th at Stroke Index 1 is best approached from a lay-up. The 18th is a tricky par 3 having a burn and out-of-bounds to add to the pain of a mis-hit. There are a lot of fine links courses in this part of the world but if you are looking for a pleasant day out, on a parkland course of character, Ardeer is well worth seeking out.

15 Irvine

Irvine Golf Club, Bogside, Irvine, Ayrshire KA12 8SN
TEL: *01294 275979* **FAX:** *01294 278209*
LOCATION: *On the A737 through Irvine to north side of Irvine, take right before High School*
COURSE: *18 holes, 6408yd/5857m, par 71, SSS 73*
GREEN FEES: *£££*
FACILITIES: *Changing rooms and showers, full catering and bar, shop, short game practice, trolley hire*
VISITORS: *Welcome weekdays and weekends although no play before 3pm Saturday and Sunday. Pre-booking is advised for Sunday*

Every hole on the Irvine course at Bogside is quite distinct. It is therefore the kind of layout where everyone has his or her personal preference. Typically links in its appearance, with narrow and undulating fairways, the ground rolls and bobs over ancient dunes, divided by gorse and heather upon a stretch of Scottish coastline that is ideal for the game of golf.

Built between the town, a racecourse and the muddy River Irvine, Irvine is also renowned for its velvet greens. Its most outstanding hole is undoubtedly the 6th, an eminent par 4 that soars over the crest of a hill before falling 40ft/12m on to the fairway and green. At 411yd/375m, it's not a monster but each stoke needs to be precisely and bravely struck.

If it is a calm day you can score well here but, perched as it is on a wide, open rise with wind seeking every corner, there is usually the important factor of the elements to be considered. One of the bonuses of golf particularly around Ayrshire is that most courses play all year round enjoying the benign waters of the Gulf Stream which help keep the greens frost-free.

The wide green with unwelcoming gorse on the 3rd hole at Irvine. This a par 4 just under 300yd/274m.

16 *Glasgow Gailes*

Glasgow Gailes Golf Club, Gailes, Irvine, Ayrshire KA11 5AE
TEL: *0141 942 2011* **FAX:** *0141 942 0770*
LOCATION: *On the A78, take the exit marked for Gailes 4 miles/6km north of Troon and south of Irvine. The clubhouse is visible on right. Out of Irvine, follow Harbour Side signs. The course is some 30 miles/50km from Glasgow*
COURSE: *18 holes, 6537yd/5975m, par 71, SSS 72*
GREEN FEES: *££££*
FACILITIES: *Changing rooms and showers, full catering and bar, pro shop and teaching pro, driving range, short game practice, trolley hire, buggy hire, club hire*
VISITORS: *Welcome weekdays and weekends after 2.30pm although pre-booking is advised*

With recent improvements to the clubhouse, Glasgow Gailes is now as attractive a proposition as any of the courses to be found on this marvellous stretch of links coast. Along the fairways the course is lined with clingy heather and springy gorse so there is good reason to stay out of the rough. But it is the luxurious rolling greens, giving subtle movements like a true links, that provide much of the action and adversity.

The 14th is a worthy par 5 of 526yd/481m, while the 15th is another testing hole, a par 3 onto a plateau green of considerable elevation with a big fall off to the left. All the greens on this course run moderately fast.

At the finish, the 18th is an excellent par 4 of 435yd/398m and plays into the prevailing wind. This slight dogleg right to left proves a difficult fairway to hit and can upset a reasonable round.

ALL IN A NAME

You may wonder why a golf club called Glasgow Gailes is over half an hour's drive from the city. The explanation is that in 1892 the original Glasgow Golf Club decided to open a second facility for its members on the Ayrshire coast to take advantage of the frost-free winter conditions. The exclusive Glasgow Golf Club also plays at Killermont in Bearsden in Glasgow, a course without provision for visitors.

🏐 *Western Gailes*

Western Gailes Golf Club, Gailes, Irvine, Ayrshire KA11 5AE
TEL: *01294 311649* FAX: *01294 312312*
LOCATION: *3 miles/5km north of Troon*
COURSE: *18 holes, 6639yd/6068m, par 71, SSS 73*
GREEN FEES: *££££*
FACILITIES: *Changing rooms and showers, full catering and bar, pro shop and teaching pro, driving range, short game practice, trolley hire, buggy hire, club hire*
VISITORS: *Welcome weekdays and weekends although pre-booking is advised. Contact in advance as this is very popular and a handicap certificate required*

The delights of Western Gailes might be in danger of being eclipsed by its very close proximity to Royal Troon and Prestwick Golf Club. However, fortunately, this is not the case. Indeed Western Gailes's reputation has grown largely by word of mouth as golfers, coming across it perhaps on a second or third trip to Ayrshire, wax lyrical about what they have discovered. Once smitten, many claim Western Gailes as their favourite course. Once you see its billowing links and the views across the wide stretches of the Clyde Estuary to the peaks of Arran. you may well agree.

The 13th at Western Gailes with the peaks of Arran in the hazy distance.

The first few holes head north, presenting heather, gorse and wispy, ensnaring rough for wayward fairway shots. The course then turns into frequent folds of high, sandy dunes interspersed with inventive, sensuous greens.

It is the 7th that sticks in most golfers' minds here. A tricky par 3, the hole plays parallel to the beach from an elevated tee into a dune-surrounded hollow with a deep, sleeper-lined bunker scaring most golfers to the right. While this might be less worrying, there are two bunkers on this side too, so the only sound approach is to land just short of the green and roll in. Three burns and a ditch cross the course at least seven times and feature more significantly from the 8th onwards, adding to the fascination of this magnificent natural layout.

The course, designed by Willie Park Sr and Jr, was remodelled only 20 or so years ago when a new road took away part of the original layout. The Club was founded in 1897, and in 1903 Harry Vardon took the prize in the first competition. Since then Western Gailes has hosted the Curtis Cup, PGA Championship, British Seniors, Scottish Championships and Ladies Home International.

🏐 *Kilmarnock (Barassie)*

Kilmarnock (Barassie) Golf Club, 29 Hillhouse Road, Barassie, Ayrshire KA10 6SY
TEL: *01292 311077* FAX: *01292 313920*
LOCATION *2 miles/3km north of Troon*
COURSE: *18 holes, 6484yd/5926m, par 72, SSS 73*
GREEN FEES: *£££*
FACILITIES: *Changing rooms and showers, full catering and bar, pro shop and teaching pro, driving range, short game practice, trolley hire, club hire*
VISITORS: *Visitors welcome Mondays, Tuesdays, Thursdays and Friday pm although pre-booking is advised*

With a recent addition of 9 holes to provide for its Open championship qualifying rounds, Kilmarnock Barassie now finds itself with a perfect product – 27 excellent, and highly agreeable links holes. Much to a touring golfer's delight, a round on the big course can be followed after lunch with a sample of the original 9 – or vice

A local Ayrshire coastal rail line from Glasgow divides Kilmarnock Barassie from its neighbour Western Gailes.

versa. Not that there was anything wrong with the original holes; in fact most of them are as graceful and challenging as any you would find along this golfing coast. But they were just a little short for championship play.

The new, 9-holes makes one 18-hole course of 6817yd/6230m from the medal tees, which is more than adequate for this area considering the frequent breezes. For visitors the layout is still quite demanding especially in a wind.

The 9-hole course measures 2756yd/2519m from the visitors' tees. The new section is quite links-like and has settled well. In 1997 when the Open was held at Royal Troon, the R&A made the course a qualifying venue. Making use of the available natural links terrain there is little evidence that the new holes have stood here for decades. Apart from more noticeable borrows, you would be hard pressed to tell the greens on the new 9 from the old.

The 4th on the new section is a 149yd/137m, par 3 with a burn running down the left from tee to green and a sleeper-lined

bunker facing. With the wind blowing almost from any direction this is a difficult target to reach successfully. The 8th is a long, true par 5 where it is not possible to cut any corners or even with a tail wind make the green in less than regulation.

19 Lochgreen

Lochgreen Course (Troon Municipal), Harling Drive, Troon, Ayrshire KA10 6NF
TEL: *01292 312464* **FAX:** *01292 312578*
LOCATION: *Adjacent to railway station, 1 mile/1.6km off the Ayr-Glasgow road*
COURSE: *18 holes, 6822yd/6235m, par 74, SSS 73*
GREEN FEES: *££*
FACILITIES: *Changing rooms and showers, full catering and bar, pro shop and teaching pro, practice area, trolley hire, club hire*
VISITORS: *Welcome weekdays and weekends although pre-booking is advised*

Lochgreen is the best and best-known of a trio of municipal courses on the east side of the popular holiday town of Troon. Each course offers an excellent golfing experience and at a fraction of the royal fee charged by their more aristocratic neighbours.

The longer course of the three, Lochgreen is a par 74 running parallel at points to Royal Troon and used for several years as a qualifier for the Open. The fairways are fairly forgiving and reasonably wide. The 6th is a par 3 of around 190yd/174m from an elevated tee and has a most eye-catching design.

Lochgreen's sibling, the Darley course at par 71, measures 6360yd/5813m but it can be quite a bit tougher than Lochgreen with tight fairways criss-crossed by burns and a lot more whins and heather. Recently it was rated the 4th hardest course in Scotland to play to your handicap. Finally, the Loop is a parkland section occurring at the most northerly point on the course where gorse bushes and rolling links gives way to rich grass and tall, mature trees.

Any of the three courses are great value for money and, considering the amount of traffic, each of them is a tribute to the greenkeeping staff. The clubhouse offers full catering facilities with upgraded changing rooms.

20 *Royal Troon*

Royal Troon Golf Club, Craigend Road, Troon, Ayrshire KA10 6EP

TEL: *01292 311555* **FAX:** *01292 318204*

LOCATION: *South side of town of Troon on coast*

COURSE: *18 holes, 7097yd/6487m, par 71, SSS 74*

GREEN FEES: *££££+ Single rounds are the same price as the Day ticket*

FACILITIES: *Changing rooms and showers, full catering and bar, pro shop and teaching pro, driving range, short game practice, trolley hire, club hire, caddy hire subject to availability*

VISITORS: *Welcome from the 1st Monday in May to the last Thursday in October – Monday, Tuesday and Thursday only between 9.30 to 11am and 2.30 to 4pm. Portland Course 9am 10.30am and 2.30 to 4pm. Please note: a letter of introduction from your club and a handicap certificate may be asked for. Visiting ladies cannot play the Old Course but can take up the option of a double round on the Portland*

ROYAL TROON
OLD COURSE

HOLE	YD	M	PAR	HOLE	YD	M	PAR
1	364	333	4	10	438	400	4
2	391	357	4	11	481	440	4
3	379	346	4	12	431	394	4
4	557	509	5	13	465	425	4
5	210	192	3	14	179	164	3
6	577	527	5	15	457	418	4
7	402	367	4	16	542	495	5
8	126	115	3	17	223	204	3
9	423	387	4	18	452	423	4
OUT	3429	3134	36	IN	3668	3353	35

7097 YD • 6487M • PAR 71

As with most clubs that have a Royal prefix, one might assume that Troon has held its honoured status for centuries but the title was not in fact bestowed until 1978, the club's centenary year. This makes Royal Troon the youngest Royal golf club in the world.

Designed by, amongst others, Willie Fernie, James Braid and Alister Mackenzie, Royal Troon is also a relative newcomer as an Open championship venue. The first Open was played here in 1923. So as you stand on the 1st tee, don't let the history or the scenery distract you. It will certainly be hard to ignore Troon's tranquil views over the Firth of Clyde to the mountains of Arran nearby and Ailsa Craig rising magnificently to the south.

Royal Troon, as many golfing legends have found, is an enigmatic course and not to be looked to for any sympathy. The first five holes are, as it happens, relatively straightforward, a typical links layout running at sea level with

high dunes offering little protection if there is a wind (and there usually is). The 6th, at 577yd/527m, is one of the longest par 5s on the Open rota. This was the hole that frustrated Bobby Clampett's efforts in 1982 when, after blazing opening rounds of 67 and 66, he took an 8 here and then watched his game go to pieces. Tom Watson steadily gained ground to take the championship.

The 8th, or Postage Stamp, is the shortest on the Open circuit and Troon's most famous

hole. For visitors it plays at around 120yd/110m. Nevertheless, from the tee, looking out to sea, it seems a long way to that little green. In a headwind, the Postage Stamp can call for a 3-iron. This is a death or glory hole, a birdie opportunity for those who hit and hold the narrow green, or a calamity for those who find themselves in one of the five deep, surrounding bunkers.

It is Royal Troon's middle holes that test a player's consistency and mental game. The 11th, perhaps not as publicised as the 8th, is a short par 5 of apparently mild temperament for members but one of the toughest par 4s in the world for pros – according to Arnold Palmer, 'the most dangerous hole I have ever seen'. By contrast, pros say the homeward stretch lacks the character that is presented in the middle six holes. However, for most players it remains very testing. The 13th, without bunkers, is difficult enough, as is the 15th with its elevated fairway partially causing a blind tee shot and a similarly impeding sight of the green. With the 18th, bunkers form the main hazard. Bear in mind, too, that out-of-bounds lies just behind the green – perhaps to provide protection for the clubhouse windows.

For the record, Troon has hosted seven Open championships won by Arthur Havers (1923), Bobby Locke (1950), Arnold Palmer (1962), Tom Weiskopf (1973), Tom Watson (1982), Mark Calcavecchia (1989) and Justin

The par 3 Postage Stamp 8th at Royal Troon (above). This is a do-or-die hole for the best in golf: Arnold Palmer scored a 7 here in 1973 while one German amateur, in competition, racked up a confounded 15. The 18th at Royal Troon (below). The course was designed with the combined expertise of Braid, Mackenzie and Fernie. Royal Troon only offers Day tickets for one round on the Old Course and one round on the Portland, which includes morning coffee and a buffet lunch.

Leonard (1997). The course record is 64, held by Greg Norman from the 1989 Open. Whatever you hope to go round in, Royal Troon will present a supreme round of golf in the classic links fashion, with danger lurking in the wind, rough and bunkers.

21 *Prestwick*

Prestwick Golf Club, Links Road, Prestwick, Ayrshire KA9 1QG
TEL: *01292 477404* **FAX:** *01292 477255*
LOCATION: *In town centre, just off A79. Prestwick Airport is 1 mile/1.6km north*
COURSE: *18 holes, 6544yd/5981m, par 71, SSS 73*
GREEN FEES: *££££*
FACILITIES: *Changing rooms and showers, full catering and bar, pro shop and teaching pro, trolley hire, caddie hire, club hire*
VISITORS: *Welcome weekdays except Thursday afternoon and pre-booking is essential*

The first Open championship to be held anywhere in the world took place here on 17 October 1860. The 12-hole course at Prestwick, laid out by Old Tom Morris in the 1850s played host to this great event and continued to do so for the following 12 years. The line-up of players following the fairways at Prestwick through these years and on into the 1920s reads like a 'Who's Who' of golf's early days: Willie Park, the two Tom Morris's, Willie Auchterlonie, Harry Vardon and James Braid to name but a few.

The championship was subsequently shared

The venerable 17th at Prestwick has remained unchanged since the 1850s with its blind second shot, its high ridge of dunes and the great Sahara bunker that waits just short of the green.

with Musselburgh and St Andrews on a rotating basis and Muirfield was included in 1892. Prestwick continued its reign as an Open venue until 1925 when, with the growing popularity of the event, it found itself unable to accommodate the ever-increasing galleries.

Although it no longer features on the Open rota, Prestwick is still a unique and challenging experience that keen golfers from around the world should long to play. Once renowned for its blind shots into deep dells, the present-day course is not quite so sporty, but it still reflects a bygone era as it dips and winds amongst the ancient sand dunes of the coast.

Of the most memorable holes, the 1st opens cheek-by-jowl with the main coastal railway. Prestwick Station is only a wire fence away to the right, and to be avoided at all costs. The 5th is noted for its massive and elongated Cardinal Bunker with subsequent danger in the nearby burn or the tall railway sleepers that loom above the bunkers. The railway sleepers are a distinctive feature of the Old Prestwick course. Should you tangle with any of these hazards it will be costly. The greatest hole on the course for many golfers though is the 17th with its massively intimidating 'Sahara' bunker.

22 *Prestwick St Nicholas*

Prestwick St Nicholas Golf Club Grangemuir Road, Prestwick Ayrshire, KA9 1SN
TEL: *01292 477608* **FAX:** *01292 473900*
LOCATION: *Towards beach from Prestwick town towards Ayr turn right into Grangemuir Road*
COURSE: *18 holes, 5952yd/5440m, par 69, SSS 69*
GREEN FEES: *£££*
FACILITIES: *Changing rooms and showers, full catering and bar, golf shop, trolley hire, club hire*
VISITORS: *Welcome weekdays and Sunday afternoon although pre-booking is advised*

Prestwick has two other courses – St Cuthbert and St Nicholas – and the latter is an excellent links course with magnificent views over the sea. Gorse bushes, which put on a dazzling yellow display in the early part of the year, are its main defence, especially for the opening and closing holes. The course is full of novel holes, some a little short but a fair challenge to most golfers. The 6th, 7th and 8th play round an old quarry while the undulating greens are usually in supreme condition and true.

23 *Belleisle*

Belleisle Golf Club, Belleisle Park, Doonfoot Road, Ayr KA7 4DU
TEL: *01292 441258* **FAX:** *01292 442632*
EMAIL: *golf@southayrshire.gov.uk*
LOCATION: *On main coast road just south of the town of Ayr in Belleisle Park*
COURSE: *18 holes, 6431yd/5878m, par 71, SSS 72*
GREEN FEES: *££*
FACILITIES: *Changing rooms, showers, full catering, bar, pro shop, teaching pro, practice area, trolley hire, club hire*
VISITORS: *Welcome everyday but pre-booking is advised*

This exceptional parkland course comes highly praised by European professionals playing at nearby Troon and Turnberry. It is set in harmonious woodlands, and has extra-long beech-lined fairways interlaced by a serpentine old burn.

The 6th tee offers views over the Firth of Clyde with Arran clearly visible. It is a downhill par 4, with two bunkers positioned at driving range. Other hazards include the well-bunkered green and woods on the right

Probably the best municipal golf course in Scotland, this is the imposing castle/hotel and 18th green at Belleisle.

hand side and snarling rough on both sides. The rough at Belleisle is particularly punishing and the James Braid 1927 designs stand up well. The 13th plays back up hill, another par 4 that has a noticeable dip that prohibits sight of the green for the approach shot. It also has a tight entrance to the green with an angled fairway bunker. This in most circumstances is a difficult green to catch. The 17th is one of five classic short holes with the 14th being the most difficult.

24 *Brunston Castle*

Brunston Castle Golf Club, Golf Course Road, Dailly, Girvan, Ayrshire KA26 9GD
TEL: *01465 811471* **FAX:** *01465 811545*
EMAIL: *golf@brunston.freeserve.co.uk*
WWW: *brunston.freeserve.co.uk*
LOCATION: *6 miles/10km south-east of Turnberry; A37 to Girvan then B741 to Dailly, well-signposted.*
COURSE: *18 holes, 6681yd/6106m, par 72, SSS 72*
GREEN FEES: *££*
FACILITIES: *Changing rooms and showers, full catering and bar, pro shop and teaching pro, driving range, short game practice, trolley hire, buggy hire, club hire*
VISITORS: *Welcome weekdays though pre-booking is advised. Members have priority from 8am to 10.30am and 12.30 to 1.30pm on Saturdays*

Opened in 1992, with an ongoing programme of improvement, this course is in superb condition. Sheltered in a valley surrounding the River Girvan, the opening holes play out and back along the river valley and are not taxing to the prudent player. The fairly wide river comes into play on the 7th, Stroke Index 1, where the narrow fairway runs parallel, pulling anything left off the tee into thick grass lining the banks or, worse still, into the river itself.

The back 9 runs over the valley side with the 12th, 13th, and 14th skirting its slopes. Back on level ground, the par-3 17th is a scary gamble for intermediate players who will find an intimidating 184yd/168m carry over a duck pond. The pond horseshoes front, left and right of a green that slopes towards the water. A confident stroke is required to the heart of the green to avoid making a splash. The closing hole climbs 20-30ft/6-9m back up towards the clubhouse.

25 *Turnberry (Ailsa Course)*

Turnberry Hotel and Golf Courses Turnberry Hotel
Turnberry, Ayrshire KA26 9LT
TEL: *01655 331000* **FAX:** *01655 331706*
EMAIL: *turnberry@westin.com*
WWW: *www.turnberry.co.uk*
LOCATION: *On A719, Ayr to Girvan route on north side of the village of Turnberry and very well signposted*
COURSE: *18 holes, 6976yd/6377m, par 69, SSS 72*
GREEN FEES: *£££££+*
FACILITIES: *Changing rooms and showers, full catering and bar, pro shop and teaching pro, golf academy, driving range, short game practice, caddie bookable in advance, club hire*
VISITORS: *To stay and play at either of the Turnberry courses, guests need to be resident at the hotel*

TURNBERRY
AILSA COURSE

HOLE	YD	M	PAR	HOLE	YD	M	PAR
1	350	320	4	10	452	413	4
2	430	393	4	11	174	159	3
3	462	422	4	12	446	408	4
4	165	151	3	13	412	377	4
5	442	404	4	14	449	410	4
6	231	211	3	15	209	191	3
7	529	484	5	16	409	374	4
8	431	394	4	17	497	454	5
9	454	415	4	18	434	397	4
OUT	3494	3194	35	IN	3482	3183	35

6976 YD •6377M • PAR 70

Looking over the wide reaches of the Firth of Clyde to the Isle of Arran and the great pudding-shaped volcanic plug of Ailsa Craig, the sumptuous Turnberry Hotel, Golf Courses and Spa could not be better positioned. The best view point must be from any one of the seaward facing rooms and from here you best appreciate the wide links that accommodates both the Ailsa and Arran courses. The hotel itself has gained some of the world's most prestigious awards.

The Ailsa course was laid out at the end of the 19th century by the Marquis of Ailsa, a captain at the Prestwick Club who, tired of travelling up the coast for his golf, decided to build a private course on his Culzean Estate. McKenzie Ross had a later hand in it and the development quickly grew in popularity.

Turnberry is the most recent course to enter the Open circuit and the event came here in 1977. It was then that the Open saw perhaps one of its most dramatic contests, the head-to-head 'Duel in the Sun' between two of the game's greatest figures, Jack Nicklaus and Tom Watson.

The Ailsa course is a jewel in the crown of Scottish links set out on land between the sweeping dunes and the solid rise of the Ayrshire hills. It opens with a soft par 4 that has been criticised in the past as being a little too easy for tournament standards, but the same can be said of St Andrews and Royal Troon. Here the course rather eases players into their game on the relatively straightforward first four holes. By the 6th the challenge is well under way with a deceptively lengthy par 3 of over 200yd/183m that can be particularly difficult in a headwind. The 9th, Bruce's Castle, with the famous Turnberry Lighthouse to its left, has one of the most photographed championship tees in the game, perched as it

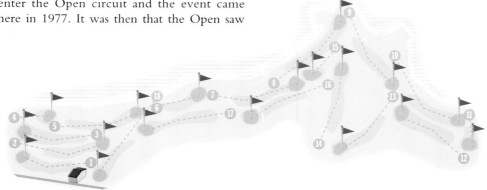

is on a chunk of igneous rock that protrudes into Turnberry Bay.

The homeward holes do not become a mental challenge until the 12th where the course turns away from the water and back towards the hotel glinting in the distance. The wind from the south-west cuts across these inward holes so there is little respite here.

The Ailsa course is as good a course as nature and architect can create (five holes redesigned by Donald Steel). There is another course available to hotel guests: the Arran, a par-72, 6457yd/5902m layout that would be even more highly regarded if it were not set next to an Open championship venue.

Goat Fell, the 8th green. During World War II the course became an airfield for bombers. Runway patterns to the east of the course can still be discerned.

Turnberry Lighthouse is visible on a headland cutting into the Firth of Forth. Far in the haze lies Ailsa Crag.

REGIONAL DIRECTORY
Where to Stay
Glasgow **Nairns** (0141 353 0707) in Woodside Crescent in Glasgow is a lovely Georgian townhouse with a five-star restaurant run by TV celebrity chef Nick Nairn and his brother Topher. The **Arthouse Hotel** in Bath Street (0141 221 6789) is a sumptuous new hotel situated in the heart of the city centre; it has contemporary styled bedrooms and a restaurant that is growing in both popularity and acclaim. On Greenhead Street, **The Inn on the Green** (0141 554 0165) has 18 rooms offering a traditional and modern touch that is distinctly Scottish. **Park House** in Victoria Park Gardens South (0141 339 1559) is a four-star B&B situated in the West End of the city, in a luxurious Victorian townhouse that is warm and friendly as well as convenient. The **Ewington Hotel** (0141 423 1152) overlooking Queens Park is secluded yet near the city centre for leisure and shopping and can offer good rates if they are not full of business people.

Outside the city of Glasgow, the **Bowfield Hotel & Country Club** (01505 705225) is a comfortable place situated in the picturesque Renfrewshire village of Howwood with easy access to both Glasgow and surrounding areas. **Makerston House** in Park Road, Paisley (0141 884 2520) is a three-star guest house situated in the suburbs with good links to surrounding courses. **Toftcombs Country House Hotel & Restaurant** (01899 220142) is in Biggar and is a four-star country house hotel offering quiet, quality accommodation and a good restaurant. **Skirling House** also near Biggar (01899 860274) is a five-star B&B in a house that is visually and architecturally stunning. **Gleddoch House** (01475 540711) overlooks the River Clyde Estuary and has its own excellent golf course near Langbank, which is around ten minutes west of Glasgow airport.

Ayrshire and Arran **Turnberry Hotel Golf Courses & Spa** (01655 331000) is no doubt the premier residence to stay and play golf in Ayrshire. The service is impeccable and the spa most relaxing. In Troon the popular **Marine Highland** (01292 314444) is less formal with fine views of the 1st and 18th on Royal Troon and it also has a swimming pool and leisure facilities. Also in Troon is the **Piersland Hotel** (01292 314747). Less expensive and most friendly is the **Kincraig Hotel** in Prestwick (01292 479480), which is ideally placed for Ayrshire's many coastal links. The **Montgreenan Mansion House Hotel** near Kilwinning (01294 557733) is an impressive residence dating back to 1817 and enjoys a tranquil atmosphere set back from the coast. Further south again in Alloway, with its strong connections to Robert Burns, is the **Brigadoon Hotel** (01292 442466). Another good bet overlooking Turnberry's rolling links is the **Malin Court** (01655 331457).

Isle of Arran The **Kinloch Hotel** in Blackwaterfoot (01770 860444) is the largest hotel in Arran and ideal for playing the nearby Shiskine course. **Auchrannie Country House Hotel** in Brodick (01770 302234) is the four-star flagship hotel on Arran with a bistro and leisure club while the **Glanartney Hotel**, also in Brodick (01770 302220) is two star yet very comfortable for its lower rates.

Where to Eat
Glasgow Glasgow is full of unusual, quirky and exciting eateries. In fact the city has often set the trends that others follow. An old favourite now is the **Ubiquitous Chip** (0141 334 5007) and even older is **Roganos** (0141 248 4055) in the city centre. 1 Devonshire Gardens (0141 339 2001) is very smart and best for formal evening meals while **Yes** (0141 221 8044), also in the centre is rather stylish. **Gamba** in West George Street. (0141 572 0899) is a new seafood restaurant gathering much praise since opening its doors while **Air Organic** in Kelvingrove Street (0141 564 5200), is a superb retro style restaurant, concentrating on contemporary food prepared with organic produce. **Groucho Saint Judes** in Bath Street (0141 352 8800) is the sister restaurant to the London establishment of the same name, offering a bold and contemporary menu with British and international influences. **Nairns** in Woodside Crescent (*see above*) is unique and a huge success in Glasgow offering an innovative and exciting menu using the finest of Scottish produce. **The Doocot** in Mitchell Lane (0141 221 1821) is situated within **The Lighthouse**, Scotland's Centre for Architecture, Design & the City.

Outside Glasgow the **Restaurant Bouzy Rouge** in Airdrie (01236 763853) is a very cosy, stylish bistro offering a gourmet menu at extremely affordable prices. **Gavin's Mill** in Milngavie (0141 956 2255) is housed in a converted millhouse. The menu features Scottish cooking with a European twist. Families are welcome, and food is also served in the mill courtyard. The **New Lanark Mill Hotel** (01555 667200) is very reasonably priced while **Gleddoch House Hotel & Country Estate** in Langbank (01475 540711) offers a variety of outdoor pursuits including golf to whet the appetite.

Ayrshire and Arran In the north of Ayrshire near Largs, **Fins Seafood Restaurant** (01475 568989) in Fairlie, is a renovated farm bistro giving traditional treatment to fresh fish of all kinds. **Scoretulloch House Hotel** (01560 323331) in Darvel, converted from a 15th century farm with superb views of Loudoun Valley, has a five star restaurant offering home cooked traditional Scottish cuisine. **The Carrick Restaurant** at the Malin Court Hotel (01655 331457) serving traditional Scottish cuisine overlooks Turnberry's two famous courses along with great sunset views over the Clyde Estuary. Near Kilwinning, **Montgreenan Mansion House** (01294 557733), is a rather splendid piece of period architecture with impeccable food and wine. **Piersland House Hotel** (01292 314747) in Troon was built for the grandson of Johnnie Walker of whisky fame. The a la carte menu is exceptional. The **Turnberry Hotel** (01655 331000), offers classical cooking in its main restaurant and the spa's **'Bay' Restaurant** has a far leaner menu for the health conscious.

Arran There is a wide range of eating places from the relaxed atmosphere of the **Brodick Bar** (01770 302169) and family appeal of **Brambles Bistro** at Auchrannie Country House Hotel (01770 302234) to the more formal setting of **Creelers Seafood Restaurant** in Brodick (01770 302810) and the **Burlington Hotel & Restaurant** in Whiting Bay (01770 700255).

What to Do

Glasgow is the most friendly of Scotland's cities with a huge variety of pubs, wine bars and other convivial places to meet the locals. There is often live entertainment and many of the pubs serve good meals. There is also a flourishing Ceilidh scene when Scotland's vigorous native music can be enjoyed both on and off the dance floor – check the local newspapers for venues or telephone the tourist office.

Glasgow's museums and art galleries are exceptional and usually free. For one of the world's finest collection of fine and decorative arts head to the **Burrell Collection**, displayed in a specially designed building in Pollok Country Park. Charles Rennie Mackintosh is one of the city's many famous sons and his distinctive architecture can be appreciated at **Glasgow School of Art**, the **Willow Tea Room**, **Scotland Street School** and the **Mackintosh House** in the **Hunterian Art Gallery. The Gallery of Modern Art** is Glasgow's newest art gallery reflecting the four natural elements of earth, fire, air and water.

The **Museum of Transport** offers a fascinating display that includes Glasgow trams and buses, locomotives, horse-drawn vehicles, Scottish-built cars and shipbuilding on the Clyde. Outside Glasgow the **New Lanark Visitor Centre** is an industrial village founded in 1785, scene of early experiments in paternalistic care for workers.

Ayrshire and Arran In the north of Ayrshire, **Kelburn Country Park** is near Largs. The **Scottish Maritime Museum** at Harbourside, in Irvine is well worth a visit. But, above all, Ayrshire is Robbie Burns country and there is a **Burns Heritage Trail** to find out about Scotland's national poet. From Irvine to Alloway there are important sites where the poet lived, loved or laboured. The **Burns Cottage and Museum** in Alloway is a must as is the **Tam O' Shanter Experience** nearby. But it is Alloway Kirk and the **Brig o' Doon** that evokes some of Burns most eloquent verse.

Isle of Arran The isle is all the incentive you need to make the short ferry crossing. It is truly a tranquil place and most visitors wish to spend a few days there. **Brodick Castle Gardens and Country Park** is 1.5 miles (2km) north of Brodick. On the west of the island looking over to Kintyre is **King's Cave**, north of Blackwaterfoot where Robert the Bruce tussled with his conscience before going on to fight for Scottish Independence. Nearby is the **Machrie Moor Standing Stones**. **Lochranza Castle** is a stark tower on the north coast of the island. The local golf course is renowned for its herd of wild red stags who enjoy the luscious grass and don't mind the golfers.

Culzean Castle and Country Park is probably one of the most popular of Ayrshire's stately piles. In south Ayrshire, the pudding bowl shape of **Ailsa Craig Island** dominates the horizon and it appears on so many golf photos but few golfers realise they can sail out and get a closer look. The 4-hour trip on the *Glorious* (01465 713219) takes in every kind of local seafaring bird as well as the occasional basking shark.

Tourist Information Offices

Glasgow Tourist Information Centre
11 George Square,Glasgow, G2 1DY
Tel: 0141 204 4400 Fax: 0141 221 3524
Email: enquiries@seeglasgow.com
www.seeglasgow.com

Greater Glasgow & Clyde Valley Tourist Board, 35 St Vincent Place, Glasgow, G1 2ER
Tel : +44 (0141) 204 4400
Email : TourismGlasgow@ggcvtb.org.uk

Ayrshire & Arran Tourist Board, Burns House, Burns Statue Square, Ayr, KA7 1UP
Tel: 01292 262555, Fax: 01292 269555
E-mail: ayr@ayrshire-arran.com

Chapter 8

Dumfries and Galloway

In the southwest of Scotland, the region of Dumfries and Galloway stretches some 100 miles/160 kilometres from east to west. The A75 is the main route through the region stringing together the charming counties of Dumfriesshire, Kirkcudbrightshire and Wigtownshire. However, most holiday golfers overlook this tranquil countryside as they head for the better-known golfing areas. But this inconspicuous south-western corner contains some glorious golf, and fewer visitors to cause crushes on the courses.

At its eastern gateway, Gretna Green has long been famous as a sanctuary for eloping young lovers eager to get legally married across the border. It is still a charming little community with a romantic air and worth breaking your journey to appreciate. The village has a 9-hole course, surprisingly long and also a 12-bay

driving range to warm up on. Nearby Powfoot Golf Club most certainly should be included in any itinerary. It has an illustrious record having held the British Seniors Open Championship as well as the Scottish Girls Championship.

Robert Burns

Dumfries, the regional capital, is a town steeped in the lore of Scotland's famous bard, Robert Burns. He resided here during his years as an excise man and also died here in 1796. The Burns Heritage Trail is a motorist's route much in evidence in this region, and well worth following. Dumfries has two well-established 18-hole courses, Dumfries and County and Dumfries and Galloway. The County is an excellent parkland course with superb greens. Meanwhile a new facility can be seen from the A75 ring-road to the north of the town. This is Pines Golf Centre, recently opened as a full 18-hole course with 20 driving bays. Moffat, Lockerbie and Lochmaben also offer engaging golf within easy driving

Left: The red sandstone ruins of Sweetheart Abbey, once home to Cistercian monks. The remains date back to the 13th century. The 14th-century Threave Castle (above) is on an island, approached only by boat.

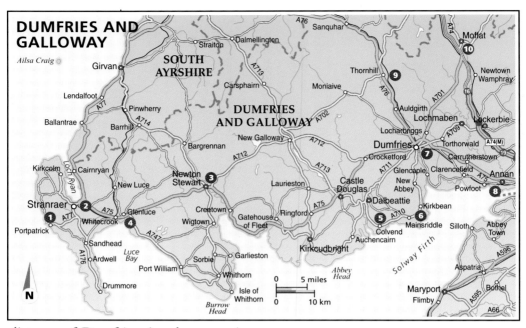

distance of Dumfries. Another gem, just 14 miles/ 23 km north of Dumfries on the A76, is Thornhill Golf Club. Set amongst the hills of Nithsdale it is an easy-walking course, and its subtle nuances make it a course golfers come back to many times.

Solway Firth

South of Dumfries is the famous Solway Firth links of Southerness. This is an internationally recognised course designed by McKenzie Ross as recently as 1947 to test the best golfers. Windy conditions add considerably to an already demanding layout. Nearby is an easier proposition that will please all levels of golfers. Colvend Golf Club has dazzling views over the expansive Mersehead Sands and Solway Firth across to the hills of the English Lake District.

Kirkcudbright and Gatehouse of Fleet both have holiday courses although Kirkcudbright is quite hilly but again, offers some stunning views. Nearby, Brighouse Bay on the Solway Firth is an interesting 6600yd/6032m par 74 course.

Dumfries and Galloway extends down to Stranraer – gateway to Ireland.

The layout of this new endeavour has all the marks of a championship venue along with an absolutely stunning setting. Ross Island and the Isle of Man are visible in the distance. One of the most attractive new courses in this area is found at Gatehouse of Fleet on the grounds of the Cally Palace Hotel. Open only to residents or those staying at one of its sister properties, the Cally Palace course is highly recommended. In the lowlands below the Galloway Hills are a surprisingly high number of quality golf clubs. Newton Stewart is one of them. Although a holiday course, it can prove quite testing with a great degree of accuracy required on almost every hole.

If you plan to stay for a few days, it is best to select two or three different bases to give yourself a relaxed way to cover neighbouring courses without long drives in between. For accommodation you can choose between charming B&Bs and luxury 4 star castles.

Wigtownshire

The ideal venue for a relaxed and unconstrained round can be found at Wigtownshire County Golf Club in Glenluce. The course stretches down to the beach with attractive wide fairways and impeccable putting surfaces. There are five good courses in this part of the county. Stranraer is the most famous and has a new clubhouse looking out over the course and Loch Ryan. To the south-west of Stranraer, Lagganmore is a new development recently extended to 18 holes. Portpatrick (Dunskey) is the other well-known course in the area, an easier test than Stranraer but, if the wind blows over those headland fairways, as it so often does, it can be very trying. To the north of this area following the A77 lie the championship links of Turnberry and Royal Troon in Ayrshire.

Gateway to Golf Pass Scheme

There are 23 courses which participate in this discount scheme. The passes offer great value for money with 3-day and 5-day passes available. They may be purchased from any Tourist Information Centres in the area, or in advance from Dumfries Tourist Information Centre – *see page 173.*

The stalwart Caerlaverock Castle dates back to the 13th Century. The imposing gatehouse fronts a triangular layout. A few minute's drive away is Caerlaverock Wildlife and Wetlands Centre for superb walking and birdwatching in well-placed hides.

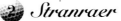

Portpatrick (Dunskey)

Portpatrick (Dunskey) Golf Club, Golf Course Road, Portpatrick, Dumfries and Galloway DG9 8TB
TEL: *01776 810273* **FAX:** *01776 810811*
LOCATION: *From Stranraer on A77 follow signs to Portpatrick or from the east follow A715, A757 then A77; on entering village fork right at Celtic Cross*
COURSE: *18 holes, 5908yd/5400m, Par 70, SSS 69*
GREEN FEES: *££*
FACILITIES: *Changing rooms, showers, full catering and bar, shop, practice area, trolley hire, buggy hire, club hire*
VISITORS: *Welcome weekdays and weekends although pre-booking is advised. Handicap certificates are required*

Above the picturesque seaside village of Portpatrick, the Dunskey course sits on an imposing headland with steep cliffs marking its western perimeter. The village and course's position on the long, rocky annex known as the Rhinns of Galloway ensures the warm benefits that the Gulf Stream brings to this area: Dunksey is playable all year round.

Set high on the cliffs, the undulating links-type course has been extended and sand bunkers introduced to give the course its fair share of tricky par 3s. The 7th is a good example. Measuring 165yd/151m it has a ledge to the left that may gather some errant shots, but it is ultimately safer to stray right. The 11th is another par 3 of 163yd/149m into a concave, gathering green whose subtle slopes make putting difficult.

The 13th offers the best sights on the course. The view of the green sitting above Sandeel Bay overlooking the North Channel to Ireland can take the breath away, as will the hike up to the 14th. Little wonder then that this friendly club has earned one golf magazine's accolade 'best holiday course in the south of Scotland.'

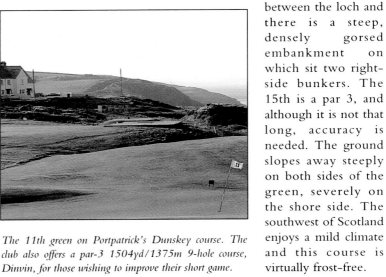

The 11th green on Portpatrick's Dunskey course. The club also offers a par-3 1504yd/1375m 9-hole course, Dinvin, for those wishing to improve their short game.

Stranraer

Stranraer Golf Club, Creachmore, Leswalt, Stranraer DG9 0LF
TEL: *01776 870245* **FAX:** *01776 870445*
LOCATION: *3 miles/5km from Stranraer on the Kirkcolm Road, the A718*
COURSE: *18 holes, 6308yd/5766m, par 70, SSS 72*
GREEN FEES: *££*
FACILITIES: *Changing rooms and showers, full catering and bar, shop, short game, practice area, trolley hire, club hire*
VISITORS: *Welcome everyday although pre-booking is advised*

With its near proximity to a sea loch you might expect links conditions at Stranraer, but it is all parkland despite two holes by the beach. Otherwise the course is laid out on rolling farmland with stands of mature trees. Set on the banks of Loch Ryan, the main route from Scotland to Northern Ireland, Stranraer is a demanding layout with the extra distinction of being the last course designed by James Braid, though he did not live to see the finished result. From the new two-storey clubhouse and the course you can survey Loch Ryan and Ailsa Craig to the north and the island of Arran beyond.

The 5th is the course's signature hole playing from an elevated tee down to the loch side. From this airy prospect, the full force of a westerly wind could play havoc with your shot. Below, the fairway is tight between the loch and there is a steep, densely gorsed embankment on which sit two right-side bunkers. The 15th is a par 3, and although it is not that long, accuracy is needed. The ground slopes away steeply on both sides of the green, severely on the shore side. The southwest of Scotland enjoys a mild climate and this course is virtually frost-free.

Newton Stewart

Newton Stewart Golf Club, Kirroughtree Avenue,
Minnigaff Newton Stewart DG8 6PF
TEL: 01671 402172 **FAX:** 01671 402172
LOCATION: *From south leave A75 at sign to Minnigaff village and follow edge of housing estate until clubhouse appears*
COURSE: *18 holes, 5903yd/5395m, par 69, SSS 70*
GREEN FEES: ££
FACILITIES: *Changing rooms and showers, full catering and bar, practice area, trolley hire, buggy hire, club hire*
VISITORS: *Welcome everyday but pre-booking is advised*

Set amongst the foothills of the Galloway Hills, Newton Stewart is a great little parkland course that, despite its appearance, is not really hilly. Apart from the hike from the 2nd green to the 3rd tee there is only a further modest elevation up to the 10th tee. The gradual rises do sometimes obscure an otherwise clear sight of the green.

Some scenic touches augment this diverse layout especially where the members have planted shrubs and flowers around the tee boxes. The course is set up for golfers to enjoy themselves and not get hung up in devastating rough – although there are patches of gorse that will catch really wild shots.

The 9th is a par-4 dogleg playing over a

DUMFRIES DETOUR

The 'Queen of the South' as this bustling town is called, makes a good base from which to explore Robbie Burns country. It lies next to the River Nith and was once an important medieval seaport. On the high street is Burns' House (open Easter to September) where Scotland's national poet died from heart complications in 1796. He came here in 1791 and wrote much of his work. Several taverns, called 'howffs', including his favourite haunt the Globe Inn, are also linked to the bard.

---

dyke to a pond. It also has a stream running diagonally across the fairway. The green is off-set and there is the option of playing over the dyke to attack the green straight on or a less hazardous route to the right. The par-3 10th, called the Gushet, also crosses the stream and is one of the original holes of this once 9-hole layout. If you don't hit the green here you will probably lose a shot. The 11th and 12th go downhill with the last six holes also providing easy walking.

A stream and paths zig zag across Newton Stewart's charming but still testing inland course.

Wigtownshire County

Wigtownshire County Golf Club, Mains of Park,
Glenluce, Newton Stewart, Wigtownshire DG8 0NN
TEL: *01581 300420*
LOCATION: *Just off the A75, 2 miles / 3km west of
Glenluce and 8miles / 13km east Stranraer*
COURSE: *18 holes, 5843yd / 5340m, par 70, SSS 68*
GREEN FEES: *££*
FACILITIES: *Changing rooms and showers, full catering and
bar, shop, practice area, trolley hire, club hire*
VISITORS: *Welcome everyday but pre-booking is advised*

Two rounds in a day at Wigtownshire would not be taxing and the invigorating coastal air makes this a relaxed and recommended golf course. The flat links course stretches down to the wide sands of Luce Bay with wide welcoming fairways. In summer the beach holes are especially eyecatching when wild flowers bloom in the machair. The course turns away from the beach after the 11th and comes back through pines trees. The 12th, a dogleg par 4, is the most demanding especially if your second shots plays into the wind. If the tide is fairly high, watch out for water, but generally this area is dry (though out-of-bounds). The 18th is a tough par 4 into the prevailing wind. A tree-lined fairway and out-of-bounds to the left also make driving very difficult.

Colvend

Colvend Golf Club, Sandyhills, Colvend, by Dalbeattie,
Kirkcudbrightshire DG5 4PY
TEL: *01556 630398* **FAX:** *01556 630495*
LOCATION: *6 miles / 10km from Dalbeattie on the A710,
Solway Coast road, between Dalbeattie and Dumfries*
COURSE: *18 holes, 5220yd / 4771m, par 68, SSS 67*
GREEN FEES: *££ per day*
FACILITIES: *Changing rooms and showers, full catering and
bar, shop, trolley hire*
VISITORS: *Welcome everyday*

What it lacks in length, Colvend makes up in cunning. Recently this 9-hole course was upgraded to 18. The 1st takes you up a steep hill of the old course but once on the upper level, there are superb views over the Mersehead Sands and Solway Firth. On a clear day the 3rd tee offers vistas over to the Lake District and the Isle of Man.

The new 9 holes are found crossing over the A710. Here there are some gentle slopes with one more difficult climb at the 12th. The 13th offers a squeeze between two ponds while a long meadow has been cut on the 14th making a long woodland-surrounded hole that also plays across a burn.

Breath-taking views of wide stretches of Solway sand and the Galloway Hills await the holiday golfer coming to Colvend Golf Club.

Southerness

Southerness Golf Club, Southerness, Kirkbean, Dumfries and Galloway DG2 8AZ
TEL: *01387 880677* **FAX:** *01387 880644*
WWW: *southernessgolfclub.com*
LOCATION: *On A710, 16 miles/26km south west of Dumfries and signposted one mile off main road.*
COURSE: *18 holes, 6566yd/6001m, par 69, SSS 73*
GREEN FEES: *£££ per day*
FACILITIES: *Changing rooms and showers, full catering and bar, shop, short game practice area, trolley hire*
VISITORS: *Welcome weekdays between 10am and 12pm and 2pm to 4.30pm; and at weekends from 10 to 11.30am and 2.30 to 4.30pm. Pre-booking is advised and a handicap certificate required*

There is little doubt that Southerness is the most challenging championship links on the Solway Firth and indeed one of the most difficult courses in Scotland. McKenzie Ross designed the course in 1947 with heather and bracken much in evidence. But it is the wind that can make this course intensely difficult so if it is gusty (and it often is) be prepared for difficulties.

The course is set on a low-lying curve of links land fringing the Mersehead Sands and Solway Firth. Although the course was designed nearly half a century ago, Southerness is still capable of testing the most skilled of players. With at least eight par 4s over 400yd/365m and the coalition of wind,

Southerness is championship links territory where heather and bracken abound. Golf skills are definitely demanded so holiday golfers looking for a more relaxed round may find playing here frustrating. Panoramic views of the Galloway Hills do not lessen the pain of a poor round.

heather, and marsh most players are happy just to keep in play and accept a score they would generally consider high.

Many consider the par-4 12th the course's best hole. It is a right-hand dogleg fringed by thick heather, marsh and grass that runs towards the sea and into the wind. Any temptation to cut the corner must be carefully considered. A detour off the fairway here will be punished in the rough.

Ross's favourite hole was, curiously enough, a par 3: the 7th is 215yd/196m and seldom is there anything other than a driver required here. The green appears to be on a small shelf and is not fully sited. The hole plays towards the sea and generally into the wind in the same direction as the 12th. With well-placed bunkers defending the green, this hole comes very high on the difficulty list.

So Southerness can be a most challenging course to play on most days and is therefore only really suitable for experienced or skilled golfers. Those with a high handicap would be advised not to take it on as they will find it discouraging as well as moderately pricey.

🏌 7 *Dumfries and County*

Dumfries and County Golf Club, Nunfield, Edinburgh Road, Dumfries and Galloway DG1 1JX
TEL: *01387 253585* **FAX:** *01387 253585*
LOCATION: *In Dumfries, 1 mile/1.6km north-east off A701*
COURSE: *18 holes, 5928yd/5418m, par 69, SSS 68*
GREEN FEES: *££*
FACILITIES: *Changing rooms and showers, full catering and bar, pro shop and teaching pro, practice ground, trolley hire, club hire*
VISITORS: *Welcome weekdays and Sundays although pre-booking is advised*

Running in part through an old estate full of established mature trees, Dumfries and County Golf Club offers some fine parkland golf. By contrast, a section of the front 9 was laid out on reclaimed, rolling farmland where the trees are less mature but allow views up towards the Lowther Hills. Generally play is controlled by the trees rather than thick rough, so misdirected balls are not lost so easily.

The 5th sticks in most visitors' minds with the River Nith on its right. It is a 374yd/342m par 4 to an elevated green which drops off to the left and rear. The river also comes into play at the par-5 7th. The 14th, Wee Yin, is a mere 90yd/82m – a par 3 surrounded by no less than five bunkers that will certainly trap the wayward shots.

🏌 8 *Powfoot*

Powfoot Golf Club, Cummertrees, Annan, Dumfries and Galloway DG12 5QE
TEL: *01461 700276* **FAX:** *01461 700276*
LOCATION: *From the A75, Annan-Dumfries Road enter Annan then to village of Cummertrees on the B724. Ignore first sign to Powfoot and turn left at the second sign*
COURSE: *18 holes, 6266yd/5727m, par 71, SSS 71*
GREEN FEES: *££*
FACILITIES: *Changing rooms and showers, full catering and bar, pro shop and teaching pro, practice area, short game practice, trolley hire, club hire*
VISITORS: *Welcome weekdays and Sundays after 2pm. Pre-booking is advised*

A superior links in Scotland's southwest, Powfoot is distinguished as a championship course that plays through a sea of gorse. While its position on the north shore of the Solway Firth would indicate a links course, it is not entirely so: 14 holes are true links but the back four holes are more parkland in nature. The gorse bushes that line many of the fairways and encircle the greens are prominent, and in spring and early summer the bright yellow colour is quite dazzling and the pungent smell intoxicating.

The 2nd is a 477yd/436m par 5, which faces south and overlooks the water. After the

The 11th tee at Powfoot offers a blind tee shot with gorse ahead and on either side of the fairway.

tee shot, the fairway tapers but, unless the wind is coming from the west, a steady stroke is needed to pass through the narrow entrance to the green. The 3rd plays along the shore in a west-to-east direction as does the 4th. However it is the 5th that is most outstanding a 265yd/242m par 3, one of the longest in Scotland and, yes, it does play into the prevailing wind. Most golfers stand and stare in disbelief here.

The back 9 can play a fair bit tougher than the front with the 10th turning straight back into the prevailing wind. While it is a fairly open hole the rough – mainly heather and grass – is thick and clinging. Play long and straight is the solution to this hole.

The 11th generally only calls for a driver and a 7-iron, but as the tee shot is blind most take a 1-iron or 3-wood for the best line left of centre. This will land you on a flatter area that offers a better line into the green. Meanwhile an enormous bank in front of the green can kill the second shot and drop the ball back into a bunker at the left-hand side.

The 15th is a tough par 3 with its green sloping left and can call for a 3-iron or drive into prevailing wind. The 16th is 429yd/392m into wind with a steep slope at about 250yd/228m, which you must clear although this is very difficult. The green is on a plateau and falls away on every side.

Set above the Nith Valley, Thornhill mixes parkland and heathland. Andrew Coltart is a member of this club.

Keir and Lowther Hills. Unusually it opens with a par 3 then plays over a flat expanse before dipping down at the 4th into a slight valley with the main Dumfries railway running past to the right. This is a good challenge requiring a sound drive to clear a ditch and reach the correct side of the dogleg then a long second shot into a raised, two-tiered green. The signature hole is the par-5 15th dogleg framed by a small loch.

Thornhill

Thornhill Golf Club, Blacknest, Thornhill, Dumfries and Galloway DG3 5DW
TEL: *01848 330546*
LOCATION: *On A76, 14 miles/22km north west of Dumfries*
COURSE: *18 holes, 6085yd/5562m, par 71, SSS 70*
GREEN FEES: *££*
FACILITIES: *Changing rooms and showers, full catering and bar, pro shop and teaching pro, practice ground, trolley hire, buggy hire, club hire*
VISITORS: *Welcome anytime though pre-booking is advised. Telephone for advance tee times, restricted competition days*

A real gem, Thornhill's Blacknest course should be on everyone's list, if not for the views then for the quality of the putting surfaces. It is the kind of course to play on a summer's evening with a hazy light over the

Moffat

Moffat Golf Club, Coatshill, Moffat, Dumfries and Galloway DG10 9SB
TEL: *01683 220020*
LOCATION: *Leave A74 at Beattock. Take A701 towards town of Moffat and signposted 1mile/1.6km on left*
COURSE: *18 holes, 5263yd/4810m, par 67, SSS 67*
GREEN FEES: *££*
FACILITIES: *Changing rooms and showers, full catering and bar, shop, trolley hire, club hire*
VISITORS: *Welcome weekdays except Wednesday afternoon and weekends although pre-booking is advised*

A well-established and popular moorland course, Moffat overlooks the town with stunning panoramic views over to Saddle Yoke and White Yoke, part of the Moffat Hills. For those more used to flat terrain, Moffat is something different and quite sporty, especially at the 5th and 9th. A few blind spots also add to the course's flavour.

The 9th is tough, playing blind, uphill and has bare rock sticking out of the turf near the green – beckoning unpredictable deflections. Rough, chiefly heather, abounds on several holes, such as at the 11th.

REGIONAL DIRECTORY
Where to Stay

Dumfries and Galloway is a wide area and in order to explore it thoroughly you may find it better to divide it with two or three nights in two or three different establishments. In the east of the region the **Auchen Castle Hotel** (01683 300407) in Beattock by Moffat is an imposing mansion set in many acres of garden with a 'Taste of Scotland' recognition for its restaurant. Further west, the **Blackaddie House Hotel** (01659 50270) in Sanquhar is a 16th-century traditional stone farmhouse whose kitchen specialises in locally grown organic produce.

In the heart of Dumfries itself the **Cairndale Hotel & Leisure Club** (01387 254111) is a good stop often with a weekend ceilidh. The **Selkirk Arms Hotel** (01557 330402) in Kirkcudbright is where Robert Burns is said to have written *Selkirk Grace*. This is highly recommended both for food and accommodation. The **Cally Palace Hotel** (01557 814341) in Gatehouse of Fleet is splendid with its own 18-hole golf course although it does seem to cater for an older set. A more economic proposition is the **Kelvin House Hotel** (01581 300528) in Glenluce which specialises in golf parties. One of the best deals is offered by the **North West Castle Hotel** (01776 704413), in Stranraer where golf packages of good value are available. In Portpatrick, the **Fernhill Hotel**

Dumfries and Galloway Golf Club is a typically engaging parkland course just north of Dumfries on the A701. Another course nearby is Dumfries and County.

(01776 810220), offers stunning views and is handy for both courses nearby.

Where to Eat

Claudio's Restaurant (01683 220958) in Moffat is set in an old police station but this is one jail you would not mind getting locked up in – distinctly Italian. The **Balcary Bay Hotel** (01556 640217) in Auchencairn near Castle Douglas offers a splendid setting and an award winning menu. For a taste of Kirkcudbright the **Auld Alliance Restaurant** (01557 330569) celebrates the area's produce at the highest level while chef Alistair is also a keen golfer. The scallops should certainly be sampled. Both the **Brasserie** and **Garden Restaurant** at the **Creebridge House Hotel** in Newton Stewart are worth seeking especially for the huge selection of malts and real ales. The **Knockinaam Lodge** near Portpatrick (01776 810471) offers truly excellent international food and is Michelin Star rated therefore you must phone well in advance.

What to Do

As you are arriving in the area from the south you may wish to stop at Gretna Green and the **Old Blacksmith's Shop and Visitor Centre** where eager, perhaps under-age elopers could tie the knot using Scotland's more lenient marriage laws. Dumfries and Galloway is as closely associated with Robert Burns as is neighbouring Ayrshire where he was born. He in fact spent much of his working life in Dumfries where he subsequently died at only 36 years old. **Burns House** in Burns Street, Dumfries is where his mistress, Jean Armor, lived. She soon became his wife and the house is now a museum to his life and works. The **Robert Burns Centre** in Mill Road is a similar evocation of the poet's elegiac existence while the **Globe Inn** just off the High Street in Dumfries centre testifies to his more temporal activities.

North of Dumfries, **Drumlanrig Castle** just off the A76, 3 miles/5km north of Thornhill is the impressive residence of the Duke of Buccleuch. For philatelists the world over nearby **Sanquar Post Office** is Britain's oldest. The **Museum of Lead Mining** at Wanlockhead is worth seeking out near the country's highest golf course. One of Scotland's most impressive medieval strongholds is found at **Caerlaverock Castle**, 9 miles/14km south of Dumfries and there is a wonderful wetland nature reserve nearby. The **Ruthwell Cross**, near Ruthwell off the B747 is a magnificent 7th century Pictish cross. **Sweetheart Abbey** in New Abbey, again a few miles south of Dumfries en-route to

Colvend and Southerness Golf Clubs is worth stopping for to appreciate its graceful masonry. **Shambellie House Museum of Costume** is also in New Abbey. The Colvend coast, aside from its golf course, offers a good walking stretch with a beautiful cove, **Rockcliffe**, well worth a detour. Near Castle Douglas, **Threave Castle** is a must if just to cross over to it via the lovely little row-boat. **Galloway Forest Park** is worth exploring if you are keen on forest and hill rambling while further arboreal distractions can be found in the southwest tip of the area at **Logan Botanic Gardens** 14 miles/22km south of Stranraer. Whithorn is perhaps the true birthplace of Christianity in Scotland and the **Whithorn Dig and Visitor's Centre** has revealed the area's important ecclesiastical connections. Guided tours around this are essential to grasp the full archaeological significance.

Newton Stewart lies beside the **River Cree**,

Set beneath the breathtaking Galloway Hills along a fine stretch of Solway Firth coastline, Colvend Golf Club has plenty of heather and gorse to punish wayward drives.

which is famous for its trout and salmon fishing, and so this is a good stopover centre, not least also for its fine golf course featured on *page 168*.

Tourist Information
Ferry Services
Stena Line
Tel: 01776 802165
Fax: 01776 802104
Stranraer-Belfast

Seacat
Tel: 08705 523523
Fax: 01232 314918.
Stranraer-Belfast

P&O European Ferries
Tel: 0990 780777

Dumfries & Galloway Tourist Board, 64 White Sands, Dumfries, DG1 2RS
Tel : +44 (01387) 253862
Email : info@dgtb.demon.co.uk
Website : www.galloway.co.uk

Index

Acknowledgements

Author's Acknowledgement:
The author would like to acknowledge the help of the many Scottish club secretaries, PGA professionals and club members who gave assistance with the research for this book.
Thanks also to Susie, Tracey and Yvonne for sorting out the slides.

Author's Note
I have attempted to make this golf guide as up-to-date and as accurate as possible. However, it goes without saying that things change: golf clubs extend their course, or add a new one, green fees change (they get dearer) and yardages are altered; new restaurants open, some close and telephone numbers change all too frequently while more clubs get a web site. And so on. Therefore, I hope you the reader – the visiting golfer – can help me to keep this book updated and accurate with your suggestions and findings as you tour the home of golf. Please address your comments to: Scotland Golf Update, New Holland Publishers, 24 Nutford Place, London W1H 6DQ or email me directly at djWhyte@sol.co.uk

Photographic Prints
Fine art, photographic prints of many of these images are available. For a full list and more information contact The Scottish Golf Photo Library Tel/Fax +44 (0) 1575 574515 or visit www.linksland.co.uk